THE
PATIO GARDEN

THE
PATIO GARDEN

HAZEL EVANS

FRANCES LINCOLN

Frances Lincoln Limited
4 Torriano Mews, Torriano Avenue,
London NW5 2RZ

The Patio Garden
Copyright © Frances Lincoln Limited 1985
Text copyright © Hazel Evans 1985
Illustrations copyright ©
Frances Lincoln Limited 1985
The copyright in the photographs is the property
of the photographers unless otherwise stated on
page 168.
Front cover photograph © Jerry Harpur
Back cover photograph by Geoff Dann ©
Frances Lincoln Limited

First Frances Lincoln Edition: 1985
Reprinted in 1986, 1988, and 1991
Second Frances Lincoln Edition: 1995
First Paperback Edition: 1996

9 8 7 6 5 4 3 2

British Library Cataloguing-in-Publication data
A catalogue record for this book is available from
the British Library.

ISBN 0 7112 1091 8

Set in Garamond 3 by Vantage Photosetting
Co. Ltd, Eastleigh and London
Printed in Hong Kong

CONTENTS

Foreword 6

PATIO DESIGN

Introduction 8 • Semi-wild Oasis Patio 18 • Patio on Two Levels 20
Roof-top Patio 22 • Tiled Courtyard 25 • Decked Patio 26
Town Patio Garden 28 • Japanese Water Patio 30 • Plantsman's Patio 32
Shady Terrace 34 • Tiny Backyard Patio 36 • Moated Patio 37
Classical Terrace 38 • Patio for Sun and Shade 40

PATIO CONSTRUCTION

Planning the Patio 42 • Paved Surfaces 48 • Wooden Decking 54
Walls, Fences and Screens 58 • Built-in Furniture 64 • Overhead Shelter 66
Containers and Raised Beds 69 • Water Features 72 • Lighting 76 • Special Effects 81

PLANTING THE PATIO

Introduction 84 • Climbers 86 • Background Plants 88 • Ground Cover 90
Flowers All Year Round 93 • Plants for Special Conditions 96 • Accent Plants 98
Water Plants 100 • Edible Plants 102 • Trees 104 • Shrubs 106
Climbers and Wall Shrubs 109 • Perennials, Annuals and Bulbs 112
Ground Cover 116 • Water and Marsh Plants 119 • Fruit, Vegetables and Herbs 121

FURNISHING THE PATIO

Introduction 124 • Tables and Chairs 132 • Benches 134
Lounging Furniture 136 • Containers 138 • Barbecues 140 • Lights 142
Statues and Ornaments 144

GENERAL CARE AND MAINTENANCE

Patio Maintenance 146 • Container Care 149 • Plant Care 154

Glossary 161 • Plants for Special Situations 162 • Index 163
Useful Addresses 167 • Acknowledgments 168

FOREWORD

As the owner of a much-loved patio garden, right in the heart of London's East End, I am very well aware of its special value in cramped city conditions. To me it is an extra outdoor room to relax in, and to entertain in, too, when I have guests. Most of all, it gives me a chance to get out of doors and to unwind, by tending my plants. I'm also constantly looking around for new ideas to improve it. This book is for people like me who feel the same way about their plot – not necessarily committed gardeners, but busy people who appreciate the extra space they have and want it to look good without being too labour-intensive, and to fit in with the style of their house.

Since indoor decoration has become a major point of pride and interest, it seems logical to me that we should give the same attention to our outdoor living space, exploiting its potential to the fullest. Nothing is quite as pleasant, on a summer evening, than to have a few friends round for outdoor drinks or supper, and to be able to enjoy their company *en plein air*, perfumed with fragrant plants, the sound and dust from nearby roads muffled by a hedge or by evergreen climbers, so that, for a moment at least, you can imagine you are in the country. I see so many sad unimaginative patios – expanses of grey concrete without interest, just a few bedraggled, wilting plants, heaps of old building materials or rubbish – and it seems such a waste not to make the most of what little space we do have.

What I have tried to do in this book is to put down some of the best ideas for creating an exciting new outdoor space. The emphasis is as much on the structure of the outdoor room as it is on the planting, largely because the construction side is such a massive outlay in terms of expenditure and effort. You can treat the planting rather as you would the furnishings of a room. Provided you don't go overboard for deep-rooted trees and shrubs, you can change it around from time to time to suit your mood, switching colours from one season to another.

To inspire you, and to encourage you to think afresh about your particular plot, I have selected a number of widely different patio gardens as an appetizer. Sketch plans and outline planting schemes are given, but they are for guidance only, as no-one can hope to copy in detail a garden that belongs to someone else; you need to add your own individual touch. There's a fairly detailed chapter on the basics of planning and constructing the garden, to get the major elements together. This is followed by a chapter which outlines some of the principal themes in planting up the patio, together with a selected list of some of my favourite patio plants. Like any other garden, the patio plot needs some maintenance if it is to look good all year round, so at the back of the book I've listed some basic advice on the most important aspects of patio and plant care – particularly the care of containers, which are bound to form an important part of any patio scheme. Also at the end you will find a list of plants for specific purposes.

I hope that this book will encourage you to take a second look at your own backyard or roof terrace and turn it into something you can really enjoy.

Getting a book like this together is very much a matter of team work, and I'd like to thank my ex-husband, and friend, Harry Evans, the editors, designers, illustrators and photographers at Frances Lincoln Limited and, above all, Susan Berry who coped not only with me and my idiosyncrasies but managed to produce a baby at the same time!

PATIO
DESIGN

INTRODUCTION

A patio, says the Concise Oxford Dictionary, is 'an inner court, open to the sky in Spanish or Spanish-American houses'. The original patio was developed by the Arab conquerors of Spain from the Roman atrium, a central courtyard, open mainly to the sky, around which the family lived in rooms that had few, if any, windows on to the street. It owes something, too, to the beautifully decorated and intricately patterned enclosed courtyards that the Persians used as their gardens in the first century AD.

This original definition of a patio has gone by the board as the word has become used more widely and now it does not necessarily refer to an enclosed space. But it seems a pity that, in borrowing the name, we do not usually take the trouble to pay the same attention to detail and decoration that formed such a feature of the original concept.

Today a patio can be anything from a raised terrace at the back of a house to an entire backyard in a town garden that has been mainly paved over. It can be a secret sitting-out place in the corner of a large garden, or just a few square metres of concrete at the end of a small one. It can be roofed in or, like its Roman predecessors, open to the sky. It may be elaborately designed with many changes of level and decorated with fountains and statues, or it could be very simple and functional – basically nothing more than a bicycle or tool store. The term encompasses roof gardens and balconies, too, which can be used as outdoor rooms.

What we are talking about, in essence, is a style of gardening, where grass is necessarily replaced by solid paving or some other inert covering and where trees, shrubs and plants are generally grown in a confined space.

These requirements call for a special kind of gardening, since you are restricted in size and scope. But for all that, surely no other type of garden can give so much pleasure from so small a space, and get so much use, all year round. That's why, if we are to make the most of it, we need to plan a patio garden as carefully as possible. In this chapter, I examine some of the major elements of design. The more specific details of planning are dealt with in the chapter on construction, on pp. 42–7.

Siting a patio *A patio garden does not have to take the form of a conventional square of terrace at the back of the house. The patio above has been created in a shady and secluded corner at the side of the house, giving it an almost 'secret garden' feel while the large open patio, right, forms part of a bold and sophisticated design which embraces the house and the entire garden. Both gardens demonstrate that lush evergreen trees, shrubs and climbers can be used very successfully to take the place of traditional flower colour without being dull or lifeless. By concentrating on an evergreen backdrop to the patio, you ensure that it looks good at all seasons – particularly important when the patio adjoins or is overlooked by the main living rooms of the house.*

CHOOSING A SITE

The aspect of the patio is one of the vital components to take into account when making your plans. There is no point in creating an exotic sunbathing terrace in a position that hardly ever receives the sun. Convention has it that the patio is right behind the house, but does it have to be? In a small plot, this may be the only option and, here, its aspect will, to some extent, dictate its function.

A terrace that gets the sun late in the day is not, for example, the best place to have breakfast, although it will be a pleasant place for afternoon tea, early evening drinks or a meal at night in summer when the patio is still warm.

Plants for a sunbaked patio will have to be chosen with care if they are not to be 'cooked' by the heat bouncing off the floor and walls. A cool, shady patio might be suitable for children to play on, but you are less likely to use it for sitting out. There are, fortunately, plenty of shrubs and climbers that will thrive in this type of situation (see p. 162). Very few gardens face any one direction squarely, and it is likely that your patio will have a combination of two aspects, giving some of the advantages and disadvantages of each.

If you have a long garden, you could consider having a patio-style sunbathing or lounging area tucked away at the sunniest end, perhaps screened by hedging on three sides, to keep out prevailing winds. Alternatively, a patio sited halfway down a long, thin plot breaks it up in an attractive way and makes it seem wider. This is also a better position if you intend to use the patio as a dining area, as it is closer to the house.

Access

If you are going to create an outdoor room next to the living rooms of the house, think carefully about access. The wider and more accessible the doorway, the easier it becomes to use the patio, and the easier it is to provide a harmonious link between the outdoor and indoor rooms. Obvious links, such as flooring materials or colour schemes, can be supplemented by using blending or matching furnishings. Indoor plants in the room opening on to the patio also help to blur the distinction between outside and inside, as does carefully designed lighting so that the intensity and quality of light at night are harmoniously balanced.

CREATING AN OUTDOOR ROOM

In this typical town plot, there are two patio areas, one at each end of the garden, but it still appears to be very narrow. In the alternative design, right, several existing features have been retained – the handsome flagstones near the house and the raised area at the end of the garden, together with two existing trees, but the garden has been divided into three distinct parts. The patio near the house has been separated from the rest of the garden with two raised beds and the paving has been given a surround of warm-toned bricks to match the existing brick boundary walls. A barbecue has been included next to the right-hand wall to make the patio near the house useful for summer entertaining, and the existing pond has been emphasized with a bubble fountain. At the far end, a pergola has been added. The new design has been planned to look good at night as well, with lighting focusing on specific features.

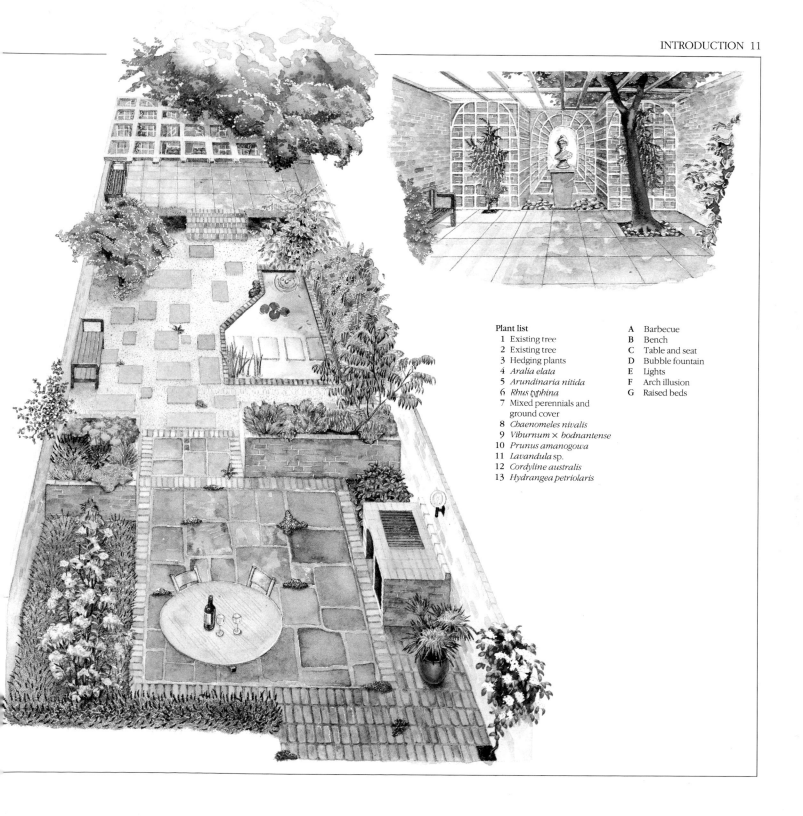

Plant list

1 Existing tree
2 Existing tree
3 Hedging plants
4 *Aralia elata*
5 *Arundinaria nitida*
6 *Rhus typhina*
7 Mixed perennials and
   ground cover
8 *Chaenomeles nivalis*
9 *Viburnum × bodnantense*
10 *Prunus amanogowa*
11 *Lavandula* sp.
12 *Cordyline australis*
13 *Hydrangea petriolaris*

A Barbecue
B Bench
C Table and seat
D Bubble fountain
E Lights
F Arch illusion
G Raised beds

Privacy

An important point to bear in mind when planning where to site your patio is privacy. Although it may not worry you that you are overlooked by neighbours, if you want to create the impression of an outdoor room, some screening will be useful. It does not have to be a solid wall; trellis or even rigid plastic netting covered with climbers gives the illusion of privacy without shutting sunlight out of the garden. In built-up areas, high rise buildings can be a nuisance, and in this situation you may find it best to roof in part of the patio in some way, even if it's only a fairly basic screening structure comprising a skeleton of posts clothed with climbers.

CHOOSING A STYLE

Many people feel perfectly at home reorganizing and redecorating the rooms in their house, but the minute they start to think about redesigning the garden, they are lost. Part of the problem is that the patio site can seem to offer too many possibilities to decide on, but if you think of it as an outdoor room, you begin to get the problem in perspective. Ideally, it should be as useful, as comfortable and probably more attractive than any room in the house.

The most common mistake made by beginners when designing their gardens is either to copy examples that don't suit the size and style of their own plot, or to try and have 'something of everything'.

Screens and shelter *Privacy, or at least the illusion of it, is important when planning a patio if you are not to feel as though you are sitting on a stage. In the patio, left, an archway separates the patio from the rest of the garden, giving a tantalizing glimpse of it while providing some shelter; the pink tiles of the patio have been carefully chosen to blend with the warm tones of the brick arch and walls. In the patio above, a carved wooden screen marks the transition between the covered patio area and the garden beyond and the screen,*

Ultimately you will enjoy the patio more, and it will certainly look better, if you limit your options a little and decide, in advance, what you really need and like.

Think carefully about the function and likely use of the patio when you are choosing a style. It would be foolish to create an elaborately raked gravel patio for a household full of children, or to construct a water feature into which small children might fall, although you can perhaps plan for such a feature in the future by installing a basic structure, and using it for plants while the children are small, only filling it with water once they have grown up or learned to swim.

If you are a keen gardener, for example, you need a scheme that allows you the maximum planting space.

As some of the garden designs illustrated on the following pages show, you can think 'vertically' as well as 'horizontally', thereby using all the available space for really lush planting. Climbing plants are particularly useful in this respect, taking up very little ground space and offering a mass of foliage and flowers.

If you are unable to spend much time in the garden and want to relax in it rather than work on it, then a design that concentrates on interesting, easy-to-maintain surfaces and on plants that look after themselves is a necessity. Such gardens certainly don't have to look hard or boring. The Japanese type of garden is a marvellous example of clean lines and surfaces that are easily maintained, although it wouldn't look right in every setting, nor would it be to everyone's taste.

Water is definitely worth thinking about in any patio, but particularly in one destined to be easy to care for. It provides a splendid contrast to the paved surfaces, bringing reflection, movement and life to the garden. Only minimal planting is needed to focus attention on it, and provided that the water is contained in suitable and interesting shapes, it really adds to the vitality of the garden. Simple channels, square ponds and very shallow water over a bed of pebbles are easy to instal and no bother to maintain. Moving water, in particular, adds interest – bubbling over pebbles into a trough, streaming into a decorative basin or dropping as a minor waterfall in one corner of the patio.

PLANTING

If you keep the basic lines of the design fairly simple, it won't mean that the patio will be dull, and you will have a lot more room for manoeuvre when you come to the planting. The bones of the patio, created by the surfacing and the walls, can be fleshed out by the planting, which in itself can be positively architectural if the right choice of plants is made. It is surprising just how the choice of planting influences the feel of the patio. Take great care when choosing any trees, since they are obviously going to be permanent features. However, pots and containers of smaller trees, shrubs and plants can be moved around to create different effects at different times of the year. More detailed suggestions on planning the planting of the patio are given on pp. 44–6 and p. 84.

hanging basket chair and floor tiles are all in similar tones, blending together to give the area a feeling of unity.
In the patio, above, plants have been used just as successfully to give an otherwise exposed balcony a little welcome privacy. The furnishings have been carefully chosen to echo the colours of the stucco walls, and the combined effect of rattan furniture, a large potted palm standing in a woven basket and a lacy tablecloth gives the patio a special period charm.

Style points

● Keep the colour theme simple and don't go for a rainbow effect unless you are very sure of your taste and style, or the result may be a confused jumble.

● Don't crowd the patio with containers dotted around it. One glorious corner of massed containers is far more effective than pots of colour scattered around the patio.

● Build in lighting at an early stage so that it can be concealed.

● Be careful not to lay a surface that is completely out of sympathy with the house. Medieval-looking brick paving may not go with a modern house unless it is in a country surrounding.

● Choose furniture that matches the style of your house and patio. Rustic chairs, for instance, can look strange in a town environment.

● Link indoors with out; if a doorframe is painted red, echo it in a pot of red tulips, then red roses, then red berries, at different seasons.

● If the patio is too small, use every trick you can to enlarge it and extend your horizons using special effects – for example *trompe l'oeil* to create a vista of another garden beyond the patio (see p. 81).

People often forget when planning the planting to think about the foliage. As many of the gardens featured in this book show, it is not only the quality of flower colour that counts, but the form of the leaves. The more they contrast – in both colour and texture, and shape and size – the more fascinating the garden and the more there is to delight the eye all year round. Don't forget, too, that some foliage is matt and dense, absorbing light, while other foliage is feathery and shiny, reflecting light. Often the filtering of light by the leaves of carefully chosen plants can bring an otherwise dull garden to life.

Since flower colour only lasts for a season at most, the actual structure of the garden must be formed from the hard surfaces and the forms of the planting. The latter should be carefully designed to give you a backdrop that looks good all year round – evergreens are an obvious choice for this reason – with splashes of colour augmenting an otherwise attractive picture at particular seasons.

SPECIAL EFFECTS

There are many special ways of creating different 'looks' to the patio. Lighting is probably a major feature since it can have a double purpose. It allows you to use the patio by night as well as by day whenever the weather is suitable. Moreover, cleverly planned and positioned it can turn even the dullest patio into one that is astonishingly dramatic. Although it is probably best to plan the lighting as a permanent feature when you build the patio, so that you can keep any cables out of harm's way, you can add to it in various ways later on, particularly using temporary lights, such as slow-burning candles and flares, for special occasions (see pp. 76–80).

With difficult or awkward sites, there are any number of ways to overcome problems, such as high walls, narrow basement areas and so on, using all kinds of 'trick' effects. In small spaces, mirrors can be used to reflect into each other, *trompe l'oeil* doorways and arbours can be painted on flat, blank walls to give interest and depth to the garden, and hedges, screens and pergolas can be cleverly positioned to break up the area to make it look much bigger than it is, by giving the impression of larger spaces somewhere just out of view.

ORIENTAL-STYLE ROOF GARDEN

The small roof terrace, below, has been principally planted with ground cover and a few rather architectural palms as feature plants. The alternative design, shown right, while retaining the low maintenance aspect of the original, has drawn attention to the beauty of the roof tiles by echoing their colour and form in the terracotta tiles used for the sitting area near the doorway. The architectural nature of the planting has been retained but given a more Japanese feel using bamboos and evergreens. The back wall has been mirrored to give the illusion of greater space.

Plant list

1 *Aucuba japonica*
2 *Arundinaria nitida*
3 *Camellia japonica*
4 *Pinus* sp. (bonsai)
5 *Hemerocallis fulva* 'Flore Pleno'
6 *Dryopteris filix-mas*
7 *Acer palmatum*
8 *Helxine soleirolii*
9 *Rhododendron* 'Keiskei'
10 *Arundinaria viridi-striata*

A Stone path
B Terracotta tiles
C Stone basin
D Cobbles
E Rattan furniture
F Bamboo and mirror screen
G Gravel

HARMONIZING WITH THE HOUSE

Wherever you decide to put the patio, it is extremely important to make sure that the patio design is in sympathy with the architectural style of the house, right down to the smallest details, including any furniture, pots and containers, and the colours of the surface and of the plants. If you don't do so, the clash in styles will create a bitty and untidy atmosphere to the patio and a slightly uneasy feeling when you use it. Far from being a natural extension to your home, making a relaxing and restful extra room, your patio will introduce a discordant note, by providing the eye with an unpleasing contrast and thus producing a disturbingly unharmonious effect.

It helps to take a look at some of the best Japanese gardens, in which the garden and the house are designed in one unit. The materials and styles flow and harmonize together in an extremely restful and pleasing way. The formality of a true Japanese garden may not be to everyone's liking, but no harm can come of following some of the main principles. Never try to crowd too much into the patio – so many seem to suffer from a surfeit of hanging baskets, too much furniture that doesn't match the house and too many pots and containers scattered all around the area. Keep the design simple, especially to begin with. If you then feel that the garden needs something more, you can always add a feature plant in a pot at a later date.

Obviously the first essentials are to look at the material used in the construction of the house and to choose a surface covering for the patio that is both practical and in sympathy with them. Although contrasts can and do work wonderfully well, it requires an expert design eye to make the right choice. Happily there is a wealth of materials to choose from nowadays (see pp. 48–57).

The gardens featured on the following pages should offer some idea of the choice of patio styles, sizes and types that can be created. Having looked carefully at your site, you can then get down to the basic planning, discussed on pp. 42–47.

Symmetry and colour

An eye for detail can make a surprisingly vivid contribution to the overall effect of the patio design. Small touches of colour in plants or furnishings can be used to emphasize a feature of the patio or draw the eye away from a less attractive part of the garden. In the photograph opposite above, the positioning against a white wall of two red chairs on either side of a white raised bed containing scarlet and white plants makes a focal point which could be easily copied in any patio. In the same garden, opposite below, the scarlet furniture and white containers have been used to great effect as a contrast with the plain grey floor tiles deliberately chosen to harmonize with the grey paint of the interior of the house. In the patio, left, the impact comes from the symmetrical arrangement of the four pots of Cordyline australis around the square water feature in front of the patio doors. With a limited range of colours, the eye is drawn to the simple architectural shapes. Another nice touch is the sympathetic use of wooden decking for the patio floor, echoing the clapboarding of the house.

SEMI-WILD OASIS PATIO

OPPOSITE *In the lushly planted central oasis, leaf colour and shape are shown to advantage – the broad leaves of* Hosta glauca, *for example, contrasting with the feathery fronds of a bamboo. This garden shows how the combination of water and planting of varying heights and forms can create visual excitement in the patio without relying on flower colour.*

BELOW *A close-up of the water feature, bisected by a decked bridge with two pots of bay trees standing sentinel. The inclusion of water in a patio also permits more interesting, stylish planting; here, stylish water lilies (*Nymphaea*) contrast with the reedy elegance of* Typha angustifolia.

A semi-wild oasis has been created in the centre of this town patio. Much of its charm derives from the contrast of the densely planted central island with the more formal paved surrounds, and from the inclusion of a large water feature divided by a decked bridge into two separate pools. The bridge helps to create the illusion of a central 'island' although, in fact, the channel of water extends down one side of the garden area only.

A water feature of this size has two virtues: it strikes a good ecological balance and is surprisingly easy to look after. In this garden the ponds are fairly deep but shallower water trickling over a bed of pebbles would achieve a similar effect more easily and cheaply. The presence of water in any garden gives it life and movement and, of course, increases the opportunity to grow different plants that need moist conditions in order to thrive.

In this garden the accent is on plants with interesting foliage of varying shape and colour. The close planting not only provides a marvellously 'natural' feel to the garden, but saves a lot of work, since the dense foliage helps to suppress weeds.

The paving used is relatively inexpensive – concrete slabs with the aggregate exposed – and the rough, textured appearance of the stones blends in well with the informality of the planting.

Tall plants have been used at both ends of the patio to give it some privacy and to enhance its 'secret garden' feel.

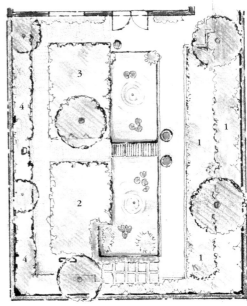

1 *Actinidia chinensis*
Agapanthus var.
Amelanchier canadensis
Iris germanica
Laburnum × 'Vossii'
Lavandula sp.
Rosmarinus sp.
2 *Alchemilla mollis*
Arundinaria nitida
Hemerocallis var.
Hosta glauca
Iris sibirica
Lythrum salicaria
Magnolia liliiflora
M. × *soulangiana*
Myrica gale
Nymphaea var.
Polygonum affine
Typha angustifolia
Verbascum × *hybridum*
V. nigrum album

3 *Arundinaria przewalskii*
Astilbe × *arendsii*
Filipendula purpurea
Laurus nobilis
Ligularia clivorum
Magnolia × *soulangiana*
Nymphaea var.
Prunus dulcis
Tradescantia virginiana
4 *Camellia* × *williamsii* 'Donation'
Cladrastis sinensis
Pieris formosa 'Forrestii'
Prunus cerasifera 'Atropurpurea'
Rhododendron 'Blue Bird'
Sambucus racemosa
Viburnum × *burkwoodii*

PATIO ON TWO LEVELS

This patio was nothing more than a junk heap when its present owner took it over. It was also completely flat and to achieve the two levels it now possesses had to be excavated to a depth of 1.2m/4ft. The task took the whole of one summer to complete as it had to be done painstakingly by hand, and the soil – five skips' full – taken through the house in sacks.

Floodlit at night by three strategically placed spotlights, the garden presents a different aspect from each floor of the house. Changes in level can be successfully used to define specific areas of the garden for particular purposes. For example, one level could be used as a place from which to serve food and drink, and another as a children's play area, as well as for concealing unsightly but necessary service items, such as dustbins. In this patio, the lower area closest to the house is used extensively as an outdoor room, and many meals are taken by the pond, watched by a collection of frogs and toads that reside there.

In a small town patio like this one, the changes of level help to create the illusion of greater space, and also permit more plants to be grown, as the additional vertical surfaces can play host to a waterfall of creeping and crevice plants, planted in purpose-built gaps in the retaining walls.

When creating a patio on different levels, particular care should be taken in the choice of paving materials, as they are likely to be more obtrusive. In this patio, York stone has been used with great success throughout, giving unity to the design.

Plants tend to stand out more in a stepped garden and in this patio the levels have been used to show off the spiky leaves of a *Phormium tenax*, for example. A patio on several levels benefits from an abundance of plants and a variety of contrasting foliage forms – tall grasses or slender-leaved plants among rounded bushy shrubs. Climbers can be used to spill over from one level to another to soften any hard edges.

RIGHT *A close-up view of the upper patio with its stone seat, showing how a profusion of plants can be accommodated in a small area to great effect. Changes of level permit a fuller planting scheme.*

OPPOSITE *Tiered walls and varying levels make good use of a standard rectangular plot and give scope for more imaginative planting. The overhead view shows the overall design – a series of overlapping and linked curves and circles. Brick and stone, softened by plant forms, make a classic partnership and blend naturally into the paving around the pool.*

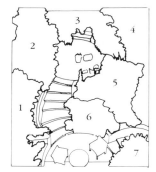

1 *Ficus* 'Brown Turkey'
Fuchsia vars.
Pelargonium (white zonal)
Pinus densiflora 'Pendula'
Prunus persica 'Peregrine'
Rosa 'Gloire de Dijon'
Senecio cineraria
2 *Ceanothus impressus*
Daphne odora
Lonicera serotina
Mahonia lomariifolia
Syringa vulgaris 'Firmament'
Viburnum tomentosum
Weigela florida 'Variegata'
3 *Camellia japonica*
Campanula portenschlagiana
Dryopteris filix-mas
Hedera colchica
Parthenocissus henryana
Pieris formosa 'Forest Flame'
Pulmonaria rubra
Viburnum tinus
4 *Azalea*
Camellia 'Leonard Messel'
Chaenomeles × *superba*
Clematis montana 'Rubens'
Helleborus sp.
Hydrangea petiolaris
Rosa sp.
5 *Chamaecyparis lawsoniana*
C. pisifera
Hedera helix 'Glacier'
H.h. 'Sagittifolia'
Lavandula officinalis 'Hidcote'
Ligularia 'Desdemona'
Myosotis sylvatica
Pachyderma terminalis
Phormium tenax 'Rainbow'
Thuja orientalis
6 *Aponogeton distachyus*
Genista lydia
Hosta lancifolia
Iris, Mimulus and *Primula* spp
Lysichiton americanus
Phalaris arundinacea 'Picta'
Primula japonica
7 *Clematis* 'The President'
Hosta fortunei
Laurus nobilis
Rosa 'Zephyrine Drouhin'

ROOF-TOP PATIO

OPPOSITE *A focal point of this roof-top patio is the minaret, one of four bought from a local antique dealer. Made of fibreglass, they were originally used to replace the real minarets that decorated the early nineteenth-century Brighton Pavilion while they were being restored.*

BELOW *An overhead view shows how white-painted posts and rails set off the many shades of foliage. The trellis surrounding the patio is almost obscured by the massed planting of mixed climbers, blurring the boundaries and helping to link the areas.*

This fascinating roof-top patio in London came into being almost by chance. Following a burglary, the owners of the house were advised to put up high walls of trellis around the roof to deter intruders. The unexpected bonus was an outdoor room on several levels. Bridges, steps and a spiral staircase were built to link the various roof areas together. Four years later, the whole effect is of a garden of delightful discoveries, with something interesting to view at every level, twist and turn. The owners' knowledge of gardening was very limited and so the plants were chosen by simply wading through a plant encyclopaedia, picking out and noting down any that took their fancy.

From the start the garden was intended primarily for use in the evening, so floodlighting was to be an important feature, as well as a useful burglar deterrent. The owners had noticed in other people's gardens that red flowers looked particularly good under artificial light, so they bought as many of those as they could, augmenting them with trees like *Liquidambar styraciflua*, the leaves of which turn brilliant orange/scarlet in autumn, *Parrotia persica* with its patterned bark and flame-coloured foliage, and *Amelanchier canadensis* with its softer autumn tints.

Plants are mainly confined to tubs and pots. The owners persuaded a local shop to sell them chipped rejects at a bargain price; as a result they now own almost 800. They shift their pots around continually, moving those that are in bloom or at their best to the forefront while 'resting' others in a less conspicuous place. Some plants, particularly azaleas, seem to thrive

1 *Hydrangea macrophylla*
Magnolia liliiflora
Pelargonium × hortorum
Syringa vulgaris
2 *Hosta glauca*
Rosa vars.
Salvia officinalis 'Icterina'
3 *Camellia japonica*
Euonymus japonica
'Microphyllus Aureus'
Fuchsia magellanica
Fuchsia vars.
Hebe sp.
Hebe × andersonii 'Variegata'
Hydrangea macrophylla
Paeonia lactiflora
Photinia 'Red Robin'
Rosa vars.
4 *Campanula isophylla*
Cotinus coggygria 'Royal Purple'
Tropaeolum majus
5 *Hedera helix*
Hosta var.

ABOVE *The delicate wrought-iron white-painted furniture blends well with the lacy patterns created by the plethora of climbers, and the white-painted bridge links this patio area with its neighbour.*

ABOVE RIGHT *In this small corner, interesting leaf shapes and colours have been chosen to contrast with each other – the silver and white of* Cornus alba *'Variegata' with the slender branches of* Cytisus scoparius *and the golden-yellow leaves of* Robinia pseudoacacia *'Frisia' in the background.*

on this, as they are moved to rest in the shade shortly after they have bloomed, until the following year's flowering season.

Half-barrels of trees and shrubs were planted in the permanent positions. The owners had no idea of how to group plants together and simply worked on the principle that plants that flowered at roughly the same time would get on well together. Although they have had a few failures, most of the groupings have been successful – in particular a tub containing variegated weigela, *Philadelphus aurea* (with pale green leaves), a purple dwarf maple and a viburnum.

No attempt is made to overwinter half-hardy plants; instead new stock is bought in each spring – a good solution if you are short of space, and have plenty of money. When growing plants in containers, you can vary the soil content as you please, depending on whether the incumbent likes or dislikes lime. Watering at roof-top level poses a special problem unless you have catered for it in your design. The owners of this patio have installed taps in all of the patio areas, each having its own short length of hosepipe.

As the garden is used a great deal in the evening, the owners have chosen plants for scent as well as colour, and are delighted with one discovery, *Trachelospermum jasminoides*, whose white flowers give off a perfume that can be quite overpowering. Plants are placed in close proximity for maximum effect, and the owners now find they have to prune drastically to keep everything under control.

Plan showing the layout of the roof

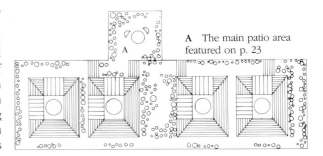

A The main patio area featured on p. 23

TILED COURTYARD

BELOW *In this tiny courtyard, the patterned tiling harmonizes well with the Moorish architecture and, a clever touch, even the pond has been tiled in a similar pattern. Few plants are necessary when the patio surface is as decorative as this.*

Ceramic tiles in black and white dominate this inner courtyard of a house in Morocco, showing how patterns rather than plants can be used as the main theme. Although of traditional Arab design, this style is easily copied and the materials are readily available. Using ceramic tiles on this scale could prove expensive so why not use just as few to form a decorative 'carpet' in the centre of a courtyard with plainer, and cheaper, tiling around the outside? Alternatively, the patterned tiles could be used to define just one area – an alcove for instance – providing a link between two tiling schemes.

Wooden shutters and seating have been used in this patio to give warmth and to soften the overall effect, although wrought iron or metal furniture would have been equally effective, and perhaps more in keeping with the surroundings.

Water in the garden is very much an Arab tradition and, in this instance, an elaborately curved shallow pool has been used as the central feature of the courtyard. In a smaller space, a raised corner pool could perform a similar function with, perhaps, water trickling from a ceramic mask on the wall above it. If you are working with highly patterned materials, it pays to keep the planting relatively simple, otherwise the overall effect may be unrestful and jazzy.

Here the plants have been reserved for the large beds around the sides, allowing the tiles and decorative pool to take the centre stage.

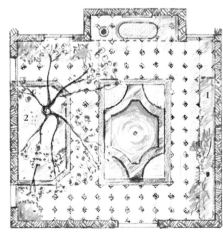

1 *Acacia longifolia*
Bougainvillea glabra
Callistemon rigidus
Clivia miniata
Schefflera actinophylla
Strelitzia reginae

2 *Cupressus sempervirens*
Datura suaveolens
Euphorbia splendens
Fremontodendron mexicanum
Jacaranda mimosifolia
Pittosporum tobira
Nerium oleander
Sansevieria trifasciata
Sparmannia africana

DECKED PATIO

OPPOSITE An extensively decked patio, designed to fit round an existing Pinus sylvestris, *shows the versatility of wood as a patio material.*

BELOW The oriental atmosphere of this same patio has been heightened by split bamboo screening and the shaped framework of the pergola. An interesting idea is the recessed seating well, which does double duty as a link to a lower level.

Surrounding one end of a country house, this decked patio overlooks a well-wooded large garden. The owner, a landscape designer, wanted a patio surface that had a very different look and feel to it, but which would be in sympathy with the natural feel of the garden. His choice of wooden decking, and of the Canadian hemlock used for it, has paid off. A 'hard' softwood, there is the double bonus that it does not splinter and also takes stain well.

The decking was also easy and quick to instal – it took just about four weeks to build. As durable as other hard surfaces, it does need occasional maintenance – a coat of preservative every few years. Another great advantage is that it can easily be built around any existing obstacles – in this patio, for example, it surrounds a very attractive fully-grown tree, transforming it into a focal point.

Built-in beds are not particularly well-suited to wooden patios but potted plants are very successful, particularly when clustered in groups both for maximum impact and for convenience, as they are then much easier to keep an eye on during the hot summer months.

If you are planning a wooden deck, take advantage of a special view. A matching wooden pergola adds to the oriental look of this patio and is a useful place to site outdoor lights, with, perhaps, an overhead vine grown for shade.

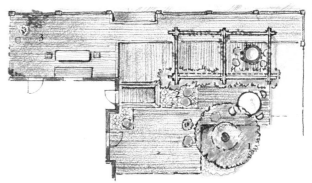

1 *Arundinaria japonica*
Campanula isophylla
Cynara scolymus
Epimedium grandiflorum
Glechoma hederacea 'Variegata'
Hebe × andersonii
Hedera colchica
Iris pseudacorus
Paulownia tomentosa
Pieris sp.
Existing *Pinus sylvestris*
Saxifraga stolonifera
2 *Arundinaria japonica*
Cyclamen neopolitanum
Fatsia japonica
Hedera helix 'Sagittifolia'
Lonicera periclymenum
Parthenocissus henryana
Paulownia tomentosa
Salvia officinalis 'Purpurascens'
Vitis coignetiae

3 *Abelia × grandiflora*
Ceanothus dentatus
Cordyline australis
Hedera colchica 'Variegata'
Jasminum nudiflorum
J. officinale 'Aureovariegatum'
Lavandula spica 'Hidcote'
Magnolia × soulangiana
Phlomis fruticosa
Robinia pseudoacacia 'Frisia'
Santolina nepolitana
4 *Acorus gramineus* 'Variegatus'
Arundinaria nitida
*Clematis × * 'Jackmanii'
C. montana 'Tetrarose'
Cyperus alternifolius
Iris sibirica
Jasminum officinale
Miscanthus sinensis 'Giganteus'
Salix matsudana 'Tortuosa'
Solanum jasminoides

TOWN PATIO GARDEN

This typical town garden is long and narrow, running straight behind a terraced house, parallel to other similar plots. Instead of the usual patio area, followed by a lawn, with, perhaps, a vegetable patch at the far end, the entire length has been paved to create an extended patio. To add interest, three different types and sizes of paving have been used, marking out each of three levels. With a very large area of paving, such a change is essential; even York stone, beautiful as it is, would look monotonous if deployed for the full length of the garden.

The present owners inherited the basic structure with a number of well-established plants, which they liked and left in place: in particular, three climbing roses, a large mahonia, and a *Cornus alba*. A *Hydrangea petiolaris* was also reprieved, as well as a lavender bush, an escallonia and the *Stephanandra incisa* which conveniently hides a large tree stump. A patch of yellow iris was also left intact, but an over-large prunus tree was removed and a *Robinia* put in its place. An empty flower bed on the right of the garden has been heavily manured and subsequently used to house plants from the owners' previous garden.

The area nearest the house is used for sitting or dining out and has a floor of flagstones, laid in random pattern, while the next level, which features a wide border, serves mainly as a corridor to the end level and is paved with old bricks. Two more steps lead up to

RIGHT *In the centre brick-paved tier of this patio garden, herbaceous border and ground cover plants have been allowed to spill over the edges of the path, helping to avoid the straight lines that would emphasize the narrowness of the plot.*

OPPOSITE *The full length of the patio seen from overhead. The walls have been completely clad with climbers, giving the garden a sense of privacy and helping to blur the boundaries.*

the highest paved area where a planted antique trough is a prominent feature.

Dividing a long garden like this up into three 'rooms' has the immediate effect of making it look wider than it actually is. And a focal point such as the trough at the far end will lead the eye towards it, making the plot appear longer. The siting of the path through from one patio to another is important as if it were to lead straight up the centre of the garden, splitting the area in half, it would only emphasize the narrowness of the plot. In this instance, the path is set to one side, with a shallow bed running alongside it, adding breadth to the design. A fence, hedge or trellis extending part of the way across the plot can be used to trick the eye and widen the appearance of a narrow garden.

1 *Agapanthus* sp.
Acanthus spinosus
Anchusa sp.
Astilbe sp.
Aucuba japonica
Berberis thunbergii
Clematis spp.
Cornus alba
Escallonia sp.
Euonymus 'Silver Queen'
Euphorbia griffithii
Galtonia candicans
Hebe 'Blue Gem'
Heuchera sp.
Hosta vars.
Iris sp.
Lobelia fulgens
Lonicera sp.
Mahonia japonica
Penstemon 'Garnet'
Rosmarinus sp.
Schizostylis coccinea
Senecio laxifolia
Viburnum tinus
Wisteria sinensis
2 *Bergenia* sp.
Camellia sasanqua
Ceanothus 'Heavenly Blue'
Chaenomeles sp.
Clematis spp.
Elaeagnus sp.
Erica sp.
Eucalyptus gunnii
Fatsia japonica
Fuchsia vars.
Hydrangea petiolaris
Mahonia aquifolium
Pieris formosa 'Forrestii'
Robinia pseudoacacia tortuosa
Rosa 'Albertine'

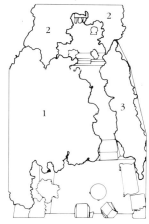

3 *Cassia* sp.
Clematis sp.
Cyclamen neapolitanum
Cytisus sp.
Daphne odora 'Marginata'
Euonymus fortunei
Hedera canariensis
Stephanandra incisa
Thymus sp.

Ground cover plants
Affonis sp.
Ajuga reptans
Epimedium sp.
Lamium maculatum
Vinca minor

JAPANESE WATER PATIO

OPPOSITE *and* BELOW *Clever use of angles makes this tiny back garden seem much larger than it actually is. Water is the main feature here, with decking over the shallower end of the pool, which finishes in a pebble 'beach'. To maintain the Japanese theme, other finishing touches have been used – split bamboo over a brick wall, Japanese pots and the deckchair made of matting. Lighting has been carefully thought out to pinpoint special features at night, focusing on a* Philadelphus, *for instance.*

The Japanese have taken the art of gardening with materials like water and stone to a point of near perfection, and this patio is an example of how Japanese style translates perfectly to a small town garden. This plot was originally a neglected backyard, filled with rubble and brambles. The new owners wanted a low maintenance garden with no lawn to mow and no flowerbeds to weed. The choice of a Japanese garden came about partly because it is easy to look after and partly because the owners already owned some very attractive ornaments from the Far East that would fit into the scheme.

The plot is typical of most city gardens – long and narrow – but by avoiding any right angles in the new design, its narrowness has been disguised. The planks of the decks were deliberately laid at different angles to form herringbone patterns, and a large stretch of decking given a focal point with a pebbled square containing an elegant bamboo, to enhance the oriental atmosphere.

Unsightly walls have been covered with inexpensive reed matting and pine decking has been installed around the large pond, which creates ever-changing reflections, making up for loss of interest from the limited planting. Although it looks as if the water runs all the way under the decking, this is, in fact, a *trompe l'oeil* – the decking simply juts out over the water.

The children in the family are old enough to cope with the dangers of water and their play needs are catered for imaginatively with a pergola at one end of the plot which doubles as a climbing frame and a support for a hammock.

The planting has been carefully chosen to emphasize the oriental feel to the garden. The bamboos and tall grass-like plants work well in these surroundings. Two original ornamental firethorns were retained but pruned back so severely that this has had an almost 'Bonsai' effect on them, unintentionally producing just the right Japanese feeling. One or two yuccas that were growing well were also left, since they fitted well into the overall design.

1 *Hosta albomarginata*
Miscanthus saccharifloris
Petasites fragrans
2 *Acacia dealbata*
Acer palmatum
Cyperus alternifolius
C. papyrus
3 *Acanthus spinosus*
Arundinaria japonica
Cyperus alternifolius
Fatsia japonica
Nymphaea var.
Scriptus tabernaemontani zebrinus
Tamarix pentandra
Vinca minor
4 *Hedera helix*
Philadelphus × 'Virginal'
Pyracantha atlantanoides

5 *Hedera helix* 'Sagittifolia'
Hosta lancifolia
Ligularia sp.
Mahonia japonica
M. lomariifolia
Yucca gloriosa

SHADY TERRACE

Large slabs of York stone laid in a random pattern and laced with ground cover in miniature – mainly mind-your-own-business (*Helxine solierolii*) – blur the transition from patio to garden proper in this imaginative design which incorporates a small pond as a feature. This patio is heavily shaded and foliage plants rather than flowers have been used to give a predominantly two-tone effect.

A small patio needs much more careful planning than a large one. In this case, the garden was originally on one level, sloping down towards the house. The owner decided to add interest by remaking the site on three levels, of which the patio is now the lowest; there is an upper lawn at the far end of the garden, also used for sitting out. The owner's original intention was to use evergreens both to edge the garden, for ground cover and for special features, so that there was something of interest all year round. The only major exception to this rule is the splash of colour provided by the dwarf *Acer japonicum* and by bold red summer flowers – pelargoniums and busy Lizzies. The latter do surprisingly well on a shady site.

A significant feature of this patio is the clever use of ground cover among the paving stones to soften their edges. The idea could be copied using other mat-forming, low-growing plants, such as chamomile in its prostrate non-flowering form (*Chamaemulum nobile* 'Treneague'), or one of the large family of creeping thymes which give off a heady scent when crushed underfoot. In this garden, ivies have also been used as

ground cover, as has a prostrate juniper (*Juniperus horizontalis*). Provided the patio is not going to be used as a seating area, nor is likely to receive a lot of foot traffic, ground cover plants can also be used successfully to disguise any unevenness in the stones.

Another idea worth borrowing is to leave out a slab of paving stone to make a small pond. In this patio this has been done using a plastic liner. By making the pond slightly larger than the visible area, the plastic edges can be tucked away out of sight under the surrounding flagstones. In this garden, two goldfish happily share the pool with an *Iris laevigata* planted at one edge.

OPPOSITE *and* BELOW *This patio has been cleverly planted using a limited colour palette, majoring on reds and greens. Heavily shaded for most of the day, it features plants that can cope with these conditions –* busy Lizzie (Impatiens *), ferns* (Athyrium filix-femina *),* Begonia semperflorens *and* Hosta fortuneii. *A simple and effective idea is the pond, created by the removal of a single flagstone.*

1 *Acer palmatum* 'Aureum'
Armeria maritima
Hedera colchica
H. helix 'Aureovariegata'
Helxine solierolii
Hosta 'Thomas Hogg'
Lonicera japonica 'Aureoreticulata'
Penstemon var.
Polystichum aculeatum
2 *Begonia semperflorens* var.
Chamaecyparis lawsoniana 'Ellwoodii'
Hedera helix 'Aureovariegata'
Helxine solierolii
Hosta fortunei
Pelargonium × hortorum
Penstemon barbatus
3 *Athyrium filix-femina*
Clematis montana 'Rubens'
Hedera helix 'Glacier'
Impatiens var.
Lonicera periclymenum
Passiflora caerulea
Pelargonium × hortorum
4 *Hedera helix* 'Aureovariegata'
Helxine solierolii
Impatiens var.
Iris pseudacorus
Juniperus horizontalis
5 *Hedera helix* 'Gold Heart'
Parthenocissus quinquefolia
Pelargonium × hortorum
Polystichum aculeatum
Sedum roseum
Wisteria sinensis

Pot grown annuals
Canna indica
Pelargonium × hortorum
Petunia var.
Salvia 'Royal Standard'

CLASSICAL STONE TERRACE

OPPOSITE *In this country patio, bricks have been used very successfully to break up the uniformity of the concrete slabs, providing a natural link with the garden proper and the surrounding old brick walls.*

BELOW *A raised area that catches the morning sun has been softened by a backdrop of* Pyracantha coccinea *and* Hedera helix. *In such an area, scented plants, such as old-fashioned roses and* Dianthus × 'Allwoodii' *grown here, provide a special bonus.*

This tranquil patio, with its border of old-fashioned flowers, has been created in a sheltered corner of a nineteenth-century garden in an area that once housed a plant nursery and kitchen garden. The terrace was made out of a combination of riven York stone for the seating area and more mundane concrete slabs, enlivened by an edging of bricks, for the remainder. A change of level divides the two areas, making a natural break between the different materials.

Near the table and chairs, a simple barbecue has been built from a single stone slab, supported on two large blocks, leaving room beneath to store fuel. But as the terrace gets the morning sun, it is mainly used for breakfast.

Around the patio a mixture of shrubs and perennials have been planted, with special emphasis on evergreens and on silvery grey foliage plants that seem to thrive in the light, fast-draining sandy soil and sunny conditions.

The colour scheme of the planting is based on a foliage framework of grey-green and silver, enhanced by related groupings of pinks and purples or yellows. The containers are planted with annuals, usually in a restricted colour scheme that varies from year to year; the most successful of all, the owners say, was in white, echoing the white-painted Chinese Chippendale style gate that was designed and built to the owners' specification.

The walls of this patio have been used to host a large number of climbing plants – in particular roses and clematis. *Pyracantha coccinea* takes pride of place on the small terrace wall near the house – it produces masses of creamy flowers in summer, and bright berries in winter. It does, however, require pruning from time to time.

1
Hedera helix
Hypericum calycinum
Laurus sp.
Lonicera sp.

2
Escallonia 'Apple Blossom'
Hedera helix 'Marginata'
Petunia var.

3
Campanula sp.
Clematis montana 'Rubens'
Petunia var.
Pyracantha coccinea

4
Alchemilla mollis
Chaenomeles sp.
Hebe sp.
Juniper horizontalis
Lavandula spica
Phlomis fruticosa
Rosa 'Constance Spry'
Rosmarinus officinalis

5
Ballota pseudodictamnus
Centaurea montana
Lysimachia punctata
Stachys lanata
Taxus baccata

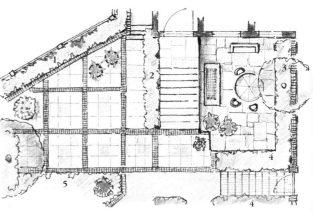

PATIO FOR SUN AND SHADE

Pebbles and granite setts have been used very imaginatively in this well-planned patio, turning what could have been a rather drab suburban plot into an unusual garden that offers sitting out areas for both sun and shade conditions.

The eye focuses upon the circular swirls of paving, helped by strategically placed decorative boulders and an old stone mill wheel. The use of both warm and cool tones for the paving has been cleverly planned to provide a link between the architecture of the house and the planting.

In this patio, which has a very modern look to it, the accent is on foliage plants rather than on flowers, sword-like leaves contrasting with the cylindrical shapes of bushy plants. A variety of foliage colours, ranging from pale green to almost amber, makes up for any loss of flower colour. The great variety of creepers and climbers clothing the walls gives the garden a very mature feel as well as plenty of privacy. The choice of plants has been particularly good.

Ground cover plants, such as ivies (*Hedera*), *Juniperus horizontalis* and *Hypericum calycinum*, have been used in the raised beds, making the garden particularly easy to maintain while providing evergreen colour to contrast with the stone surfaces.

The pergola helps to emphasize the atmosphere of an 'outdoor' room. The idea could have been extended to make a useful ceiling to the path that leads to the back door of the house, if covered with a clear material – heavyweight perspex or glass, for example – to provide shelter.

Overhead lighting fixed to the pergola, and the low lamps set amongst the pebbles, allow the garden to be used in the evening as well as in daytime.

BELOW *Although in heavy shade for large parts of the day, this patio has achieved a well-planted appearance using rhododendrons and ivies. Added interest is provided by the abundant use of climbing plants to soften harsh surfaces and hard edges.*

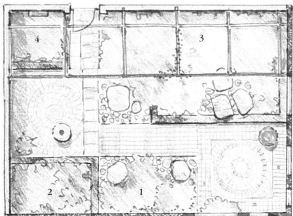

1 *Acer palmatum*
Camellia japonica
Chamaecyparis lawsoniana 'Ellwoodii'
Hedera helix
Hosta lancifolia
Iris sibirica
Juniperus procumbens 'Nana'
Magnolia × soulangiana
Pieris japonica
Sedum reflexum

2 *Armeria maritima*
Hedera helix 'Hibernica'
Magnolia liliiflora
Mahonica japonica
Pachysandra terminalis
Rhododendron sp.

3 *Aucuba japonica* 'Nana Rotundifolia'
Clematis spp.
Cotoneaster spp.
Hypericum calycinum
Juniperus horizontalis 'Glauca'
Lonicera japonica 'Halliana'
Rosa 'Aimée Vibert'
Sarocca humilis
Vitis coignetiae
Wisteria sinensis

4 *Ceanothus arboreus*
Gaultheria procumbens
Juniperus horizontalis 'Wiltonii'
Picea abies procumbens
Pinus mugo
Viburnum davidii

PATIO
CONSTRUCTION

PLANNING THE PATIO

If you are lucky enough to have a patio already, but feel that it needs major refurbishment, there is a lot you can do to improve it without going to massive expense.

The most important element is the patio paving: if it is not good quality, well-laid and in keeping with the house, then you will probably need to renew it – in which case, think carefully whether you even want the patio in that position (see p. 8). On the other hand, if only a few paving stones are loose, you could probably rebed these quite easily (see p. 147). Try to use your imagination in cases like this. If the patio has no water feature, for example, why not make a small pond in place of the removed stone, using a butyl liner (see p. 75)? Or even remove a few more, to make a simple water channel.

If the patio surface is even, but simply not to your liking – ugly concrete for example – then you could consider laying a new surface such as decking over the top (see p. 54).

Many other minor problems of an existing patio can be quite easily overcome with a little ingenuity. A high or ugly side wall, for example, could be part-mirrored to reflect more light into the garden. Alternatively, different kinds of *trompe l'oeil* effects could be created to distract attention from the wall, a special arch could be painted on it to give depth to the garden and make the wall appear to recede.

If you are not able to carry out any major restructuring (if you are in rented accommodation, for example), then you can create a surprisingly wide range of different effects with screens – both vertical and overhead – and with lighting to focus on a special plant in a container or a statue, perhaps drawing the eye away from an unattractive feature of the garden.

Even brilliant white paint can transform an otherwise unattractive wall, and makes a good backcloth for plants. If you are unable even to paint a wall, why not fix white-painted trellis to it on which you could grow a range of climbing plants. If you are a short-term tenant, grow the plants in the largest tubs you can find so that you can take them with you when you move. Alternatively, plant annual climbers like nasturtiums (*Tropaeolum*) and sweet peas (*Lathyrus odoratus*).

PLANNING A NEW PATIO

Before you get out the graph paper and start planning a patio from scratch, think fairly carefully first about the following points. When will you want to use the patio, and how many people are likely to be using it?

Do you want the patio in full sun or in partial shade, or even both? Is the area immediately behind the house necessarily the best place? If not, there is nothing to stop you having a patio at the far end of the garden.

How much time are you prepared to spend in the garden? Do you go away for periods of the year, and are the plants going to have to cope without attention during that time?

What are the principal assets of the garden as it stands? Is there a tree of singular beauty, for example, that would be worth retaining. Finally, what does your house look like? Is it modern, old, or a mishmash of architectural styles?

In answer to all these questions, it seems to me that first of all the patio *must* be functional – large enough to accommodate comfortably the people who will use it regularly; secondly, it must also be possible to use it after dark, so it should be lit in some way, and some part of it should therefore have overhead protection to enable you to use it whatever the weather. Finally, it must look as striking as possible, all year round.

Before you start, do think carefully about your own lifestyle and taste, and about the decoration, internal and external, of any building that adjoins the patio, so that you can make sure the style of the patio is in keeping with them.

The next step is to take a series of polaroids or black and white photographs of the proposed site of the patio, from as many angles as possible. Then sketch in on the photos using a chinagraph pencil any particular features you want to include to give some kind of 3D image of the new patio. Draw up the principle measurements of the patio on graph paper and mark off all the existing structures, not forgetting any drainpipes, manhole covers and so on that you may wish to disguise or equally avoid when building. Then fill in the major features, to scale: if you draw them out individually to scale first on plain paper and

This elegant and unusual patio shows how good design and careful planning make their impact. The furnishings, flooring and framework of the overhead screen are all in blending tones. The plants have been grouped together where they provide an interesting backcloth without cluttering up the main seating area, and were carefully chosen for their interesting leaf forms. An overhead vine provides welcome shelter from the sun.

For a really low maintenance patio, a combination of easy-to-care-for surfacing and ground cover plants and shrubs are essential. Raised beds – in this case large stone troughs – require less watering than smaller containers. A nice feature of this north European patio is that planting has been planned to echo the form and colours of the surrounding conifers.

Anyone who wants a truly easy-to-maintain patio should opt for flowering shrubs rather than annuals or perennials, but with a little forethought it is still possible to have something in bloom all year round. It is a good idea to start off with a skeleton of reliable evergreens, chosen with an eye for their foliage – the spikes of *Yucca gloriosa*, for instance, can be planted to contrast with the indented leaves of *Fatsia japonica* to give the patio an almost tropical appearance. Or a slender conifer, such as *Juniperus pyramidalis*, which will grow no more than 2m/6ft 6in high, can be used as a feature.

Buy your plants in containers rather than raising them from seed or cuttings. Choose specimens that are well grown, picking short, sturdy plants rather than spindly ones; they will soon catch up once they are in the ground. To keep weeding down to a bare minimum, plant them slightly closer together than is normal and underplant them with mat-forming ground-cover plants.

The general appearance of the patio should be natural and informal, with loose, rather than rigidly marked out, edges; straight, manicured ones will all too quickly show neglect. So look for trailing plants to blur the outlines of beds and containers.

High level sites

Patio gardens at high levels pose special problems. Exposure is one of the worst problems you have to contend with; prevailing winds and turbulence can play havoc with plants at this level. You may, of course, escape ordinary ground frost, but air frosts can be just as damaging and, in good weather, the sun's rays will tend to scorch the plants.

The best way to tackle air turbulence is not to have a solid wall around a roof patio, but a pierced wall or fence instead: trellis, netting or pierced concrete blocks are all suitable.

When constructing a roof garden or terrace patio there is an important factor you must take into account – the weight of the materials used. Check before you start that your roof or balcony is strong enough to take the combined weight of soil, paving, pots, furniture and so on. The weakest part of a roof or terrace is likely to be the centre, so bear this in mind when siting anything heavy. The average flat roof that

limited. The flooring is an important consideration – use large slabs or a solid surface rather than small items, such as bricks or tiles, which might lift. Avoid using gravel or granite chips because they require constant grooming and weeds have a tendency to poke their way through in the early stages before the material is compacted by wear.

Watering is one of the most time-consuming chores on a well-planted patio. It is essential to water thoroughly – too little is worse than none at all, since the roots of the plants tend to come to the surface to look for moisture, and wither and die. For the gardener who is pushed for time, an automatic watering system is the best solution.

Unless you are prepared to put in such a system, plants in small containers should be ruled out. As with gardens in strong sunlight or dry shade, an effective alternative is moisture-retaining raised beds.

High level patios can present considerable problems with strong winds and air frosts. Screening is essential from prevailing winds but should be at just the right height to protect the plants without spoiling the view. The informal and vibrant 'cottage garden' style of planting makes a good contrast with the stark forms of the buildings on the New York skyline.

has been designed to be walked on cannot usually stand more than about 30cm/12in of soil, taking into account that it becomes heavier when wet. Peat or vermiculite, which are much lighter, can be used instead of ordinary soil. Other weight savings can be made by making retaining walls out of peat blocks or tufa stone and using lightweight plant containers made of polystyrene or compressed cellulose.

The most convenient way to get soil up to a balcony or roof is to buy it already bagged, but grow bags can also be used. These can be replenished with fertilizer for two or three seasons before being discarded.

A roof garden or balcony needs shallow-rooting plants that are tenacious enough to stay put in high winds. Climbers need special care, especially clematis, which has tender roots. Of all the climbers, Russian vine (*Polygonum baldshuanicum*) grows the fastest and needs least care, though plants that cling to a structure, such as Virginia creeper (*Parthenocissus quinquefolia*), fare best in high winds once they have become established. In general, deciduous climbers tend to do better than evergreens, and are less seriously affected by winter cold and wind.

Sometimes the existing surface of the roof is covered in an unsuitable material for a patio surface – for example, bituminous compound, which tends to melt in the sun. Bearing this in mind, plus the fact that you may have to examine the structure of the roof from time to time, a good solution is to use wooden decking laid in modules which can easily be lifted (see p. 75). The decking will also help to spread the weight of any containers or furniture. Finally, remember the safety aspect when planning a roof garden. Some sort of stout guard rail, properly fixed, is essential and it will also have the advantage of enclosing the roof garden, making it less exposed and more like a room.

PAVED SURFACES

Herringbone

Basketweave

Brick patterns
When laying bricks, it is a good idea to work the pattern out to scale first on a plan, to find out if there are any obstacles. A basketweave brick pattern is relatively simple to lay successfully. Slightly more difficult is a herringbone pattern.

RIGHT AND OPPOSITE *A good demonstration of how similar materials can be used to achieve strikingly different results. With the patio, right, the formal lines of the brickwork have been used to emphasize the squared-off appearance of the patio. In the patio opposite, random patterns of bricks have been used to create an informal effect, enhanced by the 'loose' planting scheme, giving a romantic feel to the garden and breaking up a large expanse of hard surface.*

The surface of your patio is probably the single highest expenditure you will make on the garden and it is important to choose materials that blend with their surroundings. This applies not only to the texture but to the colour, too. It will pay in the long run to use the best quality paving material you can afford – it is better to pave a small area well than a large area badly. But first make sure the site is properly prepared or you may have to deal with loose or uneven paving later.

When planning the size of the patio, always make it a little larger than you think you will need. Ideally, aim to allow at least 3sq m/32sq ft per person for the first three people and 2sq m/21½sq ft for each additional person. For a family of four, this means a patio area of approximately 3 × 3.7m/10 × 12ft. If you are planning to have patio furniture other than seats, then you will have to allocate more space. If your requirements change over the years, it should be possible to extend an existing patio. The difficulties here are matching the surface levels of the original and new paving and the colour difference between the older, weathered material and the new, so be generous to start.

If your patio butts up against an existing building, take care that the top surface of the paving is at least 5cm/2in below the damp-proof course. On the

WOODEN DECKING

The use of wood for decking, walkways and bridges can give a refreshingly different, innovative look to a patio garden. A raised deck usually requires the service of professionals to build and instal but avoids many of the problems, such as excavation and level surfaces, associated with working in solid materials. It is also the best way of spanning uneven terrain of any type. Drainage does not usually cause a problem and, because small gaps are left between the wooden planking, you do not need to build in a slope to encourage water run-off.

Patio decks staggered terrace-fashion down a slope from a house can form useful areas for dining or for guests to congregate at parties. Decking installed flush with a lawned area can form a durable, low-maintenance patio that doubles as a play area for children. Using this type of material, scattered points at different levels of the garden can be brought into use with minimum disturbance to plants and trees.

Decking harmonizes particularly well with country surroundings and, especially, with houses set among trees. It is equally good as a surface for a roof garden, since it is not too heavy and the slats can be placed, on a low framework, over a bitumastic surface of the kind often found on flat roofs. Because it blends in so well with all forms of architecture it is suitable for use with both new and older properties. Wooden decking is also resilient, looks and feels warmer underfoot and yet does not become as hot as stone or concrete in strong sunlight.

The major disadvantage of decking is that, unless you live near a cheap and convenient source of timber, it can be surprisingly expensive to buy and have installed. Hardwoods, such as redwood, oak, teak or the less-expensive African hardwoods, are best. If you use softwood, it must be treated beforehand with a preservative. Whatever timber you choose, it must not only be hardwearing and relatively splinter-proof, but must also be resistant to any tendency to warp despite the adverse conditions it will face. This means buying more-expensive, well-seasoned material. Fastenings, too, can be expensive for they must be galvanized or made of copper or brass to avoid staining and discolouring the wood.

Decking can be used successfully to span several different levels. In this example it has been used as a bridge as well, linking two separate areas. Bleached by the sun, the wood blends well with the stone of the patio.

FINISHES AND ACCESSORIES

If you are planning only a small area of decking, the wood is best laid in a straightforward design, but larger areas can be built in a variety of interesting patterns. One of the most successful designs is when the planks are laid diagonally, and another is when a herringbone pattern is used. If the wood is being made up into square modules, they can be laid over the supporting timbers with the planks running alternate ways to achieve a parquet effect. The planks can also be nailed diagonally, radiating like the spokes of a wheel – this is especially pleasing when the decking is constructed around an existing tree. This same basic module construction will allow you to create a diamond pattern.

Once the decking is in place, you have the perfect platform on which to construct a range of different utility storage lockers, perhaps for garden tools or children's toys, a built-in sandpit, flower boxes, or integral seating. As well as being entirely practical, these accessories also help to break up a large expanse of otherwise plain wood. Construction of the facing boards and lid should be out of the wood used for the decking.

DECK CONSTRUCTION

Some types of decking can be built by a skilled do-it-yourselfer, but the higher the deck is raised off the ground, the more ability is required. Professional help will certainly be required if you are planning to build over sandy or water-logged soil or on any unstable base. It may then be necessary to drive piles into the ground as supports and the cost will be high, too. You will also almost certainly have to obtain local planning permission and conform to building codes or regulations. Also take into account that in some climates the structure will have to bear the weight of snow, which can be considerable.

Ground decking

Some provision must be made for air to circulate under decking laid at ground level. One way to solve the problem is to use square modules. Nail the wood of the decking on to a framework of 5 × 5cm/2 × 2in

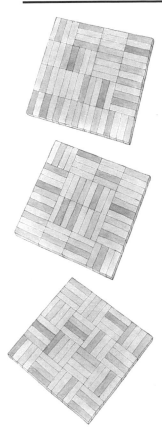

Decking patterns

Making decking up into individual modules (see opposite) gives you the opportunity of varying the appearance of your patio or terrace. Avoiding long, straight runs also means that any slight discrepancies in module construction are not so apparent, since spaces between planks will not have to align with those of all other modules.

A series of broad, decked steps creates exciting changes in level in this steeply sloping garden. Suspended as it is above the ground, the decking brings various areas of the garden into use without disturbing the planting.

This simple small-scale decking shows how modules can be used to pinpoint changes in direction. Ground-level decking like this could be constructed without professional help, and in this setting it gives a very attractive oriental look to the garden.

Constructing modules

Decking modules 53.5cm/21in square can be made from 10 × 2.5cm/4 × 1in planking on a framework of 5cm/2in square battens, and by lifting and turning them round you can change the shape or appearance of a decked area with relative ease. Utility items, built to the same basic module design and complete in themselves, can be moved around at will to make seating, planters for temporary flower displays, or children's play areas where you most need them.

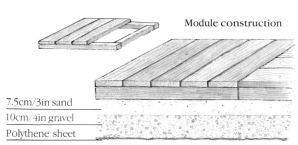

Module construction

7.5cm/3in sand
10cm/4in gravel
Polythene sheet

Storage and utility modules

These should be built out of the same material as the decking so that they blend well. Build the side panels of sand boxes, storage units and planters out of 20 × 3.8cm/8 × 1½ in wood to give you a good usable depth. If hinges are being used make sure they finish flush with the surface, and line the inside of planters with waterproof material to prevent the bottom decking from rotting.

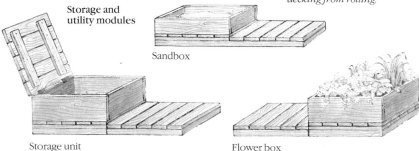

Storage and utility modules

Sandbox

Storage unit

Flower box

wood, dipped or treated with preservative. You can then lay the modules, in any of a variety of different patterns, on a bed of polythene sheeting, covered by a 10cm/4in layer of sand. If the decking is to be laid just above the ground, it is advisable to put down a sheet of thick polythene, too, both to keep constant damp off the underside of the wood and to smother any weeds that might otherwise grow up underneath and sprout between the planking.

Using wooden decking which has been pre-constructed into square modules not only makes the job of laying the deck easier, but gives you great flexibility, too, in what you do with it. If the modules are screwed rather than nailed into place on their supports, they can be taken up from time to time and switched around – giving a herringbone-style effect, for instance, if they are diagonally patterned. Modules can be switched around too, to avoid wear and tear, so that areas that get the most amount of traffic can be replaced after a while with modules that are in a corner that is seldom used. If you are working in modules, it pays to make any built-in furniture on the same scale and screw that into place so that, once again, it can be moved around to suit your changing needs (see below left).

Raised decking

Decking is usually built on joists, like domestic flooring, and these should be at least 5 × 15cm/ 2 × 6in and 46cm/18in or closer apart. The joists, in turn, are carried on beams, the number and size of which are governed by the distance to be spanned. The beams can be fixed to the house at one end and to posts at the other. Alternatively, they can be away from the house, resting on a wall or posts, which will need to be set in a deep, concrete foundation. Any deck more than 46cm/18in above ground level should have a railing around it.

Wooden rails are usually chosen to edge a deck, but for a different look, especially if you have a water feature in the garden (see p. 72), try the effect of a handrail made from heavy rope, threaded through brass eyes on wooden posts, set at intervals along the deck. This nautical look goes well with the deck planking and is all you need if the area is not used by young children.

WALLS, FENCES AND SCREENS

In many town patios you may have a mixture of wall and fencing, as in this example, and a generous planting of climbers has disguised this fact while helping to 'lose' the boundaries of the patio.

It is important to define the boundary of your patio, even if you use nothing more than a simple windbreak, otherwise you will have the feeling that you are sitting on a stage rather than enjoying at least the illusion of privacy. A solid brick wall or a close-boarded fence provides complete protection, but these can be expensive to build, shut out too much light and cause turbulence and downdraughts in certain situations. A pierced wall, slatted fence or more informal screen can be a better choice.

TYPES OF WALL

Walls of brick or stone are the strongest and last for a long time, but they are also the most expensive type to build. All walls need footings – a shallow trench with a firm, level base – to stand on. Brick and concrete block walls must have a concrete base, but a dry stone wall can be built on a compacted earth base as long as the wall is not higher than 75cm/30in.

The cost of brick walls can be kept down by using single-thickness open brickwork, which also lets in

A pale-coloured high wall looks less solid and menacing than dark brick and helps to 'bounce' light into rooms that might otherwise be dark and gloomy. By painting the wall cream instead of white, you tend to cut down on glare.

Types of wall

A solid brick wall is strongest but can cause downdraughts and eddies around its base. A better choice is often pierced brickwork. Pierced concrete is best used in small runs and, like pierced brickwork, lets in light and air to grow plants.

Solid brick

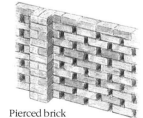

Pierced brick

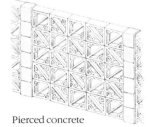

Pierced concrete

light and air. An open English bond, staggered cross openings and a honeycomb effect are all feasible designs, but if you leave too many openings, the wall will not be strong enough and may break up in a hard winter. Pierced brick walls will need piers built in them every 3–3.5m/10–12ft; solid walls will need piers every 1.8–3m/6–10ft, if you use 11.5cm/4½in wide bricks.

One way to avoid buttressing a wall in this way is to overlap or zig-zag it so that you do not get long, straight runs. In solid walls the strongest bonds are the running bond, where the outer edge of the bricks in one row meet over the centre of the bricks in the rows below and above, and English bond, where one row of bricks is laid side-on and the next row head-on.

Walls of brick or light blocks up to 1m/3ft high need a 7.5cm/3in concrete base, 30cm/12in wide. Use a 6:1 sand and cement mix for the job. Stone walls built with mortar need the same foundation as brick walls. Make sure the wall is perfectly vertical and straight; a wavy wall looks bad and is not strong. Any wall higher then 90cm/36in is best left to a professional. Walls should be capped either with bricks laid on edge or concrete coping to prevent frost damage.

Stone walling

Although difficult to lay, stone walling is very attractive in the right setting. If you are planning a stone wall of any height, it is best to obtain the services of a specialist craftsman. Dressed stone is expensive, and so most garden walls are built from rougher quarry stone instead. Dry stone walls (ones that are not held together with mortar) should be slightly narrower at the top than the bottom and the base should be at least one-third as thick as the height. The rough stones will come in all shapes and sizes and before starting to build you should sort them into piles of large, medium and small. Use large stones for the base and make it two stones thick, best set in sand on top of hardcore. As you lay the stones, ram earth behind and between

Concrete block wall

Walls made from concrete blocks are simple to construct but can look unattractive unless painted or heavily planted with climbers. The centres of the concrete blocks are hollow, allowing steel reinforcing rods to be inserted for extra strength.

Reinforcing rods

Concrete blocks

them. Put in some 'through' stones, running from one face of the wall to the other, to bind and strengthen the structure. Omit face stones every now and again to provide spaces in which to grow trailing plants or alpines. A dry stone wall more than 1m/3ft high should incorporate some mortar for extra strength. This can be done without losing the dry stone effect by using a 4:1 mortar mix for filling gaps on the inside parts of the wall where it will not show.

Concrete blocks

The cheapest and easiest type of patio wall to build is made from concrete blocks. As well as being strong and able to take a lot of weight, they are available with an ornamental rock-like face, or made from reconstituted stone. Also available are cavity blocks, known

Trellis gives at least the illusion of privacy around the patio but, at the same time, lets in air and light, which the plants beneath the wall will need. Openwork fencing of this type can also be used to hide ugly views or walls beyond.

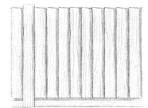

Closeboard

Picket

Diagonal board

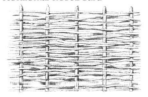

Horizontal closeboard

Wattle hurdle

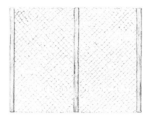

Brick with wooden trellis

Wire netting

Types of fencing
Closeboard fencing gives the most privacy but tends to be rather dull unless well planted. Picket fencing looks very orderly and has a country atmosphere about it. Wattle hurdle is not robust but it is suitable for short runs. Diagonal board fencing gives a more sophisticated look and is visually suited to long runs. Wooden trellis can be attached to fences or brick walls for additional height. Wire netting is maintenance-free, but it needs to be stretched and secured carefully.

Posts for fencing
These should be securely fixed in concrete on a hardcore base. A useful alternative is a metal spike with a 'cup' on top, into which the post is secured. This keeps the wood out of contact with the ground and so lessens the likelihood of rot. It is, however, more expensive if you have a long run of fencing to erect. The metal spike is also useful if you have to replace a rotten fence post. Instead of having to dig all the old concrete out, you can simply hammer the spike into the rotten stump and then secure the new post.

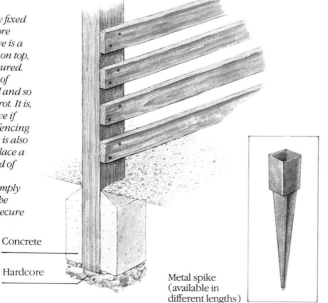

Concrete

Hardcore

Metal spike (available in different lengths)

as 'breeze' blocks, which are quick and easy to lay but rather unattractive. These, however, can be rendered smooth, or trellis, on which plants can be supported, can be fixed to cover the face. All concrete block walls require the same foundations as brick walls.

FENCE TYPES

Fences are usually much cheaper than walls but cannot be expected to last as long. Open fences – wire netting, chain link and lattice – let you see the view but also let in cold winds. Chain link is difficult to erect neatly as it is springy and tends to unravel. It comes in plain, ungalvanized metal or with coloured plastic-coated finishes. Wire netting is cheaper but sags easily and looks untidy. Lattice fencing, made from wood lathes, looks better but is not as strong as metal link.

The most usual type of open wooden fencing is the picket fence made with planks, sometimes with decorative carved tops, spaced fairly widely apart on rails top and bottom. The picket itself is supported by heavier wooden posts sunk into the ground. Palisade fencing is similar, but the planks are closer together. Both types are usually painted.

Solid fences

Closeboard, interlock and interwoven wooden fences are stronger than open fences but they are more expensive. Privacy and shelter on the patio are improved but at the cost of some loss of sunlight.

Closeboard fencing consists of made-up panels of vertical boards, each board overlapping the one next to it. This is the most expensive form of fencing and the boards are usually made of a hardwood such as oak. A much cheaper form of solid fencing is lapped panel fencing. These boards have wavy edges, which run horizontally within a frame of 2m/6ft panels. They are ready nailed and come in heights from 1m/3ft to 2m/6ft. Interwoven fence panels are made from thin strips of wood, woven like ribbon in front of and behind supporting uprights.

Wattle hurdles, usually made from willow, are another type of panel fencing. They can be used to give a very attractive rustic appearance but are not long-lasting. Hurdles are useful, however, for providing temporary shelter for a young hedge until it is fully established.

OPPOSITE White-painted trellis has been used to give the illusion of a gazebo in the corner of the patio. In fact, it consists of two simple screens linked by a mock pediment.

Fence building

Many types of fencing now come in ready-made panels or in kit form, but with a little ingenuity you can construct a really individual-looking fence for the patio. But no matter how good the fence looks, it is basically only as strong as the posts that support it. These should be made from solid hardwood – oak or larch is best – at least 7.5 × 7.5cm/3 × 3in for close boarding or 10 × 10cm/4 × 4in for open fences. The posts should be set at least 56cm/22in into a concrete foundation. If you are setting posts directly into the ground, put a little hardcore down first for drainage. There are also different types of metal slips and spikes, which can be used to drive the posts into the ground and, at the same time, protect the wood from rot. All fences need maintaining with a wood preservative that will not harm plants, and the base of any wooden posts in contact with the ground should be soaked in it before they are set up.

USING SCREENS

Screening can be used effectively either around the edges of a patio, much like a fence or low wall, in order to separate it from the rest of the garden, or actually on the patio itself. Here you can use screens to break up the patio space into dining, sunbathing or, perhaps, children's playing areas. On an exposed site, well-secured screens can also act as a very efficient windbreak, providing protection and shelter for both people and tender plants.

Another use for screens is when you want temporary effects only, or where you do not want anything that is too thick or solid. They are also convenient when you are renting the property and do not want to invest too much money in the garden.

Nearly all gardens have small unattractive areas, such as bins, storage cupboards or oil storage tanks, that could be effectively hidden from view behind a screen. Bear in mind that the nearer the screen is to

Screening can be used with great success within a patio garden to define one area and make it more intimate for, say, dining or sunbathing. Here a pergola over which climbers have been trained, together with tall plants interspersed at intervals in line with it, have been used to divide the larger expanse of the patio, creating some shelter and privacy near the house without spoiling the view of the garden.

the house, and to your eyeline, the more it will hide –
so do not erect it down at the far end of the garden.

Squared trellis (more stable than the diamond-
shaped type) can make an attractive screen, as can
split cane, but both require a solid supporting frame.
Screening, which is usually light, can behave like a sail
in high winds, so do not skimp on the supporting
structure. Probably the cheapest screening of all is
plastic-covered netting, which can be surprisingly
effective if you choose a rigid variety and then cover it
with evergreen climbers.

A much stronger, more permanent screen can be
made from pierced concrete patterned blocks, which
are available in interesting textures, shapes and
colours. Easier to erect and cheaper than pierced
brick, this type of screen looks best with modern
rather than period architecture. It is by far the most
expensive form of screening material, and should only
be considered if you want the screening permanently
in place. Pierced concrete screening is laid on a
foundation similar to brick. As a general rule, it should
have strengthening pillars (supplied with the blocks)
at 3m/10ft intervals.

Types of open screening
*Decorative open screening
need not be expensive or heavy
in its construction. Bamboo
looks very good and can be
used, too, to disguise a less-
than-perfect fence or wall.
Trellis can be painted or left
natural and makes an
attractive frame for flowers.
Battening, fixed close together,
is a more unusual choice.*

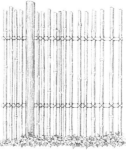

Bamboo

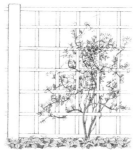

Trellis   Battening

BUILT-IN FURNITURE

Circular seat

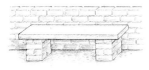

Brick and concrete bench

Built-in furniture
Simple built-in furniture for a patio could include a very useful circular seat constructed around a tree or a bench, consisting of brick supporting columns and a plain concrete slab, built against a convenient side wall.

The cost of good-quality (and therefore long-lasting) garden and patio furniture can be prohibitive. Often, a cheaper and better alternative is to integrate such items with the overall patio or terrace design by building them in right from the beginning. For maximum flexibility, however, the ideal situation is a mix of some built-in and some movable items.

PROJECT SUGGESTIONS

The success of built-in furniture depends, to a large extent, on it blending naturally with existing features. If, for example, your patio has a tree growing up through it, then a circular seat, made from slatted wood, built around it could make the tree even more of a feature – a perfect place to congregate for evening drinks or to find shade on a hot day. If you are dealing with decking (see p. 54), which is an extremely flexible material to work with, then built-in furniture seems to be an obvious choice. Benches can be built into outside rails, or even permanent eating areas designed and made from the same material as the decking itself, helping to create a practical and stylish environment.

When constructing solid side walls, it is relatively simple to build in some useful bench seating. At this stage, any brick supporting pillars can be tied into the brickwork quite naturally, creating a visually pleasing and structurally sound result. Bench seating of this type could also incorporate useful storage space, where garden tools or any other small items could be conveniently placed out of the way until needed in the garden (see p. 146).

This curved wooden seat built into a decked patio doubles as a safety rail, shielding patio users from the drop below. A seat of this type involves steaming the wooden slats to produce the curve, and you would probably need professional help.

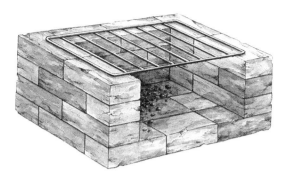

Temporary brick barbecue
An attractive temporary barbecue can be quickly put together in any convenient corner of the patio. Using approximately 35 bricks only, a barbecue about 30cm/12in
high can be built, with a grilling area of 45 × 30cm/ 18 × 12in. A suitably sized griller can be bought or made to order. Leave bricks unmortared so that the structure can be dismantled.

A permanent barbecue is not essential. A simple slab set on concrete blocks, above, makes a platform on which to site barbecue grills. This arrangement can quickly be dismantled and stored away out of season. Alternatively, a built-in barbecue pit, right, is not only safer from the point of view of fire risk but also makes a focal point in a patio, surrounded as it is, in this case, by integral seating – amphitheatre style.

A close-boarded fence constructed around a patio (see p. 58) can be used to host a series of storage cupboards. These can be built unobtrusively in front of the fence to protect such items as a bicycle or a lawnmower from the rain. To help the cupboards blend, build the fascias out of the same close-boarding as the fence. A quick-growing climber could also be trained over them in a very short time.

Possibly the simplest and most useful piece of built-in furniture is a barbecue. This could be incorporated into a side wall as soon as the patio flooring is complete. But a barbecue does not have to be built along conventional lines with permanent benches and a table tacked on almost as an afterthought. If space permits, you can construct a barbecue pit instead, with curved seating incorporated into the basic design (see left). For a smaller patio, a perfectly adequate temporary barbecue can be quickly erected from loose bricks or, better, concrete blocks, and then dismantled again afterwards. Concrete blocks are better because fewer are needed to get the barbecue up to a comfortable height for cooking on. A built-in plant trough somewhere near the barbecue area could be used to grow herbs for cooking.

Built-in furniture, provided it is properly positioned, can make the apparent size of the patio larger; a bench against an end wall, for example, takes up less space than a free-standing arrangement. It can be useful for a children's play area, too – a sandpit can easily be built into the floor of a patio, and could later become a square or rectangular pool when the children have grown up and no longer need it. A climbing frame built into the patio, provided it is sited in a corner rather than in the centre, can become a rose-covered arbour in later years.

At the very least, consider making some shelves on the patio just outside the kitchen or sitting room door. These will prove very useful if you need somewhere to deposit food or drinks *en route* from the house to the garden. Supports can be fixed to the floor if planned for at the early stages of patio construction.

OVERHEAD SHELTER

Adding some form of overhead cover to your patio immediately turns it into more of an outdoor room. A roof structure, even if it is quite an open one, will help to define the area of the patio while retaining an open, outdoor feel. If it extends beyond the bounds of the patio itself, it will make the whole area appear much larger; if it is combined with a fence or wall, it can make a charmingly secluded and private place.

An overhead shelter can be used as a visual link between the house and the patio or other areas, such as a car port. But, as with paving (see p. 48), the materials used must suit the general look of the house and garden. Rustic arches, for example, would not be ideal in the setting of an ultra-modern house.

THE STRUCTURE

Care should be taken when planning a pergola or other overhead shelter attached to the house itself. There is a danger that it will make the indoor rooms darker, especially if you cover it completely with some sort of material to keep the rain out or if you grow a heavy evergreen climber over it. On the other hand, if the rooms are particularly sunny, you may appreciate the extra shade provided by a roof shelter on hot, summer days. If more of a garden room is required, then it may be best to invest in a lean-to glass structure instead.

The simplest overhead structure to build is roofing material running from a house wall to posts set in the garden beyond the patio. Beams set across the tops of the posts are then used to support rafters.

The size and spacing of the rafters depends on what the roof is used for. If it is purely for its visual appeal, they can be light and well spaced. But once you start adding even short pieces of wood to them to form an attractive grid pattern, you increase the overall weight that has to be carried and you may, therefore, need heavier rafters or space them closer together. Bear in mind, too, that if you plan to train climbing plants over the frame, the vegetation of a mature climber can be surprisingly heavy. If you are in any doubt, err on the side of safety and make the structure stronger than you think it needs to be. As an added precaution, call in professional advice.

Any form of overhead screening immediately changes a patio into an outdoor living area. In this example, a variety of attractive climbers have been trained underneath clear plastic roofing material. Plants crammed into close proximity in this way need watching carefully for infestations of aphids, red spider or fungal diseases, which tend to spread quickly in these conditions.

Dressing the structure

A climber, such as wisteria or Virginia creeper (*Parthenocissus quinquefolia*), that drops its leaves in autumn gives you the best of both worlds when trained on an overhead structure – shade in the summer and a clear space overhead in winter to let in precious sunshine. As an alternative to climbers, or perhaps while waiting for these to become established, ceiling laths or split bamboo canes make attractive shelter overhead. The laths have a pleasant natural look about them and they can be obtained from some specialist building merchants (they are used for repairing old ceilings and walls) or from demolition sites. Being so thin, they are very prone to rotting and must be treated with a preservative. Both laths and split bamboo can be nailed to light frames and dropped into place on the roof structure in summer when you need the shade, then removed or moved around in winter to let in any sunshine. And you can turn each frame in a different direction to vary the shade pattern.

Waterproof coverings

A canvas awning makes an attractive overhead shade, but it will cut out a great deal of light. An alternative – which provides both shade and some rain protection – is heavy-duty translucent plastic sheeting material with reinforcing thread buried inside it. This material has a pleasant, slightly rough, natural look, it is relatively inexpensive, cuts out harsh sun and gives protection from rain. It is usually available in blue or white. To fix the plastic, all you need do is attach one edge to the house end of your structure, then drape it over the framework. It is then possible to fix a batten to the front edge and instal a system of pulleys and cords, so that the plastic can be pulled back at will, from ground level, when you want the roof open to the sky.

Fully rainproof shelter for a patio is best made with glass or heavy plastic sheets, although if you have plants growing on the patio you may prefer to leave part of the roof open to let the rain water them naturally. One reason for wanting this type of protective covering is to provide an area you can work in

This corner of a patio looked rather bare until a few container-grown plants were added to give it an instant mature look. Flowers grown in pots can be used in the same way to bring a splash of colour to any part of the patio, just where it is needed. Plants with a cascading habit will also tend to disguise the fact they are in pots.

Despite the fact that large containers make the most impact, small ones can be used effectively in some places – up the side of a flight of steps, for instance, or lined up on a window sill. They can be massed together, too, for an effect like a miniature garden, just where they can be seen best.

A permanent cluster of pots can even have its own self-watering system. The simplest method is to use a narrow-gauge, specially made hose that 'weeps' water in small quantities whenever a valve, with its own wick in the soil, opens to let some water through. Alter-

natively, a permanent large-scale planting around a patio could be plumbed into the water system with a fine perforated copper pipe running along a wall behind and hidden from view. This would automatically spray the plants whenever the connecting tap is turned on.

MAKING A RAISED BED

Raised beds are an effective way of decorating a patio with small plants, such as alpines, because the specimens can be easily seen when displayed in this

way. A point to remember when constructing raised beds is that proper drainage is vital if the plants are not to become waterlogged. This may mean installing weep holes – short lengths of tubing – near the base of the bed at 50cm/20in intervals to act as drains. A raised bed that is too small, however, will tend to dry out quickly and needs constant watering. The best height for a raised bed is about 45cm/18in if it is not to dominate the patio. A width of about the same measurement should give you plenty of scope for interesting planting.

Raised beds can be made from many materials. Apart from brick, stone or concrete, railway sleepers and other heavy forms of wooden planking can be used, but make sure these are treated with preservative. If weight is important, such as on a roof terrace, then peat blocks can be used instead.

The retaining wall of a raised bed has to stand up to considerable pressure from the soil behind it. If the bed is large and high, a wall made from bricks should have concrete foundations at least 40cm/16in deep, and be built with a backward slope of 1:12.

A stone trough in this setting blends in well with a raised bed behind it, giving the effect of mature planting, showing the natural affinity these materials have with plants and with each other.

Railway sleepers

Dry stone

Retaining brickwork

Sand/peat/loam mixture

Pea gravel

Concrete patio base

Types of raised bed
Railway sleepers are long-lasting and make good strong containers. Leave small gaps between the planks at the bottom for drainage. Low, dry stone walls look good when planted with small creeping plants. A retaining wall of brick round the patio can be turned into a raised bed if you build two walls, one brick thick, with a bed of soil between them. All raised beds should be filled with free-draining material and soil, as shown.

WATER FEATURES

OPPOSITE *Water has become the main feature for this small decked patio garden, with lilies and reeds providing interest in two dimensions. The overall effect is that of a lush green jungle swamp.*

There are many ways in which water can be used in a patio garden for dramatic effect. Not only does its movement provide constant interest and variety but water can also act as a mirror, reflecting the sky, neighbouring plants and, sometimes, any buildings beyond. A water feature can also have the effect of making the patio area seem larger than it actually is. When planning such a feature you can choose a simple pond or a more elaborate fountain in a basin, or an ornamental mask, perhaps mounted on a wall, from which water trickles down into a container below. Very effective also, when space is limited, is water rippling over a base of cobble stones, made possible by a hidden pump. And a narrow canal, either bisecting or edging a patio, can do much to enliven an area of paving.

Bear safety in mind when planning a water feature, especially if you have young children. You may need to build a retaining wall to surround the pond, or net the surface if you cannot be there to supervise.

Water has been used very attractively in this garden to distract the eye from its long narrow shape and to provide interest on the edge of the patio. A bridge leads into a winding path beside heavily planted beds.

LOOKING AT OPTIONS

Even the smallest patio can have a water feature – one slab on a paved terrace can be removed, for example, and the gap made into a mini-pond using a plastic liner (see p. 75). This is best done when the patio is being built. Or you could simply make a hollow in one corner in which to grow marginal plants, such as cottongrass and marsh marigold. If, however, your patio is affected by frost, a shallow pond may freeze solid and is not suitable for plants or fish. To prevent this, you could instal a pond heater during the winter months.

Anything that will hold water can be used as an instant pond, but some containers are better than others. A discarded water cistern, for example, can be set into paving, its edges softened by ground-cover plants, or could be featured in a raised bed. A half barrel, a tub or an urn can be filled with water and then planted with miniature water lilies, which will thrive in cramped conditions. Old stone sinks, too, can be plugged and then pressed into service as a shallow pool. Old coppers, on the other hand, do not make such a versatile option, since copper is toxic to both plants and fish.

On a small patio, a fountain needs to be sited with care. It is important that the cascade rises no higher than the radius between the fountain itself and the edge of the basin. A too-powerful pump will tend to shoot water over a wide area, and you may have to eschew planting water lilies for they dislike heavy spray. Fish, on the other hand, appreciate the extra oxygen that fountains give the water.

Preformed pools are a popular option, but these tend to come in ugly shapes and in colours that make them look unnatural. A better option is heavy-duty butyl lining. Made especially for pond construction, this material should last at least 10 years and you can dig out any shape pond you like – free-form or formal. Butyl is easy to instal (see p. 75) but you should line the hole first with sand, turf or even pieces of old carpet. This will make a soft bed for the vinyl and help to prevent punctures. Use butyl with the neutral, rather than the blue, side up for a more natural effect and a feeling of greater depth.

LIGHTING THE PATIO

Installing lights on a patio can transform even the dullest patio into something exciting, original and attractive and will amply repay the time, effort and expense involved, as the area can then be used not only during the daytime but also at night. Lighting outside the house has positive effects on the interior as well. By integrating these two areas a sense of increased space is created inside. But for this to work well, the relationship between the internal and external lighting schemes is most important, and the two should flow together, without abrupt changes of intensity, and harmonize. This will also help to create an illusion of extra space on the patio by minimizing the distinction between house and garden.

LIGHTING SCHEMES

Patio lighting is of several types – floods and other lamps to light up a whole area; spotlights to accent points of interest; purely functional lights to mark a door or the edges of steps; and special occasion lights such as candles and flares. Bear in mind when considering these different lights that in darkness the eye registers light more easily, and dramatic effects may be produced with minimal light output.

If you are lighting any large flat surface, the first consideration is its condition and texture. If the patio surface is made of attractive weathered bricks, for example, they will lend themselves to being washed with light. Concrete, on the other hand, unless it is textured, is a difficult material to light successfully, and so a more subdued lighting scheme might be called for. A glazed or semi-glazed patio flooring material is best lit indirectly to minimize glare.

Instead of an overall lighting scheme, another approach (and easier to achieve) is to pick out elements of the patio for highlighting – a window box, tree or raised bed, for example. Your final result will probably incorporate a combination of one or more of these methods.

Floodlights

Cleverly positioned, floodlights can be used to define one area with a wash of light. If they are fixed high up on a tree or wall, make sure they are positioned correctly from the outset as later adjustment can be difficult. Floodlights may, however, be overpowering in a confined area. Since their range is large, they must be used with care if the garden is not to look rather like a prison exercise yard. Provided your patio is large, floods can also be effective when placed low down, so that they throw light upwards to illuminate a statue or other feature.

Think carefully about what colour lamps to use with the lights. While lamps with an orange tinge may cast a warm glow on brick and stone, the colour can prove unattractively brown when directed on to green plants. Tungsten, on the other hand, which appears nearly white to the naked eye, will make even the dullest planting scheme look vivid and bright green, but may not flatter a building.

Spotlights

One of the advantages of a spotlight is that it can be adjusted and angled, as the seasons progress, to highlight different areas of particular shrubs, trees or blooms when they are at their best. Spotlights can be mounted either permanently, as with floods, or on movable stands or spikes that can be pushed into the ground. The disadvantage of the movable variety is their trailing cables, which can be unsightly and must be arranged where nobody will trip over them or chop through them with a spade.

Use spotlights so that their narrow beams shine either on the surface of a plant, to illuminate its shape and texture, or through the leaves whose translucent qualities will soften and diffuse the effect.

Take your cues from the architectural surroundings when deciding what to highlight. As with stage lighting, the light source itself should be concealed. Although basically directional lights, spotlights can be bounced, for instance, off a white-painted wall to illuminate a wider space.

Functional lighting

This type of lighting is specifically designed to mark such features as doorways and steps and is available in a wide variety of shapes and sizes. It is fixed permanently in its most effective position – over a doorway,

Live flames create an instant sense of occasion wherever they are used. If flares are used to define a path or the edge of a paved area, make sure there is plenty of room to walk between them. As well as their aesthetic use in generating a festive atmosphere, many flares have the incidental advantage of deterring the insects that are so often lured to patio lights. Flares tend to be fiercer and more torch-like, while candles give a softer, more intimate lighting effect.

INTRODUCTION

The best patio planting consists of a mixture of established shrubs and possibly trees or climbers, underplanted with a selection of perennials – all of which will more or less look after themselves – and annuals and/or bedding plants, which, although requiring more effort, do enable you to vary the decorative theme from year to year.

There should also be containers of some sort – hanging baskets, tubs or troughs – to allow you some scope to change the apparent shape of the patio by moving them to different positions. They are also important for creating spots of colour within the patio, and for providing a more flexible planting scheme. For the maximum visual impact you should plan bold massed plantings. Specimens that are dotted around rather than grouped together tend to look ineffective. Another special bonus of container planting is that you can often grow exotic plants, since they can be overwintered indoors if necessary. A sheltered wall, however, would offer the same possibility.

Scale is an important factor to take into account. It is essential to choose trees, in particular, that will not eventually overshadow the patio, shutting out the light, or that will not look over-scale and totally out of place. This does not rule out some favourites since many trees that might otherwise grow too large can be planted in raised beds or large tubs, which will have a 'Bonsai' effect on them. The spread of the branches usually matches that of the roots. However, such trees may not live as long as they normally would. Remember, too, when looking through catalogues, that many of the most popular trees and shrubs often come in a range of cultivars, with sizes ranging from miniature to giant. Another point to bear in mind is that many shrubs – the buddleia for instance – tend almost to double their size if they are grown in particularly favourable conditions – up against a sunny brick wall, for example.

Year-round appeal is an essential consideration when plant planning. You will need both evergreen and deciduous trees and shrubs if the effect is not to become monotonous. For variety, aim to present a different picture on the patio at each season of the year, and do not forget winter, for there are many attractive winter-flowering plants that add interest during the cold months.

A plant's shape is also important: you will need an attractive mix of tall and low-growing, thin and rounded shrubs for the best effect, contrasting, say, columnar conifers with the rounded shapes of shrubs and then, at a lower level, planting tall spiky plants behind lower hummocky growers such as some of the heathers. Perennials and bedding plants can be used very successfully to 'knit' the shapes together into a well-integrated whole. Plants with positively shaped leaves are invaluable to give architectural shape to your planting design to provide an interesting single feature, or to provide contrast between the various plants. Create a balance between the bold sword-leaved specimens, such as yucca (good for a tropical look) or New Zealand flax (*Phormium tenax*), and the fine-leaved or ornamental grasses, such as bamboos (*Arundinaria*) and pampas (*Cortaderia*), some of which are variegated. Against this background you can grow specimens with well-rounded leaves – the rhododendron and azalea family, camellias and ivies, and those with very small leaves such as some of the hebes. Thistle-like plants can be very striking, especially in silvery shades, and the cardoon (*Cynara cardunculus*) and its more edible relative, the globe artichoke (*Cynara scolymus*), both make a good choice.

Think in terms of contrasting colours for foliage as well as for flowers; for instance, silvery leaved plants will reflect the sun in a hot sheltered spot, and they can also cope with drought. In dark corners introduce some plants with bright yellow variegated leaves to give the illusion of dappled sunlight. In general, colour should be used with care when doing your basic planting: a chiaroscuro crammed into a small space, an unbridled mix of every colour of the rainbow, can dazzle the eye. Sometimes it is better to stick to a simpler palette: a single-colour flower scheme can look particularly effective.

If you have young children, check before buying a plant that its berries and leaves are not poisonous, and also whether the berries will stain paving slabs.

Pots and containers provide an opportunity to add extra colour or interest to a planting scheme or to enliven a dull corner of a patio with a splash of colour. Pedestal or tall containers, like this chimney pot, can be used to introduce colour at a different level, and to raise small scented plants off the ground, so that their fragrance can be appreciated.

CLIMBERS

Climbers can provide an amazing range of colours in a patio, and no other type of plants will give such value for the small amount of ground space they occupy. In fact, six vigorous climbers planted in a piece of land 30cm/12in wide by 9m/30ft long will quickly provide a glorious display of foliage and colourful flowers over 56sq m/600sq ft of wall. Climbers perform other useful functions too: disguising a less-than-perfect wall, for instance, or hiding an unpleasant view or a utilitarian building, such as a garden shed. They will also help to blend a patio boundary wall in with a nearby house wall made from dissimilar materials.

In the patio, climbers can also be used in a wide variety of ways. For example, planted in troughs and trained up a trellis or netting they can be grown as a free-standing screen. Their versatility makes it poss-ible to use them as trailing plants, grown in containers on top of a wall. Some climbers also make excellent ground cover.

Climbers have several methods of growing. Some will scramble unaided up a wall – ivy (*Hedera*) and the climbing hydrangea (*Hydrangea petiolaris*), for instance, both of which have aerial roots. Others have adhesive pads that will stick to any rough surface; Virginia creeper (*Parthenocissus quinquefolia*), for example, grows by this method. A further group of climbers will need some support – netting or frequen-tly spaced wires – if you want to avoid having to tie them in place. Among these are honeysuckle (*Lon-icera*) and the Russian vine (*Polygonum baldschuan-icum*), which twine around supports by their growing tips, and the sweet pea (*Lathyrus odoratus*), which clings by tendrils. Yet another group use their sharp thorns to spike and catch on to a compatible surface, but they may need tying back – roses are an example.

Aspect is important when you are picking climbers for the patio, for the direction in which a wall faces must be taken into account when choosing plants to grow up against it. The most accommodating wall of all is the one that enjoys the afternoon sun, for it gives the most shelter and is the best wall for trying out climbers that are not totally hardy. A wall with day-long sunshine makes an ideal host for sun-loving plants but bear in mind that the soil beneath it will tend to dry out, so choose climbers that can tolerate drought.

A cool exposed wall is the most difficult to deal with, for, although it will probably get winter sun in the morning, when combined with frost this will 'burn' the blossoms on plants such as camellias.

In addition to these general guidelines on aspect, other factors often need to be taken into considera-tion, in cities in particular: high-rise buildings and exposed sites, for example, can cause down draughts and wind funnels, and shade in places where you would least expect it, so choose plants that can cope with these factors.

On a patio it is a good idea to frame the whole area with some climbers. Evergreens are best, but they are few and far between – the most spectacular are often deciduous. However, not all evergreens are monoton-

RIGHT *Virginia creeper* (Parthenocissus) *makes a splendid self-clinging wall covering with marvellous colour in autumn, when it turns a rich rose-red. Because it climbs so easily, it can be used to clothe a high wall that might otherwise look forbidding.*

OPPOSITE *Climbers don't have to be used singly. Why not grow several together, allowing them to intertwine? Here clematis and roses make a particularly attractive partnership, which is also practical since the clematis can use the roses' thorny stems to twine around. Grown against a boundary wall, they help to disguise its straight lines, while providing the patio with welcome privacy.*

ous or unattractive. Ivy, for example, has some highly attractive variegated versions – *Hedera colchica* 'Variegata', for instance, which is edged with cream, or *Hedera helix* 'Goldheart', which is splashed with gold. *Garrya eliptica*, with its attractive trailing green catkins, is another evergreen, and both clematis and honeysuckle can be found in evergreen and semi-evergreen versions. Evergreen climbers are best planted in spring rather than autumn, so that they can get well established before being subjected to wintery conditions.

Having established some basic background climbers, you can achieve exciting results by planting other climbers with colourful flowers to scramble over them. Roses and clematis go together perfectly, and passion flower (*Passiflora*) looks good grown with wisteria or with grape vine (*Vitis vinifera*). To cover a large area rapidly, plant Russian vine (*Polygonum baldschuanicum*), which grows up to 6m/20ft in one summer but needs a hard prune in winter if it is not to take over the entire patio. Look out, too, for climbers with a bonus: some roses have very attractive hips – 'Mme Gregoire Staechelin' is one – while other climbers have a delightful scent and should be planted near the house – for instance, jasmine (*Jasminum officinale*), some kinds of clematis and, of course, honeysuckle (*Lonicera*).

When planting climbers, do not restrict the growing circle of their roots by putting them too close to a wall, which, in the case of a hot sunny wall, may also tend to 'bounce' too much heat on to their roots. Such ill-situated plants may also fail to receive adequate moisture, for the wall will tend to shield them from the rain. Check the pH of your soil first (see p. 149) if you are planting under a newly constructed wall: rubble with mortar, which contains lime, may have become crushed into the soil, and thus have increased its lime content dramatically. You may want to correct this imbalance.

Climber supports, whether trellis, netting or wires, should be chosen with care as all climbers become heavier as they mature. Supports should be kept slightly away from the wall or fence and should not be nailed straight onto it so that the climber can twist around the supports satisfactorily, and also so that air can circulate around the plant.

BACKGROUND PLANTS

The backdrop to your patio – the basic framework – should mainly be evergreen trees, shrubs and climbers. These are useful in many different ways, not only to provide some greenery all year round – a great bonus, particularly in city conditions – but also to soften the sharp edges of harsh concrete and brick walls, and to make the patio seem larger than it really is, since evergreens effectively disguise boundaries. They can also be used to improve the proportion of a plot, to change its apparent shape, and to conceal service items such as dustbins. Their eventual height needs to be considered though, as they will provide screening, privacy and shade.

Site evergreens so that you will see them from the house in winter, the time when their leaf colour is most needed. It is a good idea to include a Norway spruce if you have the space so that it can be lit up and even sprayed with fake snow at Christmas time. It can reach up to 15m/50ft when 40 years old but there are dwarf and slow-growing forms such as *Picea abies* (syn. *P. excelsa*) 'Clanbrassiliana', which remains 1m/

Ivies and a climbing hydrangea (Hydrangea petiolaris) *make an obliging green background for a small patio garden in a shady corner. Dark-leaved plants like these help to make the boundaries appear to recede.*

3ft high for many years, eventually attaining tree-like proportions, and is best for a patio.

If your patio is exceptionally cold or exposed, bear in mind that the larger-leaved evergreens (camellias and rhododendrons, for instance), which came originally from sub-tropical areas such as China, Japan or India, are less hardy than those with small leaves (conifers for example), which come from colder climates. However, some of the conifers – the *Chamaecyparis* species for instance – do suffer from browning of their foliage if scorched by icy winds.

To avoid a monotonous all-dark-green view on to the patio, seek out variegated varieties of many of the most popular evergreen trees and shrubs. Holly (*Ilex*), some of the pachysandras and even the slow-growing box (*Buxus*) can be found with yellow-splashed leaves: *Ilex aquifolium* 'Aureomarginata' and *Buxus sempervirens* 'Aureovariegata' for instance. Others have colourful foliage of a different kind: in spring *Pieris formosa forrestii*, for instance, makes bright red growth, fading as summer goes on.

When space is limited, only a few evergreen climbers, notably *Clematis armandii*, are suitable as background plants. However, a number of attractive evergreen wall shrubs can be grown instead – ceanothus and *Cistus* to name just two.

Many evergreens have magnificent flowers. Apart from the camellias and rhododendrons, there are, for instance, the beautiful blue ceanothus, Mexican orange blossom (*Choisya ternata*), which looks exotic but which is surprisingly hardy, and *Fatsia japonica*, a plant of tropical appearance that can cope well with shade and that produces creamy flowers like giant dandelion clocks in autumn.

Having selected your basic evergreens and decided on their positions, add some deciduous plants, combining the two to give interest throughout the seasons. All-year-round colour gives you an exciting basis to build on when choosing herbaceous perennials and flowers to ring the changes with the seasons. However, do not think just in terms of flowers for added interest; there are many trees and shrubs with brilliantly coloured leaves in autumn – the acers for instance and some forms of malus and prunus. If you have space for it, one of the most rewarding in this respect is the little-used mountain ash (*Sorbus*), notably *S.* 'Joseph Rock' which has fresh green leaves in spring, which then turn purple, burnt orange and copper in autumn. Its creamy yellow-amber berries do not, fortunately, attract birds.

If you prune them back well each year, the dogwoods (*Cornus*) will give pleasure in winter with their colourful red stems; *Cornus alba* 'Westonbirt' is particularly attractive. The coral bark maple (*Acer palmatum* 'Senkaki') provides an even better display,

producing striking coral red stems as well as golden yellow leaves in autumn. Alternatively, try *Rubus cockburnianus*, a little-used shrub from the raspberry family, which produces 'whitewashed' stems.

Trees and shrubs that come into leaf early in spring are another useful form of background planting. If you have space for it, the heavily scented balsam (*Populus balsamifera*) brings out its heart-shaped leaves early in spring, as does the bridal wreath shrub (*Spiraea arguta*) with its fresh green leaves on arching stems.

In this particularly lushly planted patio, creative use has been made of foliage plants, particularly trailing ones. Easy to maintain, they make an excellent backdrop to the patio. Later in the year massed pots of colourful annuals can be added to provide summer interest.

GROUND COVER

Ground cover plants are extremely worthwhile in a patio garden. They will soften the harsh lines of paving, keep raised beds and containers in good condition by retaining moisture in the soil and, if chosen properly, will add to the general colour scheme and provide extra interest underfoot. Some of the more compact ground cover plants, notably chamomile (*Chamaemelum nobile* 'Treneague'), can also give you an aromatic mini-lawn without any laborious mowing.

Successful ground cover plants should be evergreen perennials that grow densely and that need practically no attention. Avoid plants such as the perennial varieties of alyssum and aubretia – which need constant grooming – clipping off dead leaves and straggling old flowering stems. You should select something that will join up quickly to form a carpet underneath your prize plants and smother weeds before they have a chance to take hold. Choose a plant that forms a shape that is suited to its final position in the patio. Some ground cover plants form clumps, mats or hummocks. Others sprawl over the ground

Sedums, in their infinite variety, make an excellent choice for planting in the crevices between paving stones. Another option would be creeping thymes, which will create a very similar effect and are tough enough to survive being trodden underfoot.

with floppy stems, while yet another group – usually plants that are normally treated as climbers – twine or creep their way among taller plants. A further group spreads by its roots and shoots. Ground cover plants that are likely to be trodden on must be tough and springy enough to make a quick recovery.

The final size of the plant and the density with which the leaves grow are also important considerations. Therefore, always choose ground cover plants that have a suitable growth habit for the size of your patio. For example, the larger and lesser periwinkles (*Vinca major* and *V. minor*), two of the most popular ground cover plants, are not sufficiently dense to grow in a small space, and rhododendron and dwarf azalea are really only suitable as ground cover for a large site.

In colder climates, the plants will need to be hardy and should provide some extra interest, either in the changing colour of their leaves or in their flowers or fruits. An excellent ground cover plant, for instance, is the wild strawberry, which has delicious tiny fruits.

Think in an inventive way when choosing your ground cover. If the soil in the patio is not suited to the plants that you wish to grow, why not put them in a separate raised bed with custom-bought compost? It is possible to buy compost for acid-loving plants, for instance. However, make sure that your soil drains freely, especially from a raised bed, if you are planning to use any alpines – for they will not tolerate waterlogged soil.

Some climbers are excellent for ground cover, though seldom used. Ivy provides a very tough, resistant mat but it can be extremely boring to look at unless it is combined with, say, clematis in summer. It has the advantage, however, of being striking in stark modern architectural patios, and looks particularly attractive when beds with ivy ground cover are included on a patio that features carefully combed gravel. Some succulents – notably sedums and sempervivums – provide marvellous ground cover on a small scale and are almost totally resistant to weeds.

Few people think of roses for ground cover, but they can be extremely successful in spots where no-one is likely to gambol barefoot. Some are actually tough enough to be walked over – 'Snow Carpet'

To enliven an area of paving that is looked on rather than used, lady's mantle (Alchemilla mollis) *makes a bold choice for interplanting between the stones. It is seen at its best just after rain or early in the morning, when drops of moisture caught in its handsome leaves glisten like jewels.*

Ground cover plants make a useful low-maintenance surface cover. Here, a massed planting of dwarf azaleas and box makes a splendid contrast to the flat expanse of the house walls and the paving.

('Sam McGredy'), which has tiny creamy double flowers, is a real ground cover rose. Ramblers that root wherever their stems touch the soil are a good choice for a larger patio, so are the 'Fairy' group of roses developed by Harkness – 'Fairy Changeling' and 'Fairy Damsel', for instance. In a container or window box, consider using miniature roses, which can now be found in climbing versions which could trail. Since roses look relatively bare-branched and unattractive when not in flower, they need to be planted among complementary ground cover for added interest – Lamb's ears (*Stachys lanata*) would make a good foil for them as would forget-me-not (*Myosotis*) or London pride (*Saxifraga × urbium*).

Many herbs provide marvellous ground cover, an added bonus if space is restricted. The dwarf version of lavender (*Lavandula angustifolia* 'Munster') is first-rate for this purpose, as are the prostrate thymes, which form a tapestry of different colourings. Pennyroyal (*Mentha pulegium*) and the tiny Corsican mint (*Mentha requieni*) make very successful ground cover, especially in the shade.

Make sure that the site is weed-free to give your plants a flying start. To smother any weeds that come up between the plants when they are first establishing themselves, cut a hole in black polythene where needed to let the ground cover grow through. Peg down and cover with gravel.

FLOWERS ALL YEAR ROUND

Brilliantly coloured annuals, massed together, contrast well with the surrounding stonework and the silvery-grey leaves of lamb's ears (Stachys lanata) growing on the wall. Containers of different shapes and sizes always look better if grouped together, as here, rather than scattered around the patio.

Can you really have flowers in full bloom on the patio during every month of the year? The answer is 'yes', provided you choose a judicious combination of flowering trees and shrubs, perennials, half-hardy and hardy annuals and bulbs. With a little cunning, you can cheat the seasons by planting shrubs against a really warm sheltered wall, when they will come into bloom early, or by bringing on other fledgling flowers with a simple temporary greenhouse cover – a strip of stout clear polythene or indeed a sheet of glass – using the same techniques as you would with a cloche (see p. 159). However, since on a patio the plants are likely to be crammed into a small space, careful planning is required and, sometimes, the shifting of plants between a temporarily unused piece of bed acting as a nursery and their final permanent bed. There is not likely to be space, for instance, to have a special plant nursery where seedlings can be brought on, and storage space must be planned for plants that need to be lifted and stored during the winter.

To give you something in bloom for every month of the year, bulbs alone could be used. Indeed, their choice is especially attractive in a patio since most of them can be lifted and stored indoors in a cool frost-free place, once the foliage has died down, to make room for something else.

Early spring should mark the blooming of winter jasmine (*Jasminum nudiflorum*), an attractive wall shrub, while among the useful bulbs in flower at this time of the year will be grape hyacinth (*Muscari*), winter aconite (*Eranthis*) and, if you have somewhere to show it off, *Iris reticulata* with its vivid blue flowers.

Once the weather warms up a little, yellow forsythia will come into bloom – this rather sprawling wall shrub can also be grown very attractively on a frame in a container, when its growth can be corraled. Daffodils and tulips will make a bold display in containers, window boxes and beds, together with the first polyanthus. Trees in flower will include the ornamental plum (*Prunus cerasifera*) and Japanese quince (*Chaenomeles speciosa*).

By late spring the attractive smaller version of magnolia (*Magnolia stellata*) will come into bloom as will camellias, which combine so well with magnolia. Among the tulips that will still be blooming, another bulb, the lily of the valley (*Convallaria*), should start to flower. The first of the clematis (*Clematis armandii*) should be out as well as alyssum and aubretia, which look attractive in tubs of flowering tulips. Rhododendrons and azaleas also begin to offer up their first blooms around now.

Once the worst frosts have passed, all the old traditional flowers will have a chance to come into bloom. The biennial wallflower (*Cheiranthus cheiri*), for instance, gypsophila in both its annual and perennial forms, and cornflower (*Centaurea cyanus*) too, can turn the patio into a convincing cottage garden. A patch of bluebells (*Endymion nonscriptus*) can look wonderful flowering under a tree, and, with wisteria and *Clematis montana* in good form on the walls of the house or garden, the patio becomes very colourful.

By early summer there should be still more colour as the first roses come into flower together with such

big way, buying instant bright colour for the patio – off a barrow, in a street market or from a garden centre. *Begonia semperflorens*, the fibrous-rooted begonia and busy Lizzie (*Impatiens*), which now comes in a double form, are both good buys with the added bonus that they come in a range of colours and do well in shade. French and African marigolds (*Tagetes*) with their vibrant yellow, orange and red hues, make a good choice to cheer up a dull or bare corner of the patio.

By late summer herbs are in full growth – lavender and rosemary should scent the air with their blue flowers and blue-green foliage. As the bedding plants continue, some spectacular lilies are also in bloom, notably *Lilium auratum*.

In early autumn chrysanthemums and dahlias (if you have space for them) will take over, and the hardy hibiscus will give an exotic look to the scene. Meanwhile autumn crocuses (*Colchicum autumnale*) with their bare stems and delicate papery mauve flowers will make a welcome appearance among the patio greenery.

In mid-autumn, nerines, those brilliant pink lilies from South Africa, steal the show, though some of the heathers (*Erica*) should still be flowering, as will *Clematis viticella*, notably *C.v.* 'Ville de Lyon' and *C.v.* 'Ernest Markham'.

Come late autumn, *Erica carnea* should be producing pink bell-like flowers and *Fatsia japonica* its creamy clocks. Scented viburnum (*Viburnum × bodnantense*) and the late clematis (*Clematis balearica*) also start flowering, augmenting all the fruits and berries that will already be decorating the patio.

In early winter, witch hazel (*Hamamelis mollis*) will come into bloom against a warm wall, and the winter iris (*Iris unguicularis*) too. Finally, in mid- to late-winter the scene on the patio can be enriched with winter sweet (*Chimonanthus praecox*), the semi-evergreen honeysuckle (*Lonicera fragrantissima*) and *Daphne mezereum*, three wall shrubs with extra welcome perfumed blooms at this time of year. Underfoot, snowdrops (*Galanthus nivalis*) should be putting in an appearance, as may the first spring crocus and the delicate flowers of the Christmas rose (*Helleborus niger*).

bedding plants as geraniums (*Pelargonium*) and begonias possibly planted in tubs with alyssum and aubretia. This is the time, too, for daisy-like flowers – asters, for instance, or marguerites (*Chrysanthemum frutescens*).

In mid-summer the patio should be at its most glorious, with any hanging baskets and tubs ablaze with colour. The choice of flowers for hanging baskets and tubs is overwhelming, with fuchsias, geraniums (*Pelargonium*) and petunias edged by trailing lobelia, sweet peas (*Lathyrus odoratus*) and nasturtiums (*Tropaeolum*) running riot. This is one of the few periods when flowering shrubs or climbers are not really needed to add colour, but, if you have space, *Clematis* 'Nellie Moser' and sweetly scented roses will form an attractive back-up and will add interest to the patio at a different level.

This is the time to home in on bedding plants in a

PLANTS FOR SPECIAL CONDITIONS

Silvery-leaved, sun-loving plants, many of them herbs, have been chosen for a hot, dry corner of a sheltered patio garden. The handsome terracotta pot, coupled with the blonde-coloured gravel, contribute to the bright Mediterranean air.

Few plants are grown in conditions that are absolutely ideal, compromises always having to be made. If, however, you have a particular problem, such as with your type of soil, or the aspect or situation of your patio, then it is worthwhile choosing plants that can cope. If you pick carefully from the gardening catalogues, it is possible, for example, to find plants that can live, even thrive, in a polluted environment.

Soil in full sunlight, particularly if it is light and sandy, will tend to dry out quickly and only plants tough enough to tolerate some drought will survive. Silver-leaved plants are best able to cope with this situation. Sun- and drought-lovers include artemisias,

especially *Artemisia arborescens*, helichrysums, lavenders and sea buckthorn (*Hippophae rhamnoides*) with its spiky twigs and orange berries. Rosemary (*Rosmarinus*) and Jerusalem sage (*Phlomis fruticosa*) are good choices of herbs for such a site, and potentillas and the hardy hibiscus (*Hibiscus syriacus*) can also cope with dry conditions.

For a shaded area, you must first determine whether it is dry shade – that is, under a tree – or moist shade – in a damp corner – as this will affect the range of plants that can be grown. If a tree has been planted, it will tend to leach most of the moisture out of the soil and any other plants for the area must be able to cope with

An unusual use of hostas, grouped as accent plants in an urn, brings a shady corner of the patio to life. Lady's mantle, which surrounds the pot, is another good choice for a shaded site as it thrives in little or no sun.

this situation; many of the ground covering varieties do well: for instance, ivy (*Hedera*), bugle (*Ajuga*), with its pretty blue flower spikes, or lady's mantle (*Alchemilla mollis*). Cotoneasters also thrive in these conditions, as do pachysandras and pittosporums. Damp shade is ideal for ferns, astilbes and the spiny *Elaeagnus angustifolia*; *Fatsia japonica* does well there, too. To give colour in a damp corner, grow Japanese maple (*Acer palmatum* 'Atropurpureum').

A cold or windy patio will first of all need screening in some way or other; conifers are an excellent choice, providing protection all year round. *Cupressocyparis leylandii* is the fastest grower and, if planted slightly closer together than usual and if clipped at the top, will knit together to form a hedge. Another choice is *Thuya plicata* 'Atrovirens', which grows fast but does not attain quite the same height. If space is a problem, then try the smaller-growing forms of *Chamaecyparis lawsoniana* — 'Elwoodii', for instance. Deciduous screening trees for a cold or windy patio include whitebeam (*Sorbus aria*), and the dense hawthorn (*Crataegus* × *grignonensis, C.* × *lavallei* or *C. prunifolia*) and, provided the soil is not too heavy, common tamerisk (*Tamarix gallica*) will grow there.

Flowering shrubs that can cope with exposed cold conditions include deutzias, kerrias and Japanese quince (*Chaenomeles speciosa*).

On seaside sites, plants have to be able to tolerate salt-laden winds. If space is limited try pyracantha, senecios, sea buckthorn (*Hippophae*) or bamboo (*Arundinaria*). To extend the range of plants that can be grown within a seaside patio, plant an evergreen screen of hawthorn (*Crataegus*), poplar (*Populus*) or the Monterey cypress (*Cupressus macrocarpa*). Such an effective screen, plus the advantage that you are less likely to get frost by the sea, means that you can then experiment with some of the more exotic, half-hardy plants on the patio.

Some man-made problems can be particularly difficult to tackle. Pollution, for example, still exists, particularly in urban areas, despite social pressures to reduce it. A patio in a town garden or near an industrial area will need to be planted with especial care; evergreens in particular will appreciate a regular spray and sponge-down of their leaves if they are to do well in this situation. Shrubs that will thrive include both deciduous and evergreen berberis, bamboos (*Arundinaria*), which make a good choice for screening and are decorative as well, cotoneasters and camellias. For an unusual effect pick the Japanese angelica tree (*Aralia elata*), with its huge leaves, silvery blue *Eucalyptus gunnii*, which grows very quickly, or Spanish broom (*Spartium junceum*).

Noise can be a problem in urban areas, and to reduce its level successfully you need a good depth of planting around your patio. Dense-leaved specimens are effective, if only psychologically. Select any of the conifers mentioned above for exposed sites, or the thick-leaved rhododendrons or viburnums.

Vandalism, whether by animals or humans, is best tackled by edging your patio with prickly impenetrable plants or with those that snap off cleanly, rather than tear, when damaged. Berberis, firethorn (*Pyracantha rogersiana*), holly (*Ilex*), Japanese quince (*Chaenomeles speciosa*) and pernettya, with its dense wiry stems, are good deterrents, so are the prickly-stemmed plants such as *Rugosa* roses if you have space. Where damage has occurred, the best plants for a quick recovery include hebes, cotoneaster, ivies and potentillas.

ACCENT PLANTS

Ferns have been used very successfully to mirror the form of the fronds of a handsome palm in the courtyard of a house in Cordoba, Spain, providing a link between the house and the courtyard beyond. Foliage plants are particularly suitable for singling out as accent plants – their striking leaf forms make a stunning contrast with most man-made surfaces.

Accent, or specimen, plants are very important on or around the patio, often taking the place of trees as a focal point where space is limited. The plant itself can be chosen for its unusual and striking colouring – as in the case of ornamental rhubarb (*Rheum palmatum*) with its purple-red leaves – or for a particular shape – as in the case of the monkey puzzle (*Araucaria araucana*), which will actually become a hefty tree, but which grows so slowly that it can be raised in a pot. Although often grown amongst other plants in a bed – where they usually tower above the surrounding plants or stand out in contrast because of their foliage – accent plants on the whole look better when segregated in some way – in a decorative tub, for instance, or stepped up on to a different level.

Finding the right specimen plants to enhance your patio may take time if you are looking for something really distinctive, for they are not necessarily found in your local garden centre. One way to spot a likely candidate to highlight your patio is to visit some of the great gardens open to the public, where plants are very often labelled – a word with a member of the garden staff might give you an idea of where it could be obtained. Photographs in magazines can be another source of inspiration. Having decided on your plant, you may find it easier to raise it from seed than track it down through a specialist grower.

One particularly popular group of accent plants are those that give an instant tropical look. The Chusan palm (*Trachycarpus fortunei*) and *Cordyline australis*, for instance, have palm-tree-like outlines that are very distinctive and exotic. *Yucca gloriosa* and New Zealand flax (*Phormium tenax*) with their spiky leaves give a similar effect on a smaller scale.

Apart from those accent plants that are distinctive looking in themselves, others can be turned into the focus of attention by the way in which they are grown – for instance, by introducing topiary into the patio or by making ordinary plants into standards.

Using topiary, a close-knit evergreen such as yew (*Taxus baccata*), box (*Buxus*) or Chinese honeysuckle (*Lonicera nitida*) can be trained and clipped into a distinctive shape. Small-scale topiary can be done very successfully on some of the shrubbier herbs – lavender, sage and rosemary all lend themselves in this way. They can be clipped into simple shapes and at the same time provide something for the kitchen. In patio surroundings, a plant that is to be grown in this way is best put in a container or, better still, a Versailles tub, the squared-off lines of which will make a suitable foil for the outline of the clipped shrub. Small-leaved plants are best for topiary since they give a denser effect.

First choose a plant that already has a shape that looks promising for your final sculpture, then gently shape it using a mix of pruning and a little judicious wiring of branches to help it on its way. Topiary can be less time-consuming using electric hedge-trimmers rather than hand shears. Simple shapes such as cones

take two or three years to achieve; more complicated ones up to seven years.

Another quicker way of creating topiary is to make a wire frame and pack it, ideally with spaghnum moss. Then train several small-leaved climbers, such as some of the ivies, over the frame, tying them if necessary. A dog can be sculpted, for instance, by training four plants, one up each leg, over a wired shape packed with spaghnum moss. The plants will cover the wire frame in one summer.

Standards can be raised from your favourite ordinary plants such as fuchsias, geraniums (*Pelargonium*) and other woody plants such as chrysanthemums, as well as from some shrubs such as wisteria, cotoneaster and the weeping cherry (*Prunus* 'Cheals Weeping'). Mop-headed bay trees can be trained as standards (see p. 155) and, inside the house, you can raise standards with the half-hardy *Coleus blumei*, which would look good on the patio in summer but needs to be taken inside in winter in most climates.

Colour does not have to take the form of flowers. Here, a golden, reed-like clump of ornamental grass provides a splendid foil for the rich ruby-red leaves of a dwarf acer, making an eye-catching focal point in this Japanese-style planting scheme.

WATER PLANTS

Water plants are easy to look after but they must be selected with special care. The water will soon cloud over and become green if it is not planted with oxygenators. These are also known as 'submerged aquatics' and are useful but not particularly attractive plants which compete for plant food – sunlight and mineral salts – with algae, which would otherwise turn the pond water green. The leaves of oxygenators absorb carbon dioxide, which is needed for photosynthesis, and release vital oxygen into the pond water. Oxygen bubbles can be seen rising to the surface. You also need plants that float on or just below the pond surface to shade the water from strong sunlight, otherwise still more algae will form on the base of the pond.

Balancing your plants properly is all-important: even if the water is an unpleasant shade of green, the

A small pond provides an attractive focal point at the base of a series of raised beds in this stone-flagged patio. The brilliant pink flowers of the moisture-loving drumstick primrose (Primula denticulata) *make a splendid contrast with the surrounding grey stones.*

right plants will clear it – first of all a reddish ring will appear around the edge and then the water will gradually clear. How many water plants you need depends on the size of the pond. Equally, the number of deep water plants, such as lilies, grown to decorate the pond will also depend on the depth of water in which they are to grow and on the variety you choose. As an approximate guide, a pond 45cm/18in deep can take one medium-sized water lily for every 0.4 to 0.6sq m/4 to 6sq ft, or one larger variety for every 0.7 to 1.1sq m/8 to 12sq ft. When purchasing your deep water pond plants, always check the recommended planting rate.

One of the most useful oxygenating plants for all ponds is *Glodia crispa*, which sits in pots in the bottom of a pond and not only helps clear the water but provides a place for fish to spawn and some shade for them, too. It is usually sold in small bunches with little strips of lead attached to string tied around the base of the stalks. This is to help 'anchor' the plants in the pot; otherwise they would tend to float away. To go with this deep oxygenator you will need a floating aquatic – water hyacinth (*Eichhornia crassipes*), for instance, which floats just on or under the surface. Water hyacinth is simply tossed into the water and left to float where it will: no pots or other form of anchorage is necessary.

Deep water plants such as water lilies (*Nymphaea*) and brandy bottle (*Nuphar lutea*) can crown the pond. Brandy bottle has leaves that are similar to a water lily's and has bright yellow flowers like a buttercup's. Water lilies can be expensive to buy but should last for years, and they can be found in all sizes, from the very smallest, which since it needs so little water could grow in a pudding basin, to the very large varieties. If you want a water lily for a very shallow spot, look out for aquatics bearing the name *pygmaea*; these are the true miniatures.

Having established the main pond plants, add a few marginals around the edge to help disguise the plastic liner, if you have used one (see p. 75 for construction details), or the hard edge of a pre-formed pond. For a pond to be lined with plastic, cut a shelf in the soil all around the sides of the pond before draping the plastic over the area excavated. As a rough guide, plant one marginal to every 0.1sq m/1sq ft of shallow water. Marginal plants should be grown in a plastic window box in at least 10cm/4in of special proprietary soil-based potting compost and should be stood on a pile of bricks in about 10cm/4in of water. If you are building a new pond, it is a good idea to provide a special shelf for marginals.

There are a large number of marginals to choose from: *Sagittaria*, for instance, otherwise known as arrowhead because of the shape of its arum-lily-like leaves; water buttercup (*Ranunculus*); cotton grass (*Emophorum*); or marsh marigold (*Caltha palustris*). Marginals will need dividing, just like land-based plants, when they become overgrown. Depending on their rate of growth and how much sunlight they receive, this should be done approximately every two years, in an established pond.

When planting water lilies, place the container directly on the bottom of the pond. Pond experts have now found that a small water lily put in a container on the bottom of the pond will grow a long stem and find its way to the surface in little more than a week. Thus it is not necessary to keep the leaves on the surface of the water and lower the container gradually as the plant progresses.

For details on maintaining a pond or water garden, see p. 148.

Water features not only make a splendid home for aquatics, like these water lilies, but also allow you to grow a wide variety of moisture-loving plants, the striking leaf forms of which can be used to create a jungle-like appearance to the patio.

EDIBLE PLANTS

In a limited space there are numerous inventive ways in which you can grow fruit and vegetables, and you will find that, far from spoiling the general effect of the patio garden, such edible plants can be used in their own right as a decorative addition to the scene.

Until the twentieth century, runner beans (*Phaseolus multiflorus*), for instance, were grown as flowering climbers. This is not surprising since there are many decorative forms beside the ubiquitous scarlet runner – those with orange, salmon, purple or white flowers, for instance. These and other extremely edible vegetables, for example courgettes, can be grown as climbers on the patio in several different ways: they can be left to scramble over a rose against the fence; they can be tied up on strings (use decorative, coloured ones) in a lattice pattern resembling trellis; or they can be grown wigwam fashion up poles in a Versailles tub, where they take on a formal look. Alternatively, dwarf bush versions and, indeed, bush beans such as the French bean (*Phaseolus vulgaris*) can be tucked in among any flowers.

Salad crops fit happily into the patio scene – closely packed lettuces, for instance, make an excellent edging for a formal bed. The salad bowl lettuce, which does not set a heart, and other loose-headed lettuces will make an attractive frilled border, while 'Tom Thumb' and 'Little Gem' are both tiny one-portion lettuces which form neat edges to a border while growing. The feathery fronds of carrots look attractive on the edge of a bed or even fringing a tub, as they resemble an exotic fern. Another salad plant well worth growing is the Italian *radicchio* (chicory 'Rossa de Verona'), which tolerates cold weather and has very attractive ruby red leaves, which look particularly impressive among silvery senecios.

Baby bush tomatoes, such as 'Gardener's Delight', are another plant that was once grown for decoration rather than for food. Its fruits were much prized not only for the table but also to brighten up the garden in early autumn. 'Gardener's Delight', and all the other baby 'sugar' tomatoes, will grow well in hanging baskets. Another decorative tomato is the yellow version of the fruit – 'Golden Sunrise' – or the giant striped version 'Tigerella'. Any tomato plant can be made to bush if you pinch out its top shoot once it has reached the required height. Otherwise it can be placed against a wall where it will not compete with climbers, provided you keep it relatively low and in the light. Tomatoes must be kept well watered.

New potatoes, freshly dug, are so delicious that it is fun to grow a few of your own, if you have space in a corner of the patio. A potato barrel can give you a worthwhile supply of fresh young potatoes from spring right through to mid-winter if it is planted in succession (see p. 152). Raised in bedding compost in a container, potatoes are much easier to harvest than those grown in the open ground: you simply delve down, grab a handful of tubers and allow the rest to grow on. Any container that is a minimum of 75cm/2ft 6in in height and diameter will do, provided it has drainage holes. If it is to be placed out of sight, a plastic dustbin is fine, or even a heavy-duty dustbin liner; alternatively, you can use old car tyres, piling one on top of the other as the potatoes grow. If the container is going to be on show, any large decorative tub will be suitable, and in mid-summer you could top it with one or two bedding plants to make it look prettier.

Strawberry planters come in many forms. This tower planter is ideal for a patio garden as it is not only decorative but highly practical. A good crop of strawberries can be grown without using valuable ground space. Growing the plants 'vertically' has several benefits: the fruit gets plenty of sunshine, it is out of the reach of slugs and other ground pests and is not as prone to rotting in damp weather as the fruit of a conventional ground crop. For information on planting, see p. 152.

ABOVE *In the seventeenth century, colourful vegetables like chard and purple basil, shown here, were grown in tubs in formal courtyards. This pot was in an exhibition of vegetables at the Royal Botanic Gardens at Kew. The idea can be translated very easily to a patio. Some of the coloured forms of lettuce and chicory would look equally good.*

RIGHT *Runner beans, combined here in a doorway with passion flower (*Passiflora*) and black-eyed Susan vine (*Thunbergia alata*), were once grown purely as decorative plants. A good crop of runner beans could be grown in a patio, trained up strings attached to a wall or fence, or as a free-standing feature in a large container, supported on a wigwam of canes.*

Strawberry barrels can also look very attractive when flowering or fruiting and are an economic way of growing fruit on the patio. Choose varieties of strawberry that will fruit continuously from early summer until autumn: 'Ozark Beauty', for instance, 'Remont' or 'Streamliner'. Purpose-made containers can be purchased from some garden centres, but it is relatively easy to convert a wooden rainwater butt or a second-hand beer barrel. However, do remember that drainage is very important, so the barrel will need to be raised off the ground – for example, on castors or on pieces of bricks – so that the water can run away at the bottom. In the barrel sides, bore a series of holes with a minimum diameter of 2cm/¾in (see p. 152). These holes must be sufficiently large for the roots and stems of the strawberry plants to be poked through them. Bore more holes in the bottom, for drainage. It is also a good idea to make some extra holes in the sides of the barrel so you can combine

strawberries with some flowers. Pansies and primulas grow well this way as does ivy-leaved geranium (*Pelargonium*) and trailing lobelia. To produce good fruit, you must have a very rich mix of potting compost in the strawberry barrel, which must not dry out.

Two useful vegetables that also look good in a mixed bed are globe artichoke (*Cynara scolymus*) and rhubarb (*Rheum rhaponticum*), which has handsome leaves that are also striking among other foliage in a 'plantsman's' plot. Seakale (*Crambe maritima*) and Swiss chard (*Beta vulgaris*) are other plants with impresssively large leaves (if you have space to put some in) and, for pure enjoyment, do grow some flowering cabbage and kale. Although bitter to eat, they make magnificent show plants with their giant rose-like heads of pink and white, carmine and cream.

No patio kitchen garden would be complete without a selection of herbs – and where better to grow them than as near the house as you can. Marjoram, thyme and tarragon, sage too, will thrive for years in a sunny spot, while mint is better 'corseted' in some way, perhaps grown in its own container, to stop it becoming invasive. Another very decorative herb is dill, which, like basil, needs to be grown as an annual in most cold climates. Basil is best grown in a pot, but dill, with its tall feathery foliage, will mix happily among annuals in a flower bed or tub, making an attractive fern-like backdrop to their colours.

Finally, when planning plants to decorate a patio wall, do not forget that you could be growing your own fruit – delicious peaches and nectarines, for instance. All you need do is grow espaliered trees instead of conventional ones (see p. 158) and they will fit neatly in place, hosting temporary climbers, such as morning glory, or more permanent lightweight plants, such as clematis and passion flower (*Passiflora*).

A vine also makes a perfect partner for a patio, but it needs a deep bed of soil to give its roots enough room, as they can go as deep as 6m/20ft in the soil. So plant it in garden soil nearby and lead it onto the patio as it grows. Do not house the vine in a raised bed or container on the patio itself. Buy a one-year-old vine and allow just the top two buds to grow on; remove the rest. Repeat this disbudding each year until the vine has made the height that you require; then you can allow it to make lateral growth, and fruit.

TREES

ACACIA dealbata

MIMOSA, WATTLE   Tender
H: 6m/20ft S: 4m/13ft
Mimosa is loved for its heavily scented fluffy, ball-like yellow flowers, which are produced in spring, and its attractive silvery green leaves. This fast-growing evergreen may be cut back by frosts, but well-established plants quickly recover. It must have the protection of a hot, sunny wall, and is best grown in a large container in cold climates.

ACER palmatum

JAPANESE MAPLE   Hardy
H: 5m/16ft S: 2.5m/8ft
The Japanese maple is one of the most popular trees grown for their colourful autumn foliage. There are a number of named sorts, each with different colouring. A slow grower, it prefers a semi-shaded position.
CULTIVARS 'Atropurpureum': bronzy-red leaves in autumn. 'Sango-Kaku' and 'Senkaki': red bark, yellow autumn foliage.

ARBUTUS andrachne

STRAWBERRY TREE   Half-hardy
H: 6–9m/20–30ft S: 2.5–3m/8–10ft
The mature tree develops an attractive, peeling, cinnamon-coloured bark. Its white flowers appear in spring and are followed by reddish-orange, small, strawberry-like fruits (hence the common name). They are edible, but do not taste of strawberries! In fact, they have little taste at all. A slow-growing evergreen, A. andrachne thrives in a partially shaded position in acid soil.

BETULA pendula 'Youngii'

YOUNG'S WEEPING BIRCH   Hardy
H: 6m/20ft S: 3m/10ft
This slow-growing birch forms a dome-shaped tree, with weeping branches that may reach to the ground. It produces handsome foliage colour in autumn and has an attractive white scaly bark, with conspicuous black patches.

CERCIS siliquastrum

JUDAS TREE   Half-hardy
H: 5m/16ft S: 4m/13ft
This slow-growing tree is related to the sweet pea and garden pea. Its pink pea-shaped flowers appear in clusters along bare shoots in spring, before the leaves appear. They can be damaged by spring frosts and do best in a sunny position with the protection of a wall. The flowers may be followed by long seed pods that turn red when they ripen.

CHAMAECYPARIS lawsoniana

LAWSON'S CYPRESS   Hardy
H: 12m/40ft S: 3m/10ft
The normal form of this conifer grows very quickly – up to 60cm/24in a year – in good conditions. However, some of the large number of named varieties are dwarf or slower growing, with different foliage or shape; all are evergreen.
CULTIVARS 'Columnaris' (H: 5–10m/16–33ft): tall thin upright cultivar with pale grey foliage; 'Ellwoodii' (H: 3m/10ft): conical, pale grey, slow-growing; 'Ellwood's Gold': yellow foliage in spring and summer.

CORDYLINE australis

CABBAGE PALM   Half-hardy
H: 3–4m/10–13ft S: 1.5m/5ft
Although it will thrive outdoors in mild climates, the cabbage palm is usually grown in large pots, which are taken indoors in the winter. It is a small slow-growing evergreen tree with fragrant white flowers in early to mid-summer, followed by small whitish fruits. The cabbage palm is, in fact, a member of the lily family.
CULTIVAR 'Lentiginosa': leaves tinged with purple.

Laurus nobilis

LABURNUM × watereri

LABURNUM, GOLDEN CHAINS   Hardy
H: 5m/16ft S: 4m/13ft
Long racemes of fragrant bright yellow flowers, hanging from arching branches, appear in profusion in early summer. Laburnum is poisonous, particularly the seeds, so any bean-like pods must be removed if there are children about. However, this particular hybrid is largely sterile, and produces few seeds, if any. It prefers a sunny position.
CULTIVAR 'Vossii': very free-flowering, with particularly long racemes.

Acer palmatum 'Atropurpureum'

Cercis siliquastrum

LAURUS nobilis

SWEET BAY   Half-hardy
H: 7m/23ft S: 4m/13ft

Most bay trees are grown in tubs as short (2m/6ft 6in), mop-head standards, kept in shape by pruning. The height and spread given above are for a mature tree grown in favourable garden conditions. The bay, a slow-growing evergreen, is only marginally hardy when container grown and tubs should ideally be moved under cover in autumn in cold climates. The leaves, which are used for cooking, can be frost-damaged in a hard winter, although the plants usually recover. This, the true bay, prefers a sunny position and its inconspicuous flowers appear in late spring.

Magnolia × soulangiana

MAGNOLIA × soulangiana

CHINESE MAGNOLIA   Hardy
H: 7m/23ft S: 4m/13ft

One of the most popular magnolias, *M. × soulangiana* is easy to grow. It produces a mass of large waxy flowers, pinkish-purple without and white within, in early spring before the leaves appear.
CULTIVARS 'Brozzonii': very large, white; 'Lennei': rich deep rose-purple without, white within, from late spring.

M. stellata

Hardy
H: 3m/10ft S: 4m/13ft

The white star-shaped fragrant flowers appear before the leaves are out fully and may be damaged by spring frosts, so this tree should be grown in a sheltered position or against a wall. It does best in sun and is slow growing.
CULTIVAR 'Rosea': pinkish flowers.

MALUS sargentii

CRAB APPLE   Hardy
H: 2.5m/8ft S: 3m/10ft

This crab, which comes from Japan, is one of the smallest available. It can be trained as a shrub or a small tree and grows quickly. The pretty fragrant white flowers appear in late spring and are followed by small bitter 'apples', which look like large redcurrants.

PRUNUS subhirtella

FLOWERING OR ORNAMENTAL CHERRY   Hardy
H: 8m/26ft S: 3m/10ft

These small trees are grown for their pretty pink to nearly white flowers which appear in winter

Female catkin

Male catkin

Salix caprea

or early spring, according to the variety. *P. subhirtella* prefers a sunny position.
CULTIVARS 'Autumnalis': 6m/20ft, flowering in late autumn and sporadically throughout the winter; 'Pendula Rubra': branches hang from the crown, umbrella-fashon; flowers in late spring.

SALIX caprea

PUSSY WILLOW   Hardy
H: 8m/26ft S: 4m/13ft

This fast-growing, vigorous tree is adaptable to sunny or shaded sites. In very dry climates, *S. caprea* can be invasive and even destructive in its quest for water, so do not plant it near drains and pipes.
CULTIVAR 'Pendula' (H:3m/10ft) is the male form of a native pussy willow. It forms an umbrella-shaped tree with long pendant branches and silver catkins, whose stamens appear in spring.

SORBUS aria

WHITEBEAM   Hardy tree
H: 9–15m/30–50ft S: 7m/23ft

This tree has many attractive features: its leaves are silvery and the creamy white flower panicles, which appear in early summer, develop large attractive red fruits by early autumn, when its foliage changes to its autumnal tints.
HYBRID *S × bostii* (H: 3–4m/10–13ft S: 3.5m/11ft 6in): smaller than the species with compact pink flowers.

Sorbus aria

SHRUBS

ARUNDINARIA viridi-striata (Pleioblastus viridi-striatus)

BAMBOO   Hardy
H: 1.5m/5ft S: indeterminate
This bamboo is grown for its foliage, which is golden yellow with broad greenish stripes. It is evergreen but shows up best for the purplish-green canes, which are cut down in early spring. It spreads slowly by suckers, doing best in full sun, and may produce a few florets, but these are of no account. It is more correctly but less commonly known by the synonym given in brackets.

BERBERIS thunbergii atropurpurea

BARBERRY   Hardy
H: 2m/6ft 6in S: 1.2m/4ft
This quick-growing, very thorny shrub has pale yellow flowers in early summer. These are followed by attractive bright red berries in autumn, when the bronze leaves turn bright red.

BUDDLEIA 'Lochinch'

Half-hardy
H: 2m/6ft 6in S: 1.8m/6ft
Grey, downy foliage and long sweet-smelling panicles of lavender-blue flowers, which appear in mid- to late summer, adorn this shrub. Provided it is pruned hard every year, it grows quickly and prefers a sunny position.

BUXUS sempervirens

BOX   Hardy
H: 6m/20ft S: 2m/6ft 6in
A slow-growing evergreen shrub, it can be used for hedging or border edging, or can be clipped for topiary. It will tolerate both sunny and shaded positions.
CULTIVARS 'Elegantissima': smaller leaves, edged with silver; 'Suffruticosa': dwarf form long used for edging.

CAMELLIA × williamsii

Hardy
H: 10m/33ft S: 3m/10ft
These evergreen hybrids provide winter colour with flowers appearing from late autumn through to late spring. The flowers, 5–8cm/2–3in across, are single, double or semi-double. These shrubs generally are hardy but do best in semi-shade and in a sheltered spot, away from cold winds. They can grow quickly but must have an acid soil. There are a number of named varieties, coloured from white to deep red.
CULTIVARS 'Anticipation': deep rose, double; 'Citation': pale pink, semi-double; 'Donation': peach-pink, semi-double; 'J.C. Williams': bluish-pink, single.

CHOISYA ternata

MEXICAN ORANGE BLOSSOM   Half-hardy
H: 2m/6ft 6in S: 2m/6ft 6in
This evergreen shrub needs protection in cold climates. It will tolerate both sunny and shaded positions. The flowers, which appear intermittently from early summer onwards, are white and smell of orange blossom (*C. ternata* belongs to the same family).

CORNUS alba 'Elegantissima'

DOGWOOD   Hardy
H: 1.8m/6ft S: 1.5m/5ft
This thicket-forming shrub is grown chiefly for its deciduous foliage, grey-green with creamy mottling, and for its bright red stems. If these are cut in winter, the growth of fresh well-coloured shoots is encouraged. Its small white flowers appear in early summer and are sometimes followed by white berries. This suckering shrub grows quickly and will cope with a semi-shaded position.

COTONEASTER 'Hybridus pendulus'

Hardy
H: 2m/6ft 6in S: 1m/3ft
This vigorous, slow-growing, semi-evergreen shrub grows either prostrate or top-grafted on to a stem as a weeping small tree. It produces sweet-smelling flowers in early summer, followed by brilliant red fruits.

DEUTZIA monbeigii

Hardy
H: 2m/6ft 6in S: 1.5m/5ft
The undersides of the leaves are white and woolly, giving a pretty effect when stirred by the wind. The starry white flower clusters appear in early to mid-summer. *D. monbeigii* grows quickly and prefers a sunny or partially shaded position.

Berberis thunbergii atropurpurea

Arundinaria viridi-striata

Choisya ternata

Cornus alba
'Elegantissima'

Hydrangea
macrophylla
(lacecap)

Hydrangea macrophylla
(mop-head)

Fuchsia
magellanica

ESCALLONIA 'Donard Radiance'

Half-hardy
H: 2m/6ft 6in S: 1.8m/6ft
A semi-evergreen, this shrub is quick growing
and does well on limy soil, preferring a sunny
position. The large, chalice-shaped rich pink
flowers appear in early summer. This cultivar is
one of a number of vigorous hybrids available
for the garden.

FATSIA japonica

Tender
H: 2.5m/8ft S: 2.5m/8ft
Grown mainly for its foliage, this vigorous
evergreen gives the patio the appearance of a
tropical jungle. It prefers a sunny or partially
shaded site and, in colder climates, shelter by a
wall. Its mid-autumn white flowers resemble
dandelion clocks.

FUCHSIA magellanica

Half-hardy
H: 2.5m/8ft S: 1m/3ft
This semi-evergreen is probably the hardiest of
the fuchsias, and will overwinter safely in

reasonably mild climates. Elsewhere it may be
cut back, but should recover. It has typical red
and purple fuchsia flowers, which appear from
late summer to late autumn. It flourishes in the
sun in any reasonable soil. There are named
cultivars in the genus which should be
reasonably hardy in milder climates.
CULTIVARS 'Alba': white and pale rose; 'Mrs Wood':
pink, less hardy.

HIBISCUS syriacus

HIBISCUS, TREE HOLLYHOCK   Half-hardy
H: 3m/10ft S: 1.5m/5ft
The flowers, like small hollyhocks, appear in
autumn and range in colour from white to pink,
red, purple and violet-blue. *H. syriacus* needs
protection in cold areas and does best in a sunny
position.
CULTIVARS There are many named cultivars. 'Blue
Bird': large violet-blue flowers with reddish
centre; 'Woodbridge': pink with darker pink
centre; 'W.R. Smith': white, with ruffled petals.

HYDRANGEA macrophylla

Half-hardy
H: 1.8m/6ft S: 2m/6ft 6in
Hydrangeas flower in mid- to late summer and
are blue in acid soils, pink in limy conditions. An
evergreen, the hydrangea grows quickly and
does especially well near the sea, but prefers a

partially shaded site. There are large numbers of
named varieties, falling into two groups: mop-
heads (or hortensias) with bun-shaped heads of
sterile flowers; and lacecaps, with flat flower
heads, only the outer flowers being sterile.
CULTIVARS 'Hamburg': deep inky blue mop-head;
'Madame E. Moullière': white mop-head, the
petals of which turn pink as they age; 'Mariesii':
pink midway between mop-head and lacecap,
turning pale blue in acid soils.

HYPERICUM calycinum

ROSE OF SHARON   Hardy
H: 50cm/20in S: indefinite
A creeping, prostrate evergreen, it produces
large (8–10cm/3–4in) bright yellow flowers in
summer. It does well in shade or partial shade.
A fast grower, this shrub spreads rapidly to
provide excellent ground cover.

LAVANDULA angustifolia (L. × intermedia)

OLD ENGLISH LAVENDER   Semi-hardy
H: 0.8m/2ft 6in S: 1m/3ft
Lavender is easy to grow as a bush, producing
masses of aromatic leaves and purple, pinkish or
white spikes all summer through. Both the
flowers and the evergreen foliage can be dried
for use in sachets, for example. It thrives in a
sunny position. There are several cultivars, all of
which are good.

PHILADELPHUS 'Lemonei Erectus'

MOCK ORANGE   Hardy
H: 1.8m/6ft S: 1m/3ft
As well as numerous species of these deciduous
shrubs, there are also a large number of named
hybrids. All have white flowers, with the typical
heady 'orange blossom' scent, in early to mid-

summer. They grow quickly in a sunny or partially shaded site. This cultivar has a neat, upright habit of growth that avoids the untidiness of most *Philadelphus*. Another useful cultivar is *P*. 'Virginal' (H: up to 3m/10ft) which produces masses of double flowers.

PHORMIUM tenax

NEW ZEALAND FLAX, PHORMIUM   Half-hardy
H: 2.5m/8ft S: 1.5m/5ft
P.tenax is grown for its foliage; it produces clumps of long, tough, upright, sword-like evergreen leaves of varying colours. The dark red flowers, when produced, appear in mid- to late summer. *P.tenax* is hardy only in milder climates. The cultivars are even more tender and should be covered in winter against frost. They thrive in sun.
CULTIVARS 'Dazzler' (H: 80cm/30in): reddish-brown leaves marked with brighter red bands; 'Variegatum' (H: 2m/6ft 6in): leaves striped green and yellow.

POTENTILLA fruticosa

Hardy
H: 1.2m/4ft S: 1.2m/4ft
Potentillas are easy and quick to grow, their dense habit of growth making them suitable for low, flowering hedging. The flowers, of yellow, pink, red or white, are produced, dotted singly and in pairs over the shrub, throughout the summer. These shrubs can be planted in a sunny or partially shaded position and do best in limy soil.
CULTIVAR 'Jackman's Variety': large yellow flowers.

PYRACANTHA

FIRETHORN   Hardy
H: 3m/10ft S:2m/6ft 6in
Firethorns, with their white mid-summer flowers followed by masses of attractive orange fruits, thrive particularly as wall shrubs. Their fruits, which do not seem to appeal to birds, often hang on the trees right through until spring. Evergreen shrubs, they can stand a shaded position.
CULTIVAR 'Orange Glow': deeper orange fruits.

RHODODENDRON

Species and hybrids
DECIDUOUS AZALEA   Hardy
H: 3–4m/10–13ft S: 2.5m/8ft
The flowers, often very fragrant, appear in early summer, preceding the leaves, which frequently turn rich red before they fall in autumn. Azaleas prefer a semi-shaded position and must have an acid soil.
CULTIVARS 'Lemonara': apricot-yellow, flushed pink; 'Silver Slipper': white, flushed pink, with an orange flare.

Hardy dwarf hybrids

H: 1m/3ft S: 1m/3ft
The shallow roots of rhododendrons make them ideal for container growing, so even if your soil is limy, you can grow these in large pots using peat and a lime-free humus. These dwarf hybrids are evergreen and do best in a semi-shaded site. Flowers are produced in late spring to early summer, depending on the type grown.
CULTIVARS 'Blue Tit': greyish foliage and lavender-blue bell-shaped flowers. 'Scarlet Wonder': dark green leaves and red trumpet-shaped flowers.

RIBES odoratum (R.aureum)

BUFFALO CURRANT   Hardy
H: 2m/6ft 6in S:1.5m/5ft
The bright yellow spice-scented flowers appear in late spring and may be followed by attractive, large, black 'currants' in autumn, when the leaves turn yellow and orange. This shrub grows quickly in a shaded or partially shaded position.

ROSA

HYBRID TEA ROSES   Hardy
H: 1m/3ft S: 1m/3ft
There is a great choice of hybrid tea roses suitable for patios. The cultivars below are compact growing, heavily scented, not too tall, semi-evergreen shrubs. They grow quickly in a sunny position and flower throughout the summer.
CULTIVARS 'Ernest H. Morse': dark red; 'Fragrant Cloud': bright red; 'My Choice': dark orange.

ROSMARINUS officinalis

ROSEMARY   Half-hardy
H: 1.8m/6ft S: 1.4m/4ft 6in
The first of the sweet-smelling mauve flowers appear in early summer and may continue sporadically. An evergreen shrub with spiky, aromatic leaves that can be used fresh or diced as a herb, it grows quickly and thrives in a sunny position.
CULTIVAR 'Miss Jessop's Variety': lighter mauve flowers, and erect habit, which makes it ideal for hedging.

SENECIO × 'Sunshine'

Hardy
H: 1.2m/4ft S: 0.8m/2ft 6in
This semi-evergreen is grown mainly for its silvery foliage, which is very popular for flower arrangements. In early to mid-summer, it produces flowers like large, yellow daisies. This shrub grows successfully in sunny, windswept seaside gardens and is an acid lover.

SYRINGA vulgaris

COMMON LILAC   Hardy
H: 3–6m/10–20ft S: 3m/10ft
A great range of named cultivars is available, many going back to the nineteenth century. All produce very fragrant flowers – single and double – in early summer, the colours of which vary from lilac, white, yellow and blue, to red and purple and all shades in between. This slow-growing, suckering shrub prefers a sunny position.
CULTIVARS 'Congo' (H: 1.5m/5ft S: 1.2m/4ft): dark lilac-red single flowers make a rounded bush; 'Sensation': red-purple single flowers with white margins; 'Vestale': white single flowers, vigorous.

VIBURNUM × bodnantense

Hardy
H: 2.1m/7ft S: 1.2m/4ft
Dense clusters of perfumed rose-tinted flowers appear in winter. The young leaves are bronze-tinted and resist frost well.

WEIGELA florida

Hardy
H: 2–2.5m/6ft 6in–8ft S: 1.5–1.8m/5–6ft
The pink flowers, which appear in early summer on this shrub, are somewhat foxglove-shaped but smaller. A slow grower, it does best in a partially shaded position.
CULTIVARS 'Foliis Purpureis': purple-flushed leaves; 'Variegata': creamy leaf margins, compact growing habit.

CLIMBERS AND WALL SHRUBS

ABUTILON vitifolium (Corynabutilon vitifolium)

Half-hardy wall shrub
H: 3m/10ft S: 2m/6ft 6in
These semi-evergreens are best grown as container plants, or in a sunny, sheltered position, where they will survive all but the most severe winters. *A. vitifolium* produces large, exotic, white to bluish flowers from late summer.

ARISTOLOCHIA macrophylla

DUTCHMAN'S PIPE   Hardy climber
H: 6m/20ft S: 3m/10ft
This vigorous climber has distinctive, pipe-shaped yellow, green and brown flowers in early to mid-summer, and has heart-shaped leaves. Makes good cover, for example for walls and sheds, but climbs by twining, and therefore needs tying in, especially when young. It thrives in a sunny or partially shaded position.

BOUGAINVILLEA glabra

Tender
H: 6m/20ft S: indefinite
Too tender to be grown outdoors in colder climates, this vine-like climber produces a profusion of purple bracts in summer. It needs a sunny site.

CAMPSIS grandiflora

TRUMPET VINE   Tender climber
H: 7m/23ft S: 4m/13ft
This climber is grown for its profusion of large, showy, orange and red trumpet-shaped flowers which appear in late summer. A slow grower, it needs a sheltered sunny site and protection against frost, and may take time to get established. It clings with its aerial roots.

CEANOTHUS 'Autumnal Blue'

CALIFORNIAN LILAC   Half-hardy wall shrub
H: 3m/10ft S: 2–3m/6ft 6in–10ft
The evergreen Californian lilac looks splendid against an old stone wall – hence its use by the Oxford colleges. Although there are a large number of species and cultivars available of varying size, colour and flowering times, 'Autumnal Blue' is one of the easiest to grow and will flourish almost anywhere, although it does not like a very limy soil. It does best in a warm sunny position and is fast growing.

CELASTRUS orbiculatus

CLIMBING BITTERSWEET   Hardy climber
H: 10m/33ft S: 8m/26ft
Grown for its attractive fruits, this climber's leaves can take on colourful autumn tints. This species normally carries female and male flowers on separate plants, so plants of both sexes may be needed to ensure a supply of fruits. These are produced inside light brown capsules that split open in the autumn to reveal the inner surface and scarlet seeds, which usually last through the winter. A rapid-growing twiner, climbing bittersweet prefers a cool yet sunny wall and produces insignificant flowers in early to mid-summer.

CHAENOMELES speciosa

JAPANESE QUINCE   Hardy shrub
H: 2m/6ft 6in S: 2m/6ft 6in
This spring-flowering shrub prefers a cool, sunny position. On a sheltered wall, its flowers may be produced before the leaves as early as mid-winter, when they make a welcome splash of colour. A slow grower, Japanese quince often produces quite large, apple-shaped, edible yellow fruits in autumn.
CULTIVARS 'Moerloosei': flowers pink outside, white inside, tall, arching habit; 'Nivalis': (H: up to 2m/6ft 6in): white flowers; 'Umbilicata' (H: up to 2m/6ft 6in S: 2m/6ft 6in): deep pink flowers, vigorous grower.

CLEMATIS hybrids

Hardy climber
H: 3m/10ft + S: 1.5m/5ft
All clematis prefer a site with their heads in the sun and their feet either in the shade or covered by dense-growing plants. However, some cultivars, particularly the pale-coloured varieties, may look better on a cool wall where their colours do not bleach. Most will flower throughout summer. Hybrid clematis are quick growing and they climb by twining their leaf tendrils around any convenient support. They should be regularly pruned.
CULTIVARS *C.* × 'Jackmanii': purple; 'King George V': pale pink with dark pink stripe; 'Nellie Moser': large, pale mauve-pink, with distinctive dark pink stripe down centre of each petal; 'President': purple; 'Rubens': pale mauve; 'Ville de Lyon': maroon

C. montana

Hardy climber
H: 8m/26ft S: 10m/33ft
This twining climber grows very quickly and easily and may well have to be pruned annually. The flowers of the species come out in early summer and are typically white, but there are some cultivars with pink flowers.
CULTIVARS 'Elizabeth': pink, fragrant; 'Rubens': rosy-pink; 'Tetra Rose': purplish pink.

COTONEASTER horizontalis

FISHBONE COTONEASTER   Hardy shrub
H: 2.5m/8ft S: 3m/10ft
The white or pinkish flowers in early summer are followed in autumn by bright red berries, while

Aristolochia macrophylla

Chaenomeles speciosa

the glossy green leaves turn orange and red before they fall. Although it prefers a sunny site, it does well by a cool wall, and gives a welcome splash of colour in autumn and winter. The common name refers to the herringbone pattern formed by the branches of this slow-growing hardy shrub.

ECREMOCARPUS scaber

ECREMOCARPUS, CHILEAN GLORY FLOWER   Half-hardy climber
H: 3m/10ft S: 1m/3ft
This climber, which has red-orange or yellow flowers from early summer through to autumn, comes, as its English name suggests, from Chile. A vigorous plant, it clings by tendrils and is usually grown as an annual in cold climates by growing seedlings indoors or under glass and planting them out when all danger of frost has passed. Can be grown as a perennial in hot, sunny, sheltered areas, in which case any growths damaged by frost should be removed in spring before the growth starts again.

EUONYMUS fortunei

SPINDLE TREE   Hardy shrub
H: 6m/20ft S: 2m/6ft 6in
This evergreen shrub grows either creeping along the ground or erect, some sorts climbing by aerial roots. The early-summer flowers are insignificant but the fruits, in the sorts that produce them, are very unusual, with pink seeds in an attractive orange capsule. It prefers a cool position.
CULTIVAR 'Silver Queen' (H: 3m/10ft): white-edged leaves, turning pink in winter.

FORSYTHIA suspensa

Hardy shrub
H: 3m/10ft S: 3m/10ft
The brilliant yellow flowers appear all along the branches in spring, covering this rambling shrub in colour before the leaves appear. This forsythia is quick growing and has pendulous interlacing shoots, which are best kept under control by tying against a wall. The early splash of yellow is very effective against a cool, sunny wall.

FUCHSIA hybrids

Half-hardy shrub
H: 2m/6ft 6in S: 2m/6ft 6in
These can be grown as bushes or trained as standards. They are fast-growing shrubs which

produce flowers from early summer onwards. They do best in warm, sheltered gardens with the protection of a wall, when they will reach the heights given above and survive the normal winter. In less favourable conditions, they will be cut down by frost but grow again in the spring. The cultivars listed below are suitable for outdoor cultivation.
CULTIVARS 'Madame Cornelissen' (H: 1m/3ft): red and white; 'Mrs Popple' (H: 1.2m/4ft): red and purple.

GARRYA elliptica

Half-hardy shrub
H: 5m/16ft S: 4m/13ft
This vigorous evergreen is grown mainly for the silvery catkins, up to 30cm/10in long, which can cover the plant from winter to spring. The male catkins are much longer than the female ones, so you should get male plants unless you want fruits, for which both sexes are needed. This shrub grows better with the protection of a wall in most areas.

HEDERA canariensis

CANARY ISLAND IVY   Half-hardy climber
H: 4m/13ft S: 3.5m/11ft 6in
This vigorous evergreen is grown for its long leathery leaves, which may turn bronze in autumn. Its late flowers are insignificant, but good for insects. More robust and quicker-growing than common ivy, it is not so hardy, and may be cut back by a severe winter. It prefers a cool wall, in the sun or partial shade, and has self-clinging aerial roots.
CULTIVARS 'Azorica': vivid green leaves, up to 15cm/6in across; 'Gloire de Marengo' ('Variegata'): large leaves that change from green in the centre to grey, with a white margin.

HYDRANGEA petiolaris

CLIMBING HYDRANGEA   Hardy climber
H: 18m/60ft S: 4m/13ft
This climber starts slowly but, once established, will move fast, and can reach tree-top height, using its self-clinging aerial roots. A good screening plant, it prefers a shaded or semi-shaded cool wall. The leaves have an attractive downy underside. Masses of flower heads, the size of a small plate, then showy, creamy-white flowers, cover the plant in summer. It grows well by the sea.

Cotoneaster horizontalis

Hedera canariensis 'Gloire de Marengo'

JASMINUM nudiflorum

WINTER JASMINE   Hardy shrub
H: 6m/20ft S: 1m/3ft
The bright yellow flowers appear plentifully throughout the winter, although a period of cold winds will temporarily stop the flowering. Winter jasmine thrives when grown against a cool wall but needs tying in to a support.

LONICERA × americana

HONEYSUCKLE   Hardy climber
H: 10m/33ft S: 6m/20ft
The flowers of this vigorous climber are heavily scented, white, yellow and pink, and appear throughout the summer. The young stems are a pretty purple and twine around supports with their growing tips. *L. × americana* prefers a cool site.

L. × brownii 'Fuchsioides'

SCARLET TRUMPET HONEYSUCKLE
Half-hardy climber
H: 4m/13ft S: 1m/3ft
A quick-growing semi-evergreen twiner, excellent for archways and pergolas, it thrives in

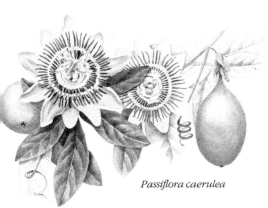

Passiflora caerulea

Pyracantha
'Soleil d'Or'

Vitis vinifera
'Purpurea'

a warm or hot sunny position. The bright orange-red flowers are produced in two flushes, at the beginning and end of summer, and in some years right through the season. They are, unfortunately, scentless.

PARTHENOCISSUS quinquefolia

VIRGINIA CREEPER Hardy climber
H: 12m/40ft+ S: 15m/50ft
This is the true Virginia creeper from North America, grown for its attractive foliage which, in early autumn, turns bright crimson. Vigorous and self-clinging – by adhesive pads at the end of its tendrils – it will climb a tall wall and hang far down the other side. This climber prefers a cool, partially shaded wall. Its flowers are insignificant.

PASSIFLORA caerulea

PASSION FLOWER Half-hardy climber
H: 5m/16ft S: 4m/13ft
This fast-growing climber does best in sunny, sheltered areas, where it is almost evergreen in mild years. In most districts, it will be cut down by frost but may grow again unless the winter has been very hard. It climbs using its tendrils to cling. The flowers, with greenish-white petals and purplish stalks on the stamens, are sweet-smelling and appear throughout summer. In favourable circumstances, they are followed by yellow, plum-shaped fruits.

POLYGONUM baldschuanicum

RUSSIAN VINE Hardy climber
H: 12m/40ft S: 10m/33ft
This, one of the fastest-growing climbers available, sometimes reaching a rate of 6m/20ft each season, is also known as mile-a-minute. A twiner, it quickly forms a dense screen of vegetation over ugly buildings, for example, but can get out of hand and be difficult to reach and to control. From late summer to autumn, it is covered with showy panicles of tiny creamy-pink flowers.

PYRACANTHA rogersiana

FIRETHORN Hardy shrub
H: 3m/10ft S: 4m/13ft
This evergreen thrives in a sunny, cool position. The creamy-white clusters of flowers, which appear in early summer, are lovely in their own right, as well as producing masses of orange-red or golden yellow berries in autumn. There are a few named hybrids, with slightly different coloured berries.
CULTIVAR 'Soleil d'Or': bright yellow berries.

ROSA

CLIMBING ROSE Hardy climber
H: 6m/20ft S: 3m/10ft
Roses flourish by a hot, sunny wall but some evergreen and semi-evergreen climbers (see below) do almost as well on a cool or cold wall. They climb by using their sharp thorns to spike onto convenient surfaces. Most are long flowering.
CULTIVARS (All sweet-smelling) 'Danse du Feu' ('Spectacular'): scarlet, semi-double; 'Gloire de Dijon': dark orange, double; 'Mme Alfred Carrière': creamy-white, large, double; 'Mme Grégoire Staechelin': pink, enormous, sumptuous, semi-double, not a repeat flowerer.

TRACHELOSPERMUM jasminoides

Half-hardy climber
H: 4m/13ft S: 1.5m/5ft
The fragrant white flowers, as the name suggests, resemble jasmine. They appear in mid- to late summer. An evergreen twiner, T. jasminoides prefers a warm or hot sunny position.
CULTIVAR 'Variegatum': leaves mottled and fringed with cream.

VITIS vinifera 'Purpurea'

GRAPE VINE Hardy climber
H: 10m/33ft S: 10m/33ft
This vigorous cultivar is grown mainly for its foliage. The leaves (which can be used for cooking) are a lovely claret colour in summer and turn wine purple in autumn. Its small, dark purple grapes are edible. Its prefers a warm sunny wall, to which it clings with its tendrils. The flowers, which appear in late spring, are insignificant.

WISTERIA sinensis

Hardy climber
H: 20m/66ft S: 10m/33ft
This is a stunning climber, producing panicles of sweetly scented, mauve flowers up to 30cm/12in long. These appear in early summer before the leaves are fully out, which adds to the dramatic effect. A second flush of blooms is usually produced in late summer. This quick-growing vigorous twiner prefers to grow in a warm or hot sunny site.
CULTIVAR 'Alba': white.

PERENNIALS, ANNUALS AND BULBS

ANEMONE blanda

Hardy tuber
H: 15cm/6in S: 10cm/4in
The large flowers of this tuberous perennial
appear throughout spring. Blue, pink, white and
mauve flowered forms can be found. These
anemones prefer a sunny or half-shaded
position.

BEGONIA × tuberhybrida

Tender tuber
H: 30–60cm/12–24in S: 38cm/15in
These popular, showy, tuberous perennials are
ideal on patios, for they can be started off in
containers indoors and moved outside when the
weather warms up. The double flowers, from
early summer through to early autumn, are up to
15cm/6in in diameter and are in both brilliant
and subtle colours, in the yellow, orange and red
range, with some white. These begonias do best
in a sunny site and grow quickly.
CULTIVARS 'Diana Wynyard': light cream; 'Festival':
gold; 'Harlequin': pink and white; 'Jamboree':
apricot; 'Mary Heatley': orange; 'Rhapsody': pink;
'Rosanna': deep pink.

CAMPANULA carpatica

BELL FLOWER   Hardy perennial
H: 25cm/10in S: 38cm/15in
These plants form clumps, topped in mid- to late
summer by masses of large, bell-shaped mauve,
purple or blue flowers. They grow quickly in sun
or partial shade.
CULTIVARS 'Ditton Blue': shorter than the species;
'White Star': white.

CHEIRANTHUS cheiri

WALLFLOWER   Hardy perennial
H: 20–56cm/8–22in S: 30cm/12in
Although perennials, wallflowers are normally
treated as biennials. Their heady scent and
showy bright colours make a welcome splash of
colour in late spring and early summer. The
species has yellow flowers, but there are
numerous cultivars in the red and orange colour
range. Wallflowers grow rapidly in a sunny
position.
CULTIVARS 'Golden', 'Orange', 'Scarlet Bedder': all
dwarf; 'Blood Red', 'Carmine King', 'Cloth of
Gold', 'Eastern Queen' (pink): all tall.

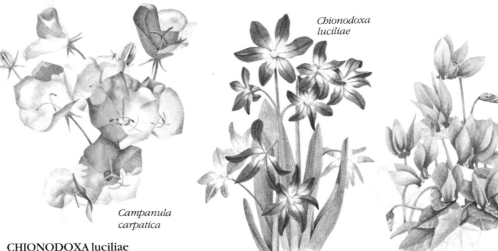

Campanula
carpatica

Chionodoxa
luciliae

Cyclamen
hederifolium

CHIONODOXA luciliae

GLORY OF THE SNOW   Hardy
H: 15cm/6in S: 8cm/3in
The six-petalled flowers, blue with a white
centre, open wide in mid- to late-spring to form a
star shape. These perennials flourish in the sun.
CULTIVARS 'Alba': all-white; 'Rosea': pink.

COLCHICUM autumnale

AUTUMN CROCUS   Hardy corm
H: 23cm/9in S: 23cm/9in
Each corm produces several lavender-coloured
crocus flowers throughout autumn. Superficially,
this plant looks similar to a crocus; however its
all-green leaves are much thicker and more
conspicuous than the grass-like leaves of the true
crocus, which grows in clumps and has six, not
three, stamens. It does best in partial shade.
CULTIVAR 'Album': white.

CROCUS chrysanthus

Hardy corm
H: 8cm/3in S: 8cm/3in
This species is bright yellow, but it has a number
of named offspring, which cover the full range of
crocus colours: white, blue, mauve, purple and
orange as well as yellow. Although it will grow in
partial shade, this corm responds and opens to
early spring sunshine.
CULTIVARS 'Blue Bird': mauve and white; 'Blue
Pearl': blue and white; 'Ladykiller': purple and
white; 'Zwanenberg Bronze': orange and bronze.

CYCLAMEN hederifolium (C. neapolitanum)

Hardy tuber
H: 10cm/4in S: 10cm/4in
The pink or white flowers, which are produced
in late summer and throughout autumn, have
reflexed petals. The leaves are very attractive,
with conspicuous markings above and a pink
underside. This tuberous plant does best in a
semi-shaded position.
CULTIVAR 'Album': white.

DIANTHUS × allwoodii

PINK   Hardy perennial
H: 30cm/12in S: 30cm/12in
Modern pinks are excellent for containers,
where they thrive and often produce so many
flowers that they can be cut for the house. They
are sweet smelling and appear from early
summer through to mid-autumn. They like lime
and do less well in acid soil so, if they are grown
in a peat-based compost, some chalk should be
added. They grow rapidly and prefer a sunny
position.
CULTIVARS 'Cherry Ripe': light cerise; 'Diane':
carnation pink; 'Doris': very pale pink; 'Ian':
crimson; 'Startler': bright red.

D. barbatus

SWEET WILLIAM   Hardy perennial
H: 30–45cm/12–18in S: 23cm/9in
Although the sweet William is a perennial, it is
treated as a biennial. There is a wide range of
varieties, mainly in the red colour group, and
with single or double flowers: these come out in
early summer. There are also dwarf cultivars,
with a height of 25cm/10in. Sweet Williams thrive
in the sun.

Dicentra spectabilis

DICENTRA spectabilis

BLEEDING HEART   Hardy perennial
H: 60cm/24in S: 45cm/18in
The red and white, heart-shaped flowers, which
open out in early summer, hang down along the
shoots. This perennial is quick growing.

ERICA carnea

Hardy perennial
H: 30cm/12in S: 45cm/18in
This is one of the few heathers that can be grown
in chalky soil. The flowers, which appear from
late autumn through to late spring, are small,
bell-shaped, crimson, dark to pale pink and
white. Like all heathers, this evergreen does best
in full sun.
CULTIVARS 'Aurea': pink with yellow-bronze leaves;
'King George': pink, early; 'Springwood White':
white, wide-spreading.

GALANTHUS nivalis

SNOWDROP   Hardy bulb
H: 25cm/10in S: 30cm/12in
Snowdrops are surprisingly difficult to establish
but are worth persisting with for the sight of
their nodding, bell-shaped, white flowers, single
and double, which appear in wintery
surroundings as the first sign of spring. They do
best in partial shade.

HELLEBORUS niger

CHRISTMAS ROSE   Hardy perennial
H: 25cm/10in S: 23cm/9in
From late winter to early spring, large white
flowers, rather like a single rose, are carried at
the top of short thick stems, above stalked
fingered leaves. This evergreen does best in a
partially shaded position.
CULTIVAR 'Potter's Wheel': larger flowers.

Helleborus niger

Impatiens wallerana

HESPERIS matronalis

DAME'S VIOLET   Hardy perennial
H: 1m/3ft S: 45cm/18in
The small, cross-shaped flowers, mauve or white,
are carried on long racemes in early summer.
They are most strongly scented in the evening.
Dame's violet grows quickly given a sunny
position.
CULTIVARS 'Nana Candidissima': white, double,
dwarf; 'Purpurea plena': purple, double.

HYACINTHUS orientalis

HYACINTH   Hardy bulb
H: 23cm/9in S: 15cm/6in
Bulbs that have been specially treated will open
indoors from mid-winter; untreated bulbs flower
later, in spring. Hyacinths, all highly scented, are
available in a great variety of colours.
CULTIVARS 'Amsterdam': light red; 'Bismarck':

blue; 'City of Haarlem': biscuit yellow;
'L'Innocence': white; 'Princess Irene': pink.

IMPATIENS wallerana (I. sultanii)

BUSY LIZZIE   Tender perennial
H: 60cm/24in S: 45cm/18in
Plants sold by nurserymen as Busy Lizzie for
outdoor use may be of uncertain parentage, but
the above names are correct. The five-petalled
flat flowers bloom right through from late spring
to early autumn. They can be red, orange, purple
or white. This perennial grows quickly given a
sunny site.
CULTIVARS 'Harlequin Orange': bright orange;
'Liegnitzia': purple, dwarf.

IPOMOEA purpurea

MORNING GLORY   Half-hardy annual
H: 25cm/10in S: 30cm/12in
A fast-growing twiner, *I. purpurea* produces
large, trumpet-shaped purple flowers from mid-
summer to early autumn. It prefers a sunny
position and will very readily run riot in
favourable climates.

IRIS reticulata

Hardy bulb
H: 15cm/6in S: 8cm/3in
The purple, blue or reddish flowers appear at
the top of short stems in early to mid-spring.
This bulbous plant does well in sun or partial
shade. There are a number of named cultivars
with larger flowers and different colours.

LATHYRUS odoratus

SWEET PEA   Hardy annual
H: Up to 2m/6ft 6in S: 15cm/6in
The sweet pea climbs by its leaf tendrils, and so
must be provided with wire or netting support. It
grows rapidly. Modern varieties, with sweet-

scented, colourful large blooms, can provide flowers for the house from mid-summer until early autumn.
CULTIVARS 'Carlotta': light red; 'Larkspur': light blue; 'Leamington': lavender; 'Princess Elizabeth': pink; 'Royal Flush': pale pink; 'White Ensign': white.

LILIUM longiflorum

EASTER LILY Half-hardy bulb
H: 75cm/30in S: 23cm/9in
This lily is ideal for container growing and it is easily raised from seed. In mid- to late summer, it produces headily perfumed, white, 15cm/6in trumpet-shaped flowers with bright yellow-tipped anthers. It thrives in full sun or partial shade. It derives its common name from the fact that, when forced, it will flower early, around Easter time.

LOBELIA erinus

Half-hardy perennial
H: 20cm/8in S: 60cm/24in
The trailing sort of lobelia makes an effective splash of colour throughout summer and autumn when planted in hanging baskets. Although a perennial, it is sold by nurserymen as a half-hardy annual; such plants are usually called 'trailing lobelia', although there are named cultivars. Lobelia prefers a sunny site.
CULTIVARS 'Blue Cascade': light blue; 'Red Cascade': red with white eye; 'Sapphire': blue with white eye.

MATTHIOLA incana

STOCK Half-hardy perennial
H: 30cm/12in S: 23cm/9in
Fragrant stocks come in a great variety of shapes and sizes. The most suitable for patio gardening are dwarf, large-flowering stocks, which are 'ten-week' stocks. They are short and compact and their early-summer blooms, single and double, are produced in many different colours – white, yellow, pink, red and mauve. These fast-growing perennials, treated as annuals, flourish in a sunny or half-shaded position, and do particularly well in limy soil.

NARCISSUS

DAFFODIL Hardy bulb
H: 16–60cm/6–24in S: 15cm/6in
Daffodils are available in a huge range of sizes and forms. The dwarf varieties illustrated below are most successful in containers and on patios. The flowers of most varieties, double or single, appear from spring through to early summer and come in various shades of yellow and white. Quick-growing, they do well in partial shade, and will naturalize well, particularly if lifted and divided every few years.

NEMESIA strumosa

Half-hardy annual
H: 20–36cm/8–14in S: 15cm/6in
This annual produces masses of small, funnel-shaped flowers in a wide colour range, from early to late summer. They can be raised easily from seed and planted out after danger of frost has passed. They are usually available in packets of mixed colours.
CULTIVARS 'Grandiflora': larger flowers; 'Nana Compacta': dwarf form; 'Suttonii': mixed colours.

NERINE bowdenii

Half-hardy bulb
H: 60cm/24in S: 15cm/6in
The unusual pink flowers with their thin, curving-back petals in broad heads, come out in autumn on stems carried well above the foliage, which often follows the flowers. *N. bowdenii* grows best by a sunny wall.
CULTIVAR 'Fenwick's Variety': darker pink.

PELARGONIUM

GERANIUM Tender perennial
H: and S: variable
Pelargonium is the correct botanical name for the plant most commonly known as a geranium. There are three sorts useful to patio gardeners: ivy-leaved, regal and zonal. All are evergreen and produce flowers from early summer through to the first frosts in autumn. Ivy-leaved geraniums have long trailing stems which fall gracefully from wall containers and baskets. Their flowers are mainly in the mauve and pink colour range. Regal geraniums are about 45cm/18in high when mature and their blooms are usually marked with

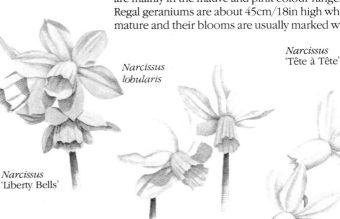

Lathyrus odoratus

Lilium longiflorum

Narcissus lobularis

Narcissus 'Liberty Bells'

Narcissus 'Tête à Tête'

darker shades. Zonal pelargoniums are stouter plants with rich flowers, mainly in shades of red.

PETUNIA × hybrida

Half-hardy perennial
H: 15cm/6in S: 15cm/6in
Petunias, which are now also available as F_1 hybrids, cover every imaginable flower colour and combination. Although perennials, these vigorous plants are usually grown as annuals and have flowers from early summer through to autumn. They flourish in the sun. The 'Multiflora' group has large numbers of relatively small flowers, and includes many named F_1 varieties. The 'Grandiflora' group has larger flowers, but fewer of them, and also includes a great many named F_1 hybrids. The 'Pendula' group comprises trailers, producing flowering stems up to 90cm/36in long.

PRIMULA denticulata

DRUMSTICK PRIMROSE Hardy perennial
H: 25cm/10in S: 20cm/8in
The spherical flower heads carried on stout erect stems give this perennial its common name. The small flowers, many to each head, appear from mid- to late spring. Their colours run from mauve to purple and pink to red and white. This primrose can grow in partial shade.
CULTIVAR 'Alba': white.

Nemesia strumosa

P. × polyantha

POLYANTHUS Hardy perennial
H: 20cm/8in S: 20cm/8in
Polyanthus make excellent container plants. Bright, quick-growing perennials, they flower in mid- to late spring, and do best in a sunny position. Many hybrids have been bred in recent years, offering a great choice of colours and far removed in appearance from the native primrose and cowslip from which they were originally developed.

SALVIA splendens

Half-hardy perennial
H: 30cm/12in S: 30cm/12in
Although a perennial, this vigorous plant is usually grown as an annual, because, like petunias and other bedding plants, it cannot overwinter out-of-doors. The flowers and bracts are typically red, but a number of varieties are available with purple, pink and white flowers, all produced from mid-summer through to autumn.
CULTIVARS 'Blaze of Fire' and 'Carabinière': bright red.

SAXIFRAGA granulata

MEADOW SAXIFRAGE Hardy perennial
H: 23cm/9in S: 23cm/9in
The flowers, white and bowl-shaped, open in early summer. An easy plant, it does best in full sun. Its leaves die down in summer, and it overwinters by its bulbils.
CULTIVARS 'Bathoniensis': red, larger; 'Plena': white, larger, double.

Sternbergia lutea

SCHIZOSTYLIS coccinea

KAFFIR LILY Half-hardy tuber
H: 75cm/30in S: 30cm/12in
Small, waxy, bright-red star-shaped flowers are carried in racemes in mid- to late autumn. The Kaffir lily does best in a warm, sunny border.
CULTIVAR 'Mrs Hegarty': pink.

SCILLA sibirica

Hardy bulb
H: 15cm/6in S: 8cm/3in
Each bulb has several flower stems, with bright blue, bell-shaped flowers in mid-spring. These bulbs can also be grown indoors and put out later in a sunny or semi-shaded site. They are easy to grow.
CULTIVARS 'Alba': white; 'Spring Beauty': dark blue.

STERNBERGIA lutea

LILY-OF-THE-FIELD Half-hardy bulb
H: 15cm/6in S: 15cm/6in
These bulbous plants resemble crocuses. The bright yellow flowers are carried on a short stem, from mid-autumn. They do best in sun, in rather heavy soil.

TULIPA

TULIP Hardy bulb
H: 15–45cm/6–18in S: 15cm/6in
Tulips are available in a wide variety of colours and sizes. The dwarf forms illustrated below are particularly successful for a patio. The natural flowering season is from late spring onwards, but early tulips can be forced indoors and planted outside later. They do best in a sunny position.

ZINNIA angustifolia

Half-hardy annual
H: 30cm/12in S: 15cm/6in
Daisy-like orange flowers are carried on the ends of erect stems in mid- to late summer. This annual likes plenty of sun.
CULTIVAR 'Persian Carpet': double flowers, bi-coloured in variations on orange and brown.

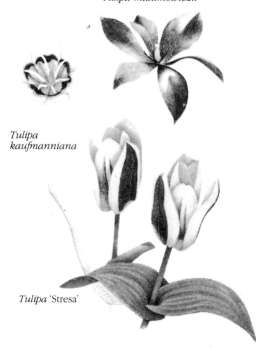

Tulipa maximowiczii

Tulipa kaufmanniana

Tulipa 'Stresa'

GROUND COVER PLANTS

ACAENA microphylla

NEW ZEALAND BURR   Hardy
H: 3–5cm/1–2in S: 60cm/24in
Effective ground cover, and also suitable between paving stones. This species has delicate, bronze, evergreen leaves and insignificant flowers from early summer to early autumn. The burrs are red and spiny. This quick-growing perennial does well in both sun and shade.

AJUGA reptans

BUGLE   Hardy
H: 20cm/8in S: 20cm/8in
Erect flowering shoots bear whorls of blue flowers in early summer. There are a number of decorative cultivars in which the leaf colour varies. This vigorous evergreen provides excellent ground cover in both sunny and shaded sites.
CULTIVARS 'Atropurpurea': purple foliage; 'Burgundy Glow': red, gold and bronze foliage; 'Multicolor': bronze, yellow and red foliage; 'Variegata': cream and green foliage.

ALCHEMILLA mollis

LADY'S MANTLE   Hardy
H: 30cm/12in S: 38cm/15in
This plant forms mounds of down-covered leaves, and prefers a sunny or partly shaded site. Branched flower heads carry tiny yellow-green blossoms in early to mid-summer, and look well long after. It is prolific self-seeder in many gardens.

ALYSSUM saxatile

GOLD DUST   Hardy
H: 30cm/12in S: 45cm/18in
The greyish evergreen foliage forms clumps which are covered in late spring and early summer with masses of gold-yellow flowers.
CULTIVARS 'Citrinum': lemon yellow; 'Compactum' (H: 15cm/6in): smaller than most; 'Plenum': double.

ANTHEMIS cupaniana

Hardy
H: 23cm/9in S: 38cm/15in
This evergreen forms cushions of foliage. The fragrant white flowers, on erect stems, come out in summer. It needs full sun to do well.

Ajuga reptans 'Burgundy Glow'

ARMERIA maritima

THRIFT   Hardy
H: 8cm/3in S:15cm/6in
Thick cushions of foliage with pink round flower heads are produced from late spring to mid-summer. A sun lover, this evergreen perennial grows slowly.
CULTIVARS 'Alba': white; 'Vindictive': rose-crimson.

ARTEMISIA brachyloba

Hardy
H: 10cm/4in S: 8cm/3in
In autumn, this evergreen has minute yellowish flowers in racemes, which rise above small cushions of silvery leaves.

AUBRIETA deltoidea

AUBRETIA   Hardy
H: 10cm/4in S: 45cm/18in
This vigorous perennial produces a mat of evergreen foliage, covered by a mass of light purple flowers from mid-spring to early summer. It likes lime and needs a sunny position.
CULTIVARS A large number of named cultivars are available with larger flowers in different colours, and some have different leaves: those named 'Aurea' are gold-edged; 'Variegata' denotes white-edged leaves. 'Dr Mules': violet flowers; 'Tauricola': deep purple flowers.

BERGENIA × schmidtii

ELEPHANT EARS   Hardy
H: 30cm/12in S: 30cm/12in
Large, broad, bright green leaves provide good evergreen ground cover. This plant does well in sun and partial shade. Heads of clear pink flowers are produced on short stalks from mid- to late spring.

Aubrieta deltoidea

BRUNNERA macrophylla

Hardy
H: 40cm/15in S: 30cm/12in
Brilliant blue forget-me-not-type flowers come out in early summer. A herbaceous perennial, it grows quickly, preferably in partial shade, and has large, heart-shaped, matt green leaves.
CULTIVAR 'Variegata': less tall and vigorous, with green and cream leaves.

CAMPANULA PORTENSCHLAGIANA

Hardy
H: 10cm/4in S: 38cm/15in
A graceful creeping ground cover, *C. portenschlagiana* has deep blue-purple flowers in summer and grows easily on most well-drained soils. It will toleate partial shade.

CHAMAEMELUM nobile (Anthemis nobilis)

CHAMOMILE   Hardy
H: 15cm/6in S: indeterminate
This evergreen perennial can make excellent ground cover in a sunny position and can be used as a low-maintenance substitute for grass. Its foliage is aromatic when crushed. The flowers, which look like daisies, appear in summer.
CULTIVAR 'Treneague': non-flowering, but very tough.

CONVOLVULUS sabatius

Half-hardy
H: 10–15cm/4–6in S: 60cm/24in
C.sabatius bears blue trumpet-shaped flowers throughout summer and early autumn. The leaves make a dense clump of foliage, but this quick-growing Italian species, native to chalky soils, is reliably hardy only on a sheltered site.

Dianthus deltoides

COTULA squalida

WORM WEED   Hardy
H: 5cm/2in S: 60cm/14in
Bronze-green ferny foliage provides not very dense ground cover in sun or shade. It forms a fast-growing mat, running and rooting at the node, and can be used as a lawn substitute. In dry weather, this semi-evergreen loses colour which it recovers after rain. In autumn, some of the foliage turns pink.

DIANTHUS deltoides

MAIDEN PINK   Hardy
H: 20cm/8in S: 10cm/4in
The dark green mats formed by this plant are ideal for filling crevices in paving. Its flowers appear from early summer to early autumn and their colours range from white to pink and red. A vigorous perennial, it likes a sunny site.
CULTIVARS 'Alba': white; 'Brilliant': rose pink; 'Flashing Light': scarlet; 'Wisley Variety': carmine.

FRAGARIA vesca

WILD STRAWBERRY   Hardy
H: 8cm/3in S: indefinite
This perennial is known for its delicious, tiny fruits. An early-summer-blooming evergreen, it spreads quickly by runners and thrives in shade.

GERANIUM renardii

Hardy
H: 23cm/9in S: 75cm/30in
A good clump-forming ground cover, *G. renardii* has five-lobed leaves that are silvery on their undersides. A profusion of white flowers with purple veins appear in early summer. It will tolerate semi-shade.

Fragaria vesca

HELIANTHEMUM nummularium

ROCK ROSE   Hardy
H: 13cm/5in S: 60cm/24in
Ideal for crevices in paving and for banks in full sun, this evergreen perennial flowers in early to mid-summer and needs an acid soil.
CULTIVARS 'Beech Park Scarlet': crimson with yellow centre; 'Ben Nevis': deep yellow and orange; 'Firedragon': orange-red; 'Jubilee': yellow, double; 'Wisley Pink': pink, with grey foliage; 'Wisley Primrose': yellow.

HOSTA sieboldiana

Hardy
H: 45cm/18in S: 45cm/18in
This plant does well in fairly heavy shade and is grown mainly for its handsome foliage; the grey-green leaves are up to 30cm/12in long. Lilac flowers protrude above the leaves in early to mid-summer.
CULTIVARS 'Aureomarginata': yellow-edged leaves; 'Elegans': corrugated leaves.

H. 'Thomas Hogg'

Hardy
H: 60cm/24in S: 45cm/18in or more
This cultivar has large oval leaves with frilled, cream-edged leaves. Lavender-blue flowers appear on slender spikes in early summer.

LAMIUM maculatum

SPOTTED DEADNETTLE   Hardy
H: 20cm/8in S: 60cm/24in
Fast-growing ground cover, *L. maculatum* has pointed oval silver leaves with narrow edging of green. Small heads of pale reddish-purple tubular flowers are produced during most of the summer.

Helianthemum nummularium 'Wisley Pink'

LIRIOPE muscari

Hardy
H: 30cm/12in S: 38cm/15in
Grassy leaves provide long-lasting evergreen ground cover. A slow grower, this perennial thrives in sunny positions. The lilac-coloured inflorescences, about 10cm/4in long, appear in late summer to mid-autumn, and have a similar form to those of grape hyacinth, hence the name *muscari*.

LYSIMACHIA nummularia

CREEPING JENNY   Hardy
H: 3–5cm/1–2in S: indefinite
A trailing waterside plant that can also be grown on ordinary soil, where it usually provides excellent perennial ground cover. The prostrate stems, carrying opposite leaves, creep along the ground. Single yellow flowers bloom in early to mid-summer. This quick-growing evergreen does well in shade.
CULTIVAR 'Aurea': yellow leaves.

MENTHA requienii

CREME DE MENTHE MINT   Hardy
H: 10cm/4in S: 60cm/24in
This semi-evergreen mint has long self-rooting stems that spread quickly to form a dense mat. Spikes of pale lilac flowers are produced in summer, giving off a strong aroma of peppermint. *M. requienii* needs some controlling as it can be invasive, but it provides good ground cover in a semi-shaded position.

PACHYSANDRA terminalis

Hardy
H: 30cm/12in S: 45cm/18in
This is a vigorous ground covering plant for shady areas. The mid- to deep-green leaves make rosette-shaped whorls. Insignificant flowers are produced in spring.
CULTIVAR 'Variegata': leaves are margined with white.

PHLOX amoena

ALPINE PHLOX Hardy
H: 23cm/9in S: 30cm/12in
This vigorous perennial produces small tufts of hairy leaves. Purple flowers, about 3cm/1in across, appear in clusters from early summer onwards.
CULTIVARS 'Rosea': pink flowers; 'Variegata': variegated leaves.

PULMONARIA angustifolia

LUNGWORT Hardy
H: 30cm/12in S: 30cm/12in
Ideal for ground cover in the shade. It is easily cultivated and propagation is by division. The flowers open in spring and are blue. There are a number of named cultivars of this perennial, some of which are a different blue, others pink or red in colour.
CULTIVARS 'Mawson's Blue': deeper blue than the species.

PULSATILLA vulgaris (Anemone pulsatilla)

PASQUE FLOWER Hardy
H: 30cm/12in S: 38cm/15in
Hairy buds are followed in late spring by large purple flowers with a boss of prominent yellow stamens and, later, by feathery fruits. A perennial with delicate foliage, it needs full sun and acid soil to grow well.
CULTIVARS 'Alba': white; 'Albicyanea; bluish-white; 'Budapest' and 'Rubra': redder than the species; 'Mallenderi': deep purple; 'Mrs Van der Elst': pink.

ROSA × 'Max Graf'

Hardy
H: 15cm/6in S: indefinite
A hybrid between *R. rugosa* and *R. luciae*, this prostrate, quick growing rose forms dense ground cover. The flowers are rich pink, borne in clusters, and bloom from early summer onwards.

SAXIFRAGA moschata

Hardy
H: 5cm/2in S: 45cm/18in
The foliage of the saxifrages resembles hummocks of moss. The flowers are creamy white and appear in early summer. The species, however, is rarely grown – one of the many hybrids or cultivars being more usual. A quick-growing perennial, it prefers semi-shade.
CULTIVARS 'Beauty of Letchworth': pale pink; 'Cloth of Gold': white, with gold leaves.

SEDUM spurium

Hardy
H: 8cm/3in S: 38cm/15in
This perennial forms a mat of fleshy, dark green leaves. The flat flower heads are pink and open out in mid- to late summer. It does best in sun.
CULTIVAR 'Album': white.

SENECIO compactus

Tender
H: 60–120cm/24–48in S: 60–120cm/24–48in
This compact shrub is noted for its silver-grey foliage rather than its yellow daisy-like flowers, which appear in summer. A sun-loving evergreen, this ground cover looks particularly good when contrasted with dark-leaved plants.

TELLIMA grandiflora

Hardy
H: 45cm/18in S: 45cm/18in
This evergreen thrives in shaded or semi-shaded conditions. The name 'grandiflora' is misleading, as the pale greenish-yellow or reddish flowers, carried on stems above the leaves, are small. They emerge in late spring and early summer.
CULTIVAR 'Purpurea': purplish foliage.

THYMUS herba-barona

Hardy
H: 10cm/4in S: 38cm/15in
This slow-growing woody herb, which grows wild in the Mediterranean, smells of caraway when crushed. The foliage, which forms a mat, grows well in the sun. The mauve flowers appear in mid-summer.

T. serpyllum

WILD THYME Hardy
H: 5–8cm/2–3in S: 75cm/30in
Wild thyme, which sounds so poetic, is often disappointing as ground cover, with tiny grey-green aromatic leaves and insignificant pale flowers, in mid- to late summer. However, there are a number of named cultivars available, which are ideal for garden use. All are excellent between paving stones. This perennial does well on lime and in sun.
CULTIVARS 'Albus': white; 'Annie Hall': pale pink; 'Pink Chintz': pink.

TRIFOLIUM repens 'Purpurascens Quadriphyllum'

WHITE CLOVER Hardy
H: 8cm/3in S: 60cm/24in
This evergreen ground cover adds nitrogen to the soil and spreads by runners. The purple leaf colour is best when the plant is grown on a sunny site. Its white flowers appear in early summer.

TROPAEOLUM majus

NASTURTIUM Hardy
H: 2.5m/8ft S: 38cm/15in
Smooth, circular mid-green leaves with wavy edges make excellent backcloth for the large bright yellow or orange spurred flowers that appear from mid-summer to early autumn. The leaves and stems have a pungent smell when crushed.
CULTIVARS 'Jewel Mixed': early flowering, mixed colours; 'Empress of India': scarlet; 'Gleam': semi-double, yellow.

VINCA minor

PERIWINKLE Hardy
H: 8cm/3in S: 90cm/36in
This small evergreen spreads quickly and does especially well in shade. The lilac-coloured flowers start in late spring and often continue intermittently until mid-summer. There is a range of named cultivars with different coloured flowers, some double.
CULTIVARS 'Alba': white; 'Atro-purpurea': purple; 'Burgundy': red; 'La Grave'; dark blue.

VIOLA labradorica 'Purpurea'

LABRADOR VIOLET Hardy
H: 10cm/4in S: 38cm/15in
This perennial has dark purple leaves, nearly all of which come true. A ground cover plant that grows quickly in many gardens, it is a typical violet with purple flowers that appear in late spring.

WATER AND MARSH PLANTS

ACORUS

SWEET FLAG   Hardy
H: 60cm/24in S: 30cm/12in
This marginal water plant has aromatic iris-like leaves. White, horn-like flower spikes protrude from the tops of the stems in mid-summer. It does best in full sun.

APONOGETON distachyus

WATER HAWTHORN   Hardy
H: 30cm/12in S: 45cm/18in
From mid-summer through to late autumn, this aquatic produces fragrant creamy-white flowers, about 8cm/3in wide, just above the water's surface. The leaves are fleshy, with brown markings. It does best in a sunny position, 23–60cm/9–24in deep in the water, but it will tolerate partial shade.

ASTILBE chinensis pumila

Half-hardy
H: 30cm/12in S: 30cm/12in
Slender spikes of rose-lilac small flowers rise from mid-summer to autumn above the ferny mid-green foliage. A good marsh plant, it also makes excellent ground cover in moist, semi-shaded conditions.

AZOLLA caroliniana

FAIRY MOSS   Half-hardy
S: indefinite
This quick-growing carpeting plant floats on the water surface and can be killed by frost. It has no flowers, but its foliage turns red in autumn.

BUTOMUS umbellatus

FLOWERING RUSH   Hardy
H: 45–90cm/18–36in S: 23cm/9in
This marginal will flower more readily if the water is shallow, so plant around the edge of ponds, 5–15cm/2–6in deep. It has typical rush-like leaves; the mid- to late summer blooms are rose-pink in umbels.

CALTHA palustris

MARSH MARIGOLD   Hardy
H: 30cm/12in S: 30cm/12in
The species is a quick-growing marginal plant, in water up to 15cm/6in deep, and carries masses of deep yellow, cup-shaped flowers that come out in late spring. The lush deep green leaves are lightly toothed at the edges.
CULTIVARS There are a number of named cultivars, which are not as big as the species plants. 'Alba': white; 'Plena': yellow, double.

CERATOPHYLLUM demersum

HORNWORT   Hardy
S: indefinite
This trailing oxygenator has dark green leaves, similar to coarse fern, and insignificant flowers. It anchors itself in the mud, 30–90cm/12–36in deep, and grows rapidly.

EICHHORNIA crassipes

WATER HYACINTH   Tender
H: (above water level) 15–25cm/6–10in
S: 30cm/12in
Rounded glossy dark green leaves are attached to short inflated stalks that act as floats. It produces short spikes of lavender blue orchid-like flowers from mid-summer. This free-floating perennial, which is vigorous and readily reproduces by means of stolons, prefers a sunny position. Its roots, which dangle in the water, are useful for fish to lay their eggs on.

ELODEA canadensis

CANADIAN PONDWEED   Hardy
S: indefinite
This trailing, quick-growing, deep water oxygenator should be planted 15–48cm/6–18in deep in the water. Small semi-translucent leaves grow in whorls, and its grey-white flowers are insignificant.

E. crispa

Hardy
H: 30–60cm/12–24in S: 30–60cm/12–24in
This attractive trailing pond weed fulfils several purposes: it oxygenates the water; feeds on waste material that drops to the pond bottom, thereby clearing the water; and provides nests for young fish. It grows quickly, is more robust than *E. canadensis*, and its leaves are rolled back in complete rings. The insignificant flowers appear in summer.

GLYCERIA aquatica 'Variegata'

Hardy
H: 60cm/24in S: 45cm/18in
A marginal aquatic, this plant is grown mainly for its clumps of handsome, stripy, grass-like leaves. It grows vigorously and, if planted in a small pond, will need thinning once a year.

HOTTONIA palustris

Hardy
H: (above water level) 13cm/5in S: 30cm/12in
This floating plant is quick growing and has feathery leaves. Its pale lavender flowers are produced in early summer. A rare native.

IRIS kaempferi

Hardy
H: 90cm/36in S: 45cm/18in
A marginal plant, *I. kaempferi* has slender deciduous foliage and deep purple flowers in

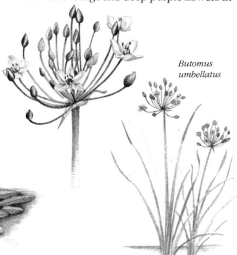

Aponogeton distachyus

Butomus umbellatus

*Iris
laevigata*

Nymphaea × marliacea
'Albida'

mid-summer. It is ideally suited to growing in
moist soil.
CULTIVARS There are several with colours ranging
from white to red-purple, lavender and pink.
'Higo': large flowers in a wide range of colours.

I. laevigata

Hardy marginal
H: 45cm/18in S: 45cm/18in
A first-rate marsh plant, it grows best in 5–13cm/
2–5in of water. Each stem carries three royal
blue flowers, which open in early summer.
CULTIVARS Named cultivars have variously
coloured flowers and leaves. 'Alba': white;
'Monstrosa': white with blue blotches;
'Variegata': light blue, with striped leaves.

LYSICHITON americanus

YELLOW SKUNK CABBAGE   Hardy
H: 90cm/36in S: 60cm/24in
A clump-forming marsh plant, *L. americanus*
has arum-like golden yellow flowers from early
to late spring and long, leathery bright green
leaves. It does best in sun or semi-shade.

MIMULUS luteus

MONKEY MUSK, BLOTCHED MONKEY FLOWER   Hardy
H: 38cm/15in S: 30cm/12in
A marsh plant, *M. luteus* has oblong mid-green
leaves and open-mouthed yellow flowers with
maroon spots, from early to late summer.

M. ringens

LAVENDER WATER MUSK   Hardy
H: 75cm/30in S: 38cm/15in
A marginal aquatic, it has dark green pointed
leaves and lavender blue flowers from mid-
summer to early autumn. It grows best in a water
depth of 10cm/4in.

MYOSOTIS palustris (M. scorpioides)

WATER FORGET-ME-NOT   Hardy
H: 23cm/9in S: 23cm/9in
This evergreen marsh plant thrives when just its
roots are in wet soil. The sky-blue yellow-eyed
flowers last from late spring through to mid-
summer.

NUPHAR lutea

BRANDY BOTTLE, YELLOW WATER LILY   Hardy
H: 60cm/24in S: 45cm/18in
The round yellow flowers of this floating aquatic
rise clear of the lush growth of large leaves from
spring to summer. It does best in a large pool in
a 60cm/24in depth of water.

NYMPHAEA × marliacea 'Rose Arey'

WATER LILY   Hardy
H: 45cm/18in S: 60cm/24in
The multi-petalled, sweet-smelling pink flowers,
10–15cm/4–6in wide, are carried in summer
well clear of the water. This vigorous fast grower
produces a great deal of vegetation; its leaves,
which float on the water's surface, are wide and
circular. A deep water plant, it prefers a sunny
position in about 45cm/18in of water.
CULTIVAR 'Albida': white, scented.

N. odorata 'Froebelii'

WATER LILY   Hardy
H: 30–75cm/12–30in S: 60cm/24in
This medium-sized slow-growing water lily
needs a water depth of 30–75cm/12–30in. The
sweet-smelling dark red flowers are about 10cm/
4in wide and appear from early to late summer.
The deep green leaves are flecked with red.
CULTIVARS 'Minor': dark green leaves and narrow
petalled, faintly scented smaller white flowers,
water depth of 30–38cm/12–15in; 'Rosea':
fragrant pale pink flowers, water depth of
30–60in/12–24in.

RANUNCULUS aquatilis

WATER CROWFOOT   Hardy
H: 75cm/30in S: 45cm/18in
This oxygenator produces two types of foliage,
carried on stems about 75cm/30in long: the
submerged leaves are in thin strips; the floating
leaves are like those of the land buttercup. Small
white flowers appear from late spring to mid-
summer, and the plant needs thinning regularly.
Plant in a water depth of 15–35cm/6–14in.

SAGITTARIA sagittifolia

ARROWHEAD   Hardy
H: 60cm/24in S: 38cm/15in
The aerial leaves, which grow on erect stems, are
arrow-shaped, hence the common name. The
underwater leaves are long and thin. In mid- to
late summer, pink and white flowers are borne
on thick stems. Quick-growing, it prefers a sunny
position in about 15cm/6in of water.

STRATIOTES aloides

WATER SOLDIER   Hardy
H: (above water level) 30cm/12in S: 30cm/12in
The sword-shaped leaves normally lie just below
the water surface, but rise above when it
produces its white flowers in late summer. It
grows rapidly, developing small plantlets.

TYPHA minima

DWARF REEDMACE   Half-hardy
H: 45cm/18in S: 45cm/18in
A marginal aquatic, it has long strap-shaped light
green leaves, and forms dense clumps of
foliage. It grows best in a water depth of
5–20cm/2–8in. The macelike brown flower
heads appear above the leaves from mid-
summer.

FRUIT, VEGETABLES AND HERBS

FRUIT

FICUS carica

FIG   Half-hardy tree
H: 3m/10ft S: 3.7m/12ft
Fig is grown for its rounded to pear-shaped, green, brown or purplish, fleshy edible fruit, in summer or early autumn. It has insignificant flowers and does well trained against a hot, sunny wall or fence. Plant in a 30cm/12in container, which will restrict the roots and force the plant to produce fruit. Do not feed until the tree starts producing fruit, otherwise too much vegetation and no fruit is produced. The fig is usually free of pests and it should be given some protection against frosts in severe winters. Prune only to maintain the tree's shape. Propagate in early autumn from stem cuttings, which should have a heel.
CULTIVARS 'Brown Turkey': less hardy; 'Brunswick': does best outdoors; 'White Marseilles': pale, green fruit.

FRAGARIA x ananassa

STRAWBERRY   Hardy perennial
H: 15cm/6in S: 20cm/8in
Grown for its juicy, red, edible fruit, usually in early summer. This low-growing plant has white or reddish flowers in spring. There are three types: early summer fruiting; late summer to early autumn fruiting; and alpines, which fruit from mid-summer to early autumn. Strawberries are generally trouble free, but must be netted against birds. Propagation is from runners, which form during summer, or for alpine varieties, which do not form runners, from seed.
CULTIVARS 'Baron Solemacher': alpine; 'Cambridge Favourite'; 'Sweetheart': small alpine plants which can be grown from seed.

MALUS sylvestris

APPLE   Hardy tree
H: 1.8m/6ft S: 1.2m/4ft
M. sylvestris is grown for its round, green-, yellow-green or red-skinned, fleshy, edible fruit, which is produced in summer to early autumn. Its white to pink flowers appear in early summer. Buy trees grafted on to a dwarfing rootstock, which will keep down their size and bring them into fruit bearing earlier. Ensure fruit by planting

two or more varieties that blossom at the same time and so can cross-pollinate. Where space is limited, plant a 'family' tree, which has more than one variety grafted on to it, or grow the trees as cordons (see p. 158). For disease-free fruit, spray with a pesticide at petal fall, then again in mid-summer.
CULTIVARS Dessert: 'Charles Ross', 'Cox's Orange Pippin', 'Sunset'. Cooking: 'Early Victoria', 'Grenadier'.

PRUNUS persica

PEACH   Half-hardy tree
H: 3.7m/12ft S: 4.7m/15ft
Grown for its large, round, yellow to yellow-flushed crimson-skinned, edible fruit in summer to early autumn. This self-fertile tree produces pale pink flowers, solitary or in pairs, in early summer. When the fruits have set, thin to leave them 18–20cm/7–8in apart, removing unwanted fruitlets when approximately the size of a pea. P. persica does best when fan-trained against a warm, sunny wall. Encourage the production of young, fruit-bearing wood by pruning out the old, hard spent wood in late spring. Spray against peach leaf curl, using a copper fungicide.
CULTIVARS 'Duke of York': best for flavour; 'Peregrine' and 'Rochester': easier to grow.

VITIS vinifera

GRAPE   Hardy climber
H: 2.5m/8ft S: 3.7m/12ft
Grown for its round, pale yellow or blue-black-skinned, green-fleshed, usually seeded fruit, which ripens in late summer to early autumn. It has clusters of insignificant greenish flowers in early summer. Grapes are self-fertile and do not need a pollinator. Pinch off surplus fruitlets, leaving only two to three bunches of fruit per shoot to swell. Do not feed, otherwise masses of vegetation and no fruit will be produced. V. vinifera does well in mild climates but prefers the protection of a wall. It flowers and fruits on the previous year's growth, which should be removed in winter after it has produced the fruit. Spray with zineb against downy mildew, and dust with sulphur against powdery mildew.
CULTIVARS Black: 'Brandt': autumn foliage; 'Pinot Noir'; White: 'Madeleine Sylvaner'.

VEGETABLES

CICHORIUM intybus

CHICORY   Hardy perennial
H: 20cm/8in S: 30cm/12in
Although a perennial, chicory is grown as an annual for its leaves, which are eaten in autumn and winter salads. Both green- and red-leaved types are excellent. One of the best-known green-leaved chicories is the 'Sugar Loaf' type, which forms pointed heads, similar to cos lettuce. Sow from early to late summer, depending on when the crop is needed.
CULTIVARS 'Red Treviso' and 'Red Verona': leaves turn red in autumn; 'Sugar Loaf': can also be cropped as immature seedlings.

CYNARA scolymus

GLOBE ARTICHOKE   Hardy perennial
H: 1.2m/4ft S: 30cm/12in
This thistle-type plant with its beautiful grey foliage has edible flower buds. Plant rooted suckers in a sheltered, sunny position in late spring. Do not try to crop the first year and remove any flower heads that appear. After a few years, take suckers from the plant and start again.
CULTIVARS 'Camus de Bretagne': large heads, but difficult to grow; 'Gros Vert de Lyon': the most popular; 'Purple Globe': attractive flowers.

LACTUCA sativa

LETTUCE   Tender annual
H: 23cm/9in S: 30cm/12in
The Salad Bowl type of lettuce is best for patios, as the pretty, edible, frilled leaves can be picked individually as required. They can be cropped regularly to give a continuous supply throughout the season. Plant seeds in pots or growing bags from late spring to mid-summer. Do not transplant.
CULTIVARS Salad Bowl type: red and green oak-leaves; 'Green Lollo' and 'Red Lollo' (deeply curled leaves). Hearting type: 'Little Gem' (small).

LYCOPERSICON lycopersicum

TOMATO   Tender annual
H: from 45cm/18in S: 30cm/12in
Grown for its red, yellow or striped, edible fruit, which is globular, pear- and plum-shaped.

Propagate from seeds, started indoors in mid-spring. Plant outdoors in a sunny position once frost risk has passed. Remove the inter-nodal side shoots as soon as they appear. Feed fortnightly when the fruits appear, and remove growing tip after four trusses have set.
CULTIVARS 'The Amateur': dwarf sort; 'Gardener's Delight': sweet, bite-sized fruits.

PHASEOLUS coccineus

RUNNER BEAN   Tender annual
H: 2.5m/8ft S: 30cm/12in
With its light green foliage and red, pink or white flowers, the runner bean not only makes an attractive screening plant but also produces edible seed pods. It needs a support up which to twine. Sow the beans in rich soil in early summer, and pinch off the tips when the plants reach the tops of their supports. Pick the pods regularly while they are young.
CULTIVARS 'Mergoles': white; 'Painted Lady': red and white; 'Scarlet Emperor': red; 'Sunset': pale pink, self-fertilizing.

P. vulgaris

FRENCH BEAN   Tender annual
H: 1.5m/5ft S: 20cm/8in
Grown for its edible pods, the French bean likes warm conditions and is killed by frosts. The climbing varieties give much larger yields than the bushes. Purple-podded climbers look especially decorative, their pods turning green when cooked. Propagate from beans sown in early summer. For earlier crops, sow under cloches in late spring. The beans will neatly climb up netting fixed to a wall or fence.
CULTIVARS 'Blue Lake': can also be dried and used as haricots; 'Garrafal Oro': very long pods.

SOLANUM tuberosum

POTATO   Tender annual
Grown for its edible tubers, which must not, however, be consumed if they show any patches of green on them. S. tuberosum produces mauve or creamy-white flowers. There are three main types: first early, second early and maincrop. The first early varieties are best for growing in barrels on the patio. For details, see p.152.
CULTIVARS 'Arran Pilot': kidney-shaped tubers, floury flesh; likes the light soil and good drainage of a barrel; 'Maris Baird': oval tubers, waxy flesh, very early variety.

HERBS

ALLIUM schoenoprasum

CHIVES   Hardy bulb
H: 30cm/12in S: 23cm/9in
Clump-forming herb with grass-like leaves, sometimes called the 'poor man's onion'. It grows very well in pots and makes an attractive edging to a raised bed. Chives can be grown from seed but propagation is usually by division in autumn, planting out clumps of up to six bulbs. To encourage growth and ensure a constant supply, cut the plants down to about 5cm/2in at regular intervals.

ANETHUM graveolens

DILL   Hardy annual
H: 1m/3ft S: 60cm/24in
This attractive feathery herb needs space and sunshine to thrive and is best grown in a bed rather than a pot. Given an undisturbed patch, it will self-seed from year to year but should otherwise be treated as an annual. Sow seed in early spring, thinning the plants as they come up so that adult plants are far enough apart not to touch each other. Seed that is not being kept for culinary use can be saved from year to year.

FOENICULUM vulgare

FENNEL   Hardy perennial
H: 90–150cm/36–60in S: 45–60cm/18–24in
This clump-forming sun-loving herb has aromatic, finely cut, green leaves, which are used raw to season fish, cheese and meat dishes. Its stems can be cooked. A decorative bronze-leaved variety is also available. Fennel produces tiny yellow flowers, in flattened heads, in summer and will readily self-seed. Propagate in spring by division or from seeds.

MENTHA

MINT   Hardy perennial
H: 60cm/24in S: 30cm/12in
Very easy to grow culinary herb, ideal for pots, which restrict the plant's invasive habit. The best variety is apple mint (*M. rotundifolia*), which has a more delicate taste than spearmint (*M. spicata*). To encourage the plant to continue producing leaves into autumn, remove the flower spikes as they appear. Propagate from seeds, cuttings taken in early summer, or pieces of the creeping rhizomes with a shoot on each.

PETROSELINUM crispum

PARSLEY   Tender biennial
H: 45cm/18in S: 30cm/12in
This herb has an undeserved reputation of being hard to grow, mainly because its seeds can take up to eight weeks to germinate. Usually grown as an annual, it is actually a biennial, although its leaves are tougher and less pungent in its second year. It looks attractive grown in a 'parsley pot' with pockets of plants in the sides. Make two to three sowings a year to keep up the supply, the first one being in spring in shallow drills. Parsley prefers a moist soil and can tolerate some shade.

SALVIA officinalis

SAGE   Hardy shrub
H: 40–60cm/16–24in S: 40–60cm/16–24in
A woody evergreen shrub that usually has green leaves but also comes in a red, gold and variegated form. Once planted, it should flourish from year to year without any trouble. Sage can be grown in pots or in an open bed, the tricolour version being less hardy and needing shelter in winter. It is usually propagated in autumn by hardwood cuttings with heels on them and these are planted in a mix of peat and sand. Sage can also be grown from seed, but this tends to be a slow process.

THYMUS

THYME   Hardy shrub
H: 20–30cm/8–12in S: 40cm/16in
A whole family of aromatic species with pungent leaves, thyme can be found in upright or creeping (*repens*) form, and with leaves ranging from dark green to golden yellow and silver. *T. vulgaris* is the best variety for general culinary use. Cut the plants back in autumn to avoid straggly growth, particularly in the creeping varieties. Old woody plants should be replaced by propagating from seeds or cuttings.

FURNISHING THE PATIO

INTRODUCTION

The finishing touches to your patio – the furniture, lighting and decoration – need to be chosen with great care and, before you buy, there are some questions you need to ask yourself. First, does the style go with the house and garden? This factor is particularly important if the furniture is to remain out of doors throughout the year. If it is used occasionally and folded away when not in use, then a clash of styles, although better avoided, is not such a problem.

Lounging and dining furniture needs to be of a colour, material and period style that complements, rather than fights with, its surroundings. Rustic furniture, for example, seldom seems appropriate in strictly town surroundings unless the whole patio has been designed to look like a country garden. Fancy wrought iron 'period' garden furniture is a tempting buy but looks strangely ill at ease in functional surroundings – though with a little extra searching you may find some examples of classic garden designs from the past that will blend – the less fussy lines of Chinese Chippendale, for instance.

Strictly functional garden chairs (tables are less noticeable) look best in modern surroundings and would spoil a patio that has been planned in a romantic vein. Sometimes you will face a decision between good looks and comfort – some of the most luxurious lounging chairs could not be described as attractive. If a compromise has to be made, and comfort wins, then you could consider painting the furniture in a colour that helps it to blend better with its surroundings or recovering any upholstery in more muted colours.

Secondly, have you shopped around enough? Attractive garden furniture, lights and containers are not to be found only at the garden centre – many of the larger stores stock them, too, as do specialist furnishing shops. Don't forget to look in the back pages of home and garden magazines. Some very attractive items, many of them imports from abroad, are available only by direct sale; a phone call could bring you a huge array of specialist catalogues. Antique shops and street markets may well be a source of splendid ornaments, statues, lights and special items of furniture.

You should take as much time and trouble over furniture and light fittings for the garden as you would when buying for the house. It is better to carry a table and chairs outside when needed while you search for exactly the right furniture for the patio, rather than make an expensive mistake. Wherever possible, if a room opens on to the patio, consider the decoration and furnishings for both room and patio together.

Thirdly, is the colour right? Do you mind if the furniture attracts attention at the expense of surrounding plants and trees? Any white furnishings will inevitably stand out, so the design needs to be chosen with great care. Bright white furniture has other disadvantages apart from being conspicuous; it will need frequent cleaning, especially in city conditions, and a flat table surface, for example, can reflect an uncomfortable amount of glare when the sun is strong in summer. If this occurs, you may have to reposition the furniture or use a coloured cloth over a table, or shade it with a parasol or some form of awning.

Brightly coloured furniture can look gay and attractive, but you may tire of it after a few years. Vivid shades, such as red and blue, can be toned down to some extent by linking them with bedding plants of the same colour. If you want bright colours, consider using them for cushions which you can change when you opt for a different colour scheme.

Fourthly, will it stand up to wear and tear? Furniture, containers and light fittings for outdoor use must be robust and well made if they are to stand up to exposure to the elements all year round. Check that screws, bolts, hinges and fittings are well made in rust-proof materials and check also that containers for plants are frost-proof. Don't be tempted to buy anything that looks good if it is flimsy – its life outdoors will inevitably be short. Umbrellas and upholstery should be made in weather-proof and fade-resistant materials.

Some garden furniture can, of course, be stacked away when not in use, and need not be as robust as the type that is left out all year round. Storage space, however, may then be a problem. You could possibly use it inside the house, perhaps in the kitchen, and some garden furniture could do double duty in a playroom.

FURNITURE CONSTRUCTION

Each of the four main categories of garden furniture – wood, metal, cane and synthetics – has its own specific advantages and disadvantages. It is up to you to choose the material that best suits your circumstances. All-year-round furniture is usually made from synthetics (including fibreglass), metal or hardwood. Less-robust furniture includes rattan, cane and softwood. Into this category, too, comes anything that is permanently upholstered in non-waterproof fabrics, rather than items that have removable cushions, which can be taken indoors if rain threatens.

Wooden furniture

Two points need to be considered before buying wooden furniture – the type of timber used and the strength of the construction. Hardwoods, such as elm, teak or oak, are best for furniture that is to be left permanently outside. Softwoods will not last

CREATING A THEME

Patio and garden will both benefit from being unified by a common theme. In the example here, the Japanese atmosphere has been carefully created through the use of wood, cane, bamboo, stone and gravel, as well as an oriental planting scheme.

1 Stone grouping
2 Bamboo fence
3 Raked gravel
4 Parasol
5 Rattan furniture
6 Maple
7 Bamboo
8 Azalea
9 Tsukubai, or water basin
10 Decking
11 Stone lantern
12 Stone path

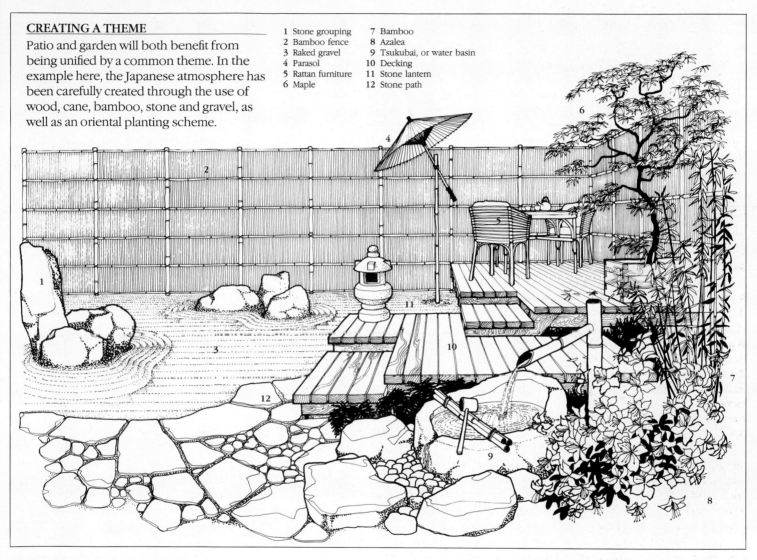

as long, and must be painted frequently or treated with preservative. Even when treated, they are inclined to warp and buckle after a few years. Softwood furniture is, of course, much cheaper and there is a case to be made, in the short term, for buying odd chairs and a table cheaply, lacquering them in bright colours, and then using them outside until either they fall apart or you tire of them. Furniture that has been glued

together, rather than properly jointed, has a particularly short life-span used this way – perhaps one season only.

Purpose-built wooden furniture for the garden is necessarily bulky and solid looking and, unless it is very plain, looks best in an informal patio or in a larger country style one. When you are buying, check that the furniture is well made – the joints should not 'give' when rocked, and should be well fixed

together, dovetail or mortise-and-tenon fashion, or with pegs or wedges. Any metal fittings should be made from non-corrosive steel or brass. Avoid polyurethane finishes on wood for outdoor use as it soon peels off.

Maintain wooden furniture by feeding and nourishing it once a year with teak oil, or its equivalent, to keep it in good condition. Metal fittings on wooden furniture should also be oiled, otherwise they tend to 'bleed'.

FURNITURE AND ACCESSORIES

You need to pay as much attention to furnishing your patio as you would to any room inside the house. Obvious items, such as tables and chairs, should, of course, suit the surface they stand on. But don't neglect the incidental accessories, such as pots and containers, statues and sun umbrellas – these, too, should be in style.

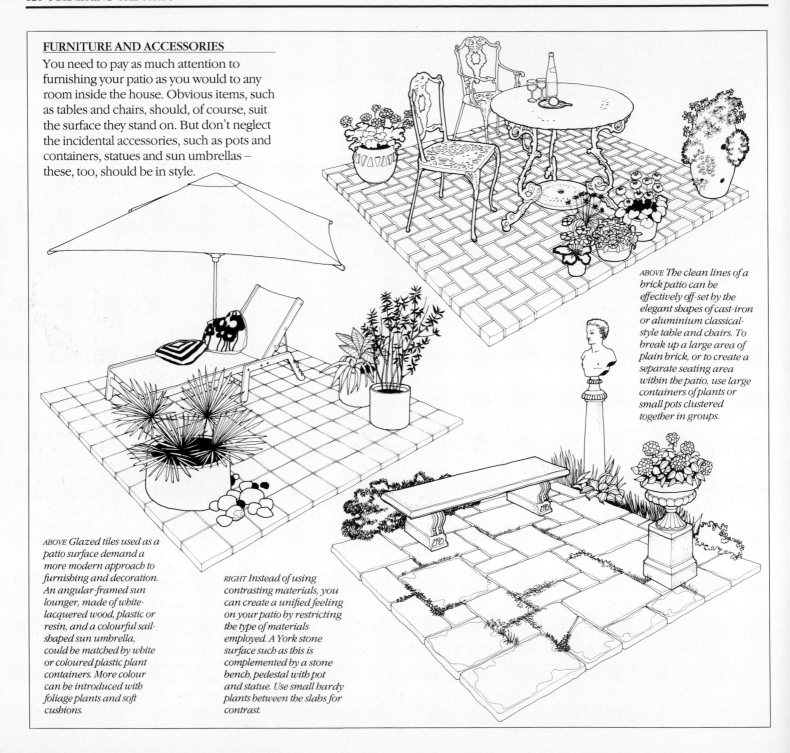

ABOVE *The clean lines of a brick patio can be effectively off-set by the elegant shapes of cast-iron or aluminium classical-style table and chairs. To break up a large area of plain brick, or to create a separate seating area within the patio, use large containers of plants or small pots clustered together in groups.*

ABOVE *Glazed tiles used as a patio surface demand a more modern approach to furnishing and decoration. An angular-framed sun lounger, made of white-lacquered wood, plastic or resin, and a colourful sail-shaped sun umbrella, could be matched by white or coloured plastic plant containers. More colour can be introduced with foliage plants and soft cushions.*

RIGHT *Instead of using contrasting materials, you can create a unified feeling on your patio by restricting the type of materials employed. A York stone surface such as this is complemented by a stone bench, pedestal with pot and statue. Use small hardy plants between the slabs for contrast.*

Metal furniture

This must be made from top-quality materials if it is to last any length of time outdoors, and the enemy in this case is usually rust and corrosion. Because of its strength, it often looks less clumsy than wooden furniture, but it should be heavy-weight enough to cope with situations, such as being sited on uneven paving, without twisting and distorting.

The heaviest metal furniture is cast iron or cast aluminium, which is often used for reproduction nineteenth-century furniture. It looks very handsome in the right surroundings and can withstand the weather well as long as it is painted when necessary. The main disadvantage is that it is usually very heavy to move around, and dragging it across a patio could damage the paved surface. Cast-iron reproductions are also inclined to be uncomfortable to sit on – many of them have shallow seats, usually, made from unyielding, extremely hard lattice. This problem can be partly overcome by the addition of slim cushions.

Modern metal furniture can be very elegant indeed and much more comfortable to sit on. For ease of maintenance, look out for designs that have been coated with plastic, since these will not need repainting.

Cane and rattan furniture

Furniture made of this material is very easy to live with and it has the great advantage of being lightweight, so it can be moved around the patio with the minimum of effort. This, however, turns out to be a problem on an exposed site where it could well be blown about in high winds. Cane and rattan often looks good inside the house, so, although usually bulky in construction, it could be brought indoors if the weather becomes too wet and blustery.

Furniture of this construction does tend to· deteriorate quickly if alternately soaked with rain and then dried out in the hot sun.

Ideally it should be sited in a conservatory or under an awning of some type and taken outside only in good weather. Even one sharp shower will tend to take off its sheen and make it more vulnerable to rot.

To keep cane and rattan in good condition, you need to brush or vacuum clean it regularly to remove the small particles of grit and dirt from the crevices where they tend to lodge. Wipe the furniture over occasionally with a damp cloth unless it is protected by varnish – a coat of polyurethane applied to the furniture when it is brand new will help it to withstand the elements much better.

Synthetic furniture

Manmade materials have not yet been exploited to their full potential in the garden. It is a pity that at the moment the market is flooded with cheap, flimsy furniture made from plastics, especially the rather nasty copies of period designs which have given synthetics a bad name. Modern shapes can be moulded very well in synthetics of all types – notably fibreglass, which is stouter than most – and bright colours are easy to achieve. When buying, make sure that the furniture itself is heavy enough to withstand high winds and that tables are steady and unlikely to be knocked over accidentally. Plastics, in general, have a static quality that attracts dust, and they will therefore need cleaning regularly, especially in town and cities. Don't use a scouring preparation, however, that might scratch the surface, or the furniture will become dull and unattractive very quickly. When buying, always check chairbacks and legs to make sure that there are no moulding faults or hairline cracks – otherwise the furniture is likely to snap when any strain or weight is applied to it.

TYPES OF GARDEN FURNITURE

Not all furniture used in the garden or on the patio need be new. Second-hand furniture bought at auctions or picked up in junk

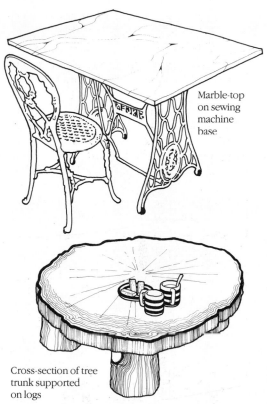

Marble-top on sewing machine base

Cross-section of tree trunk supported on logs

shops can look very effective – a selection of different types can soon be 'knitted' together into a matching set if you paint them all the same bright colour or, indeed, white. It pays to look also for large slabs of marble. These can often be found on old-fashioned wash-stands and they make very attractive permanent table tops if set on top of a base from an old treadle sewing machine, for example, or on a single heavy pedestal. Film director chairs, which are readily available new or second-hand, make good patio seating – an attractive compromise between a dining and a lounging chair. Their canvas seats and backs can be replaced easily with ones in bright colours. Second-hand deckchairs, too, can be given a new lease of life if their woodwork is painted in a bright colour and they are given a new, brightly patterned canvas sling.

On a more rustic level, a large flat section, sawn from a trunk of a tree, will make a good occasional table if set on low legs. A large piece of polished stone will serve a similar function, and these can sometimes be found as off-cuts in a stonemason's yard. You could also consider building, or having built, your own custom-designed furniture in wood – if a large tree forms part of the patio, a very convenient seat can often be constructed around it by a carpenter (see p. 64).

Dining furniture

This must be chosen in a scale to suit the patio on which it is to sit. Remember, too, that if you are dealing with a small space you must check that there is enough room not just to accommodate the dining chairs around the table, but for the chairs to be drawn back when the diners stand up. If space is at a premium, you can site the table in a corner, and build seating in around it on two sides in the form of benches.

You must allow approximately 0.75sq m/ 8sq ft to take the average dining table and four chairs. If you are in any doubt, before buying the furniture chalk the area that each item will cover on the patio itself or draw it in on a scale plan. Provided there is enough room to sit down at the table, you can cut down on the amount of space the dining area takes up when not in use by choosing a table with flaps and chairs that stack or fold.

Lounging furniture

As its name implies, this furniture must be comfortable above all else. It must also be well balanced and easy to use – some designs, for example, tend to tip up when you sit on them, and some rocking chairs are suitable only on a perfectly smooth and level surface. It is an advantage to choose wheeled models if you are using large lounging chairs on the patio, since they can be very heavy to move around. Comfort is also the main consideration when choosing upholstery.

Hammock supported between trees

While plastic-coated fabrics sound a sensible choice, they are most unpleasant in hot sun, when bare skin tends to stick to them. They are also likely to fade rather quickly. Lounging chairs anywhere near a swimming pool, however, will almost certainly have to be covered with waterproof material.

If you have little or no space on the patio for lounging chairs, consider installing a hammock, slung between two posts or trees. In a confined space you could also use airbeds of the type you take to the beach as temporary sun loungers. Alternatively, consider using giant inflatable plastic cushions, which can be deflated and stored away when not in use, and beanbags, which take up very little room on the patio.

Occasional furniture

This can be used with great success to highlight part of the patio, turning a corner, for example, into something special – possibly with a piece of pergola built overhead

to make it into an arbour. Here, a robust type of material must be used for the bench or garden seat, since it needs to be out all year round, and wood or metal is the usual choice. Good looks vie with comfort for occasional seats. Since they are not likely to be sat on for long periods of time at a stretch, good looks are almost more important. A bright colour, or white, in this case is a good choice, since it will make the feature more noticeable – unpainted hardwood tends to blend into the background and be less attractive in these circumstances. When buying occasional furniture, consider a small, low table – almost footstool height – to go with it. This is useful to take a drink or book or, in the evening, a piece of lighting equipment if you are having an outdoor party.

CONTAINERS AND POTS

Like attractive ornaments in the house, containers and pots can do a tremendous amount to set the scene and improve the look of any patio. Once again, as with furniture, the overall style of the area should be taken into consideration when you buy – terracotta pots, for example, which are very attractive in their own right, can look sadly out of place in, say, a period town patio, where handsome stone urns would be more appropriate. In the same way, wooden tubs and clay pots usually blend in better with country-style surroundings.

The larger the container the better, for not only will you be able to plant more impressive displays, but the plants will be more likely to survive and thrive, and need watering less often. It is important, however, to make sure that really large pots are sturdy enough to take the weight of the quantity of damp soil that they will contain.

Containers for the patio now come in an infinite variety of shapes and sizes, and you can choose between boxes, bowls, urns, tubs, and barrels, made in an ever-increasing range of materials, too.

Plastic containers

Containers made of plastic are the cheapest and most versatile. Plastic is light to handle, bends rather than breaks and, since it is not porous, keeps the soil inside moist. Plastic containers can be found with water reservoirs built-in – ideal if you go away for a few days, since water can be provided when the plants need it. In addition to the usual shapes, plastic can be found moulded into special planters, such as tower pots, which fit on top of one another and are used for growing bedding plants or strawberries. On the negative side, plastic does not stand up to indefinite use, and after a year or so exposed to strong sunlight it will tend to become brittle and is then likely to crack.

Glass fibre containers

Containers made of this material are more expensive than those made of plastic, but they are stronger. You will often find them moulded into classic shapes, such as decorative troughs and urns, and the material can be used very successfully to imitate lead, stone, or even wood. The main drawback with glass fibre containers is their substantial initial cost.

Concrete containers

Concrete plant containers are most usually found in modern designs – cones, bowls or squares – and it is extremely heavy to handle (even when empty), so it is wise to make sure of your site before putting the container in place and planting – moving it afterwards will be quite an operation. New concrete containers should be left out to weather for a few months if lime-hating plants are to be put in them.

Reconstituted stone containers

Ideal for facsimiles of traditional urns and troughs, reconstituted stone is made from powdered stone in a concrete mix. Once again, it is too heavy to move around easily and is not really suitable for balconies unless they are particularly substantial. As with concrete, new reconstituted stone containers should be weathered before lime-hating plants are put into them.

Wooden containers

Wood makes a particularly sympathetic material for containers because it keeps the roots of growing plants warmer than plastic or stone. Of all the containers, wood requires the most maintenance – it does tend to deteriorate quickly and will, therefore, need varnishing, painting or treating with a wood preservative that is not toxic to plants. Wooden containers can be in the form of half-tubs, squared-off Versailles tubs (which look particularly good in formal surroundings) or troughs. Wooden containers are the easiest to make yourself. Always stand wooden containers off the ground, raised a few inches on bricks or something similar, to allow air to pass underneath and stop the timber from rotting.

Terracotta containers

This material makes extremely attractive pots and containers if used in the right setting – ideal if you are aiming at a Mediterranean or tropical look on your patio. The problem with terracotta is that it is a naturally brittle material and cracks and breaks very easily. It is also porous and so plants tend to dry out more quickly and roots of plants may suffer from frosts during winter. Some convincing, and cheaper, imitations of terracotta are now appearing made out of plastic.

Resin-bonded cellulose fibre containers

This material has recently made its appearance as a short-term container – it was used originally as a lining material for hanging baskets but can now be bought in the form of free-standing pots. It cannot, however, be expected to last more than one summer. Large containers made from cellulose fibre become flimsy when filled with garden soil, and they should only be used with soil-less compost. Containers of this material make extremely good 'inners', if, for example, you want to plant up a decorative copper or some other container that is not really designed for plants.

Unusual containers

Growing bags are another form of temporary container well worth considering for the patio. Suitably well-disguised with a mini unmortared brick wall around them, and with peat or pebbles scattered over the top, they become a useful temporary flower bed that can be discarded when a change of plan is wanted.

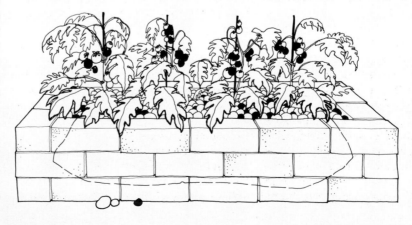

Growing bag in unmortared, brick-built raised bed

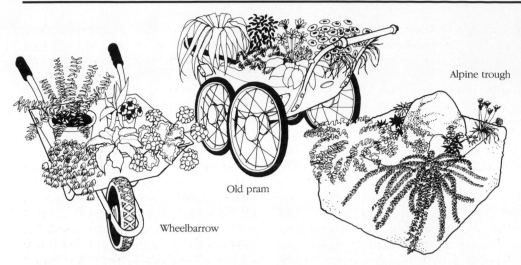

Wheelbarrow

Old pram

Alpine trough

Look around also for other unusual containers for plants on the patio – an old doll's pram or a wheelbarrow makes a good holder, when painted up, for a clutch of plants in pots. Old-fashioned stone sinks, too, make excellent plant troughs, especially for alpines. An old kitchen copper, with a cellulose fibre liner, makes an excellent container, too, if you can find one.

PATIO LIGHTING

Lighting for the patio comes under two headings – temporary and permanent. When choosing permanent electrical lighting, once again it is important to consider what style is appropriate for the site. Nothing looks more out of place than an eighteenth-century lamp in modern surroundings. If you are planning lighting on any scale, it is a good idea to seek out a specialist firm and go through their catalogue – your choice may be somewhat limited in ordinary garden centres and shops.

Garden lights that are meant to be seen, rather than hidden, range from coach lamps and lanterns and copies of old street lights to simple globes and small safety lights for steps and doorways. Then there are floodlights and spotlights, which are used to illuminate a wall, tree, statue or seating area.

These can be found with wall fittings, on posts or fitted with spikes, which are pushed into the soil. To go with them comes a range of accessories – coloured filters, interchangeable coloured bulbs, louvres to reduce glare and directional hoods.

Temporary lighting

In this category are fairy lights, flares and candles. Particularly attractive for barbecues, outdoor parties and dinners, flares come in decorative shapes mounted on bamboo poles and burn for approximately two hours. They can be pushed into a bed or the lawn or even into a large tub. Heat and light of any kind will tend to attract insects, but it is possible to buy candles that actually discourage insects. Garden candles burn from about 40 to 75 hours, depending on their size, but they do not produce as much light as flares.

There may be times, especially if you have a large area to deal with, when you need temporary lighting of a higher level than can be provided by candles, flares or decorative fairy lights. You may, for example, have to temporarily light some steps that the family are familiar with, but might be troublesome for guests at a party. For these occasions, 'chains' of linked lights are available. Each

chain can contain up to four lampholders mounted on ground spikes, and all wired to the same mains plug.

Underwater lights

For both safety reasons and for decoration, any garden water feature benefits from being well lit. Underwater lights are very specialized, need to be professionally installed and can only be used underwater. The lampholders themselves are completely sealed and made from corrosion-resistant stainless steel. Underwater lights can also be fitted with colour filters, but make sure the colour suits your water and marginal plants.

If you are planning to light a pond or pool right from the beginning, lights are better recessed into a side wall or floor, so that the safety glass sits flush with the mounting surface. If, however, lights are an afterthought, surface-mounted units can be installed. The range of styles of underwater lights is not large, since they are not intended to be on view. Better types feature an anodized aluminium reflector for maximum reflectance.

SCREENS AND ACCESSORIES

A screen should be chosen with the use to which it will be put firmly in mind – if it is purely decorative then it is possible to use much flimsier materials than if it is free-standing or acting as a fence. Once again the appropriateness of the material to the patio should be the first consideration.

Wood is the most usual material for screening. For a rustic look there is a choice between hurdles, interwoven or lapped wood fencing, wattle or reed. For a more open look, cleft chestnut fencing is relatively cheap, or picket fencing can look very attractive. Other open types of screening can be made from trellis and it is ideal for an area where privacy is not paramount. You can, of course, create your own trellis – and your own patterns, or treillage, by buying wooden battens and fastening them together or on to a wall. Bamboo, split or otherwise, also makes an effective background screening for a modern patio garden, and goes particularly well with water gardens, too. Another good form of modern screening can be made from planks set on edge to form louvres – a job that needs to be done on site, usually by a carpenter.

Pierced concrete blocks come in a wide range of patterns and make a more permanent type of screening, though they tend to look pretty ugly used over a large area. Bricks can also be laid in a bond with occasional gaps to make a pierced wall, particularly suitable when the screening needs to link into, say, the walls of a house or a general garden wall.

There are many other types of screening materials available, including chain link, decorative stone balustrades, post and rail or even wrought iron, so finding the right style to blend in with your patio and house should not be too much of a problem.

Awnings and umbrellas

Whether used for overhead or background screening, awnings must be secured to a strong structure if they are not to flap about. They will also need to be dismantled in winter unless made from particularly strong, waterproof material. In places where sunny days are few and far between, there is a form of awning material available made from canvas faced with a reflective substance that helps you to tan. In situations where the opposite applies, look out for material, and sun umbrellas, too, which filter out harmful rays but allow you to tan normally.

Umbrellas and other accessories that also act as screens need to tone in with the general colour scheme of the patio. Sun umbrellas can be found that are free-standing, usually with a weighted base, which slot into the centre of a table, or which stick into the ground by means of a spike. Choose one that is as stable as possible, especially if your patio is at all exposed.

Barbecues

If the patio is large enough, a barbecue looks best built in to the actual structure of the patio (see p. 65), but often there is insufficient space for a permanent cooking area and a free-standing barbecue has to be used instead.

Free-standing barbecues fall into two categories – small models that stand on an existing surface, such as the floor or a table top, and those that come with a stand of some sort. The simplest barbecue is the Hibachi (Japanese for fire box), a simple single or double sized box with space for a charcoal fire in the bottom and a removable grid above. The grid on which the food is cooked can usually be moved to one of three levels above the fire. The basic Hibachi is the best choice when you are barbecueing for the first time, to see if you enjoy outdoor cooking. Later on you can graduate to a larger, more elaborate set-up if you wish. The single Hibachi will cook only enough food for four people at most, but there are double and triple versions available. It can also be found in a round version on a wheeled base.

Spend more money and you can invest in a grill-brazier, which very often has a rotisserie built in to it. These types are always free-standing and choose a model that has sturdy rigid legs, especially if the patio surface is at all uneven. Some models have a very useful lower storage shelf for plates, meat or tools. The most elaborate grill-braziers not only have a motorized spit but a hood and an area built in on which to prepare food.

Hibachi barbecues are not designed for indoor use but the most sophisticated ones, operated by gas or electricity instead of charcoal, can sometimes be used safely under cover.

To go with a barbecue there is a whole range of accessories – tongs, kebab sticks, wire grill baskets and some made especially for fish, which often breaks up when cooking. Skewers, spatulas and tongs are also useful, as is a set of bellows if you are relying on charcoal for the fire.

Statues and ornaments

These are very much a matter of personal taste – not everybody would want to sit under the shadow of a replica Venus de Milo, for instance. Scale plays an important part here – too large a statue looks ludicrous, while one that is too small will be lost. There are a number of 'pop' statue designs that are seen all over the world – the boy with the dolphin, for example, and it is difficult to find anything new that looks genuine and different, short of commissioning something from a sculptor. A look round a local art school, however, at exhibition time may yield a pleasant and relatively inexpensive surprise. Otherwise, keep an eye out for suitable figures in country antique shops and, if the space available is small, think perhaps in terms of a wall mask or a small creature instead of a human figure – heraldic lions, for example, go well with many different types of patio settings. If you are buying second hand, make sure that the material from which the statue is made is suitable for constant outdoor exposure. Modern pieces are usually made in reconstituted stone or concrete.

TABLES AND CHAIRS

Heavy-duty furniture

1. and **2.** Classic design, cast-aluminium outdoor dining furniture. The rectangular table measures 109 × 74cm/ 43 × 29in and is 71cm/28in high. The round table has a diameter of 81cm/32in and is 69cm/27in high. The grape design carver chair is 84cm/ 33in high and the circular-seat chair is also 84cm/33in high.

3. Rattan chair and matching, glass-topped occasional table. Approximate sizes for the chair are: height 90cm/36in and width 45cm/18in. The table measures 90 × 43cm/ 36 × 17in.

4. Solid teak circular table standing 65cm/26in high and with a diameter of 1.07m/ 3ft 6in. The matching teak chair is 84cm/33in high.

5. Available with both a round and oval top, this attractive modern table and matching seating are made of white-lacquered expanded resin.

6. Attractive and very functional bench and matching dining table in either a natural wood or white-painted finish. Bench is available in two sizes: 1.65m/ 5ft 5in and 2m/6ft 6in. The table measures 140 × 78cm/ 55 × 31in.

Lightweight and fold-away furniture

7. Casual and well designed, this style of lightweight fold-away chair is available in bright red. Splayed legs provide extra stability and the unusual, spade-shaped seat is comfortably deep. The accompanying black metal table also folds away for easy storage.

8. Well-strutted for a rock-steady footing, this matching table and chair set is ideal for any patio or balcony. Light-weight metal framing is complemented by a deeply recessed upholstered seat sling.

9. Clean lines are a feature of this dining set. The all-aluminium table and chair frame is weather-proof – a theme carried through to the chair with its very durable back and seat slings made of vinyl coated polyester mesh. The chair is 85cm/33in high and 58cm/23in deep; the table stands 68cm/27in high and has a diameter of 1.17m/3ft 10in. Available in brown, black and white.

10. Sturdy yet simple, this fold-away chair has a comfortable body-contoured seat and back. The chair and table frame are available in either white or dark brown and the table comes with a cream-coloured, marble-effect top. Table height is 70cm/28in and diameter 60cm/24in.

11. A director's chair made of hardwood and available with a range of brightly coloured back and seat slings. The equally informal slatted wood table measures 95 × 60cm/37 × 24in.

12. Elegant, slim, metal-framed matching table and chair. The chair has a thin, padded cushion and the table is available in two sizes: 110 × 110cm/43 × 43in and 120 × 80cm/47 × 32in.

BENCHES

Functional seating

1. Solid teak, heavy-duty garden bench, available in seat lengths of 1.8m/6ft and (with a centre leg) 2.5m/8ft. The bench is 50cm/20in deep and 96.5/38in high.

2. An attractive 3-seater bench with a slatted hardwood seat and back and with wrought iron sides and legs. Length is 1.23m/4ft, depth 60cm/24in and height 75cm/30in.

3. Teak garden bench with a Chinese-style, lace-patterned back, often associated with Chippendale. Length is 1.5m/5ft, depth 74.5cm/29in and height 89cm/35in.

4. Antique Regency angle seat. This delicate-looking piece of outdoor furniture was made between 1800 and 1820 out of wrought iron and it was designed to fit round a tree.

5. An eye-catching decorative stone seat with vine and scroll-work supports. Length is 1.29m/4ft 3in, depth 75cm/30in and height 44cm/17in.

6. Attractive 2-seater bench, made of white-lacquered wood and completely weatherproof. Length is 1.12m/3ft 10in, height 75cm/30in and depth 53cm/21in.

7. Elegant 2-seater wooden bench. A traditional design, the slatted back is high enough to act as a head-rest.

Decorative seating

8. Elaborately worked, arch-backed garden seat, available in both solid teak and white-painted pine options. It comes in lengths of 2.5m/8ft, 1.9m/6ft 3in, and 1.7m/5ft 6in; depth is 55cm/21½in and height 105cm/41in.

9. Ideal for a formal setting, this 2-seater has a slatted hardwood seat and a fern leaf design, cast-iron or aluminium back and legs. Length is 1.12cm/3ft 10in, depth 56cm/22in and height 86.6cm/34in.

10. Early Victorian, 19th-century garden seat. This beautiful Gothic-style piece of furniture was made of cast iron and is now in a private collection.

11. High-backed rattan settee suitable for a sheltered outdoor area. The 3-seater version is 2m/6ft 6in long, 53cm/21in deep and 1m/3ft 3in high. Separate seat cushions are supplied at extra cost, covered either in calico or fabric of your own choice.

Informal seating

12. A simple bench suitable for a picnic table set. The metal legs and struts fold flat against the hardwood seat for easy stacking and storage. Length is 1.8m/6ft and height 40cm/16in.

13. Lightweight and comfortable, this hardwood and metal-framed seat is ideal for moving about to follow the sun or placing in the shade during the midday heat.

14. Suitable for a more modern patio setting, this style of bench is informal and is available in a range of bright colours, as well as white and natural. Length is 1.5m/5ft.

LOUNGING FURNITURE

Heavy-duty loungers

1. Adjustable, semi-reclining armchair in white-lacquered or marine-varnished wood. Height of chair when upright, 95cm/ 38in, and depth 65cm/25½in.

2. Fully reclining lounger with adjustable leg-rest and sunshade. This model has an all-metal, white-lacquered frame and is available with four deeply filled cushions.

3. Solid, low and very comfortable, this rattan lounger has an adjustable head-rest and a separate mattress and pillow. This model does not have wheels and is heavy to lift and reposition. Length is 1.95m/6ft 5in; width 75cm/ 30in.

4. Heavy solid-teak lounger, adjustable to seven positions. It is fitted with unobtrusive wooden wheels and a mattress is available as an optional extra. Overall length is 2m/6ft 6in.

5. Solidly made teak lounger. The basic model does not include the mattress and armrests (not shown). Overall length is 1.8m/6ft and width 60cm/24in.

6. All tubular steel with a weatherproof coating, this seven-position lounger has large plastic wheels and a deep, 10cm/4in filled mattress and head-rest.

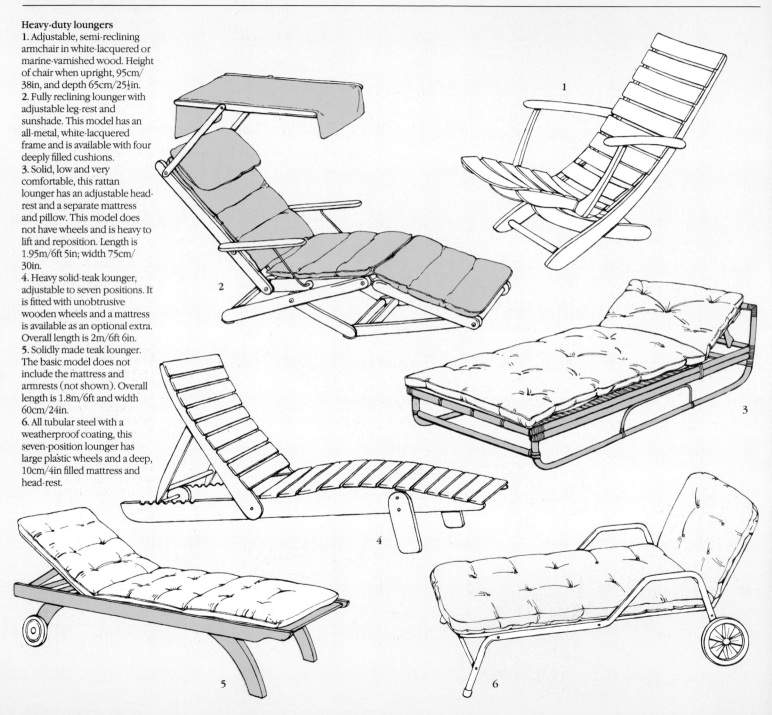

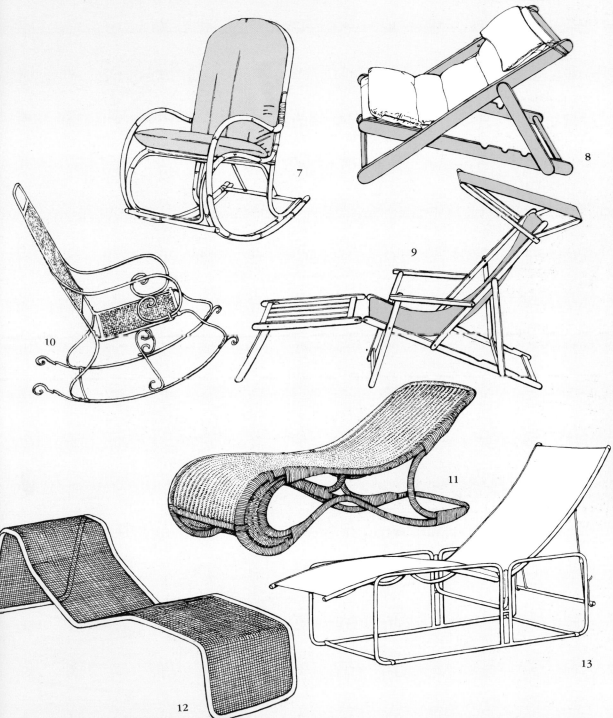

Lightweight loungers

7. Bent bamboo rocking chair, which can be taken outside and used as a lounger whenever the weather permits. Foam-filled cushions are available as an optional extra.

8. This luxury-version deckchair is made of solid teak. The heavy-duty fabric sling supplied can be supplemented by a deeply filled segmented cushion and head-rest.

9. A stretched-version deckchair with the addition of an adjustable legrest and sunshade. Overall length of the lounger is 1.62m/5ft 4in; the width is 58cm/23in.

10. Delicately shaped, this antique rocking chair would look beautiful in any outdoor setting. Although fragile-looking, its all-metal frame makes it surprisingly robust. Rockers such as this can only be found by touring second-hand and antique shops.

11. This sun lounger looks heavy but is, in fact, quite light. It is not completely weatherproof and so would need to be brought indoors in bad weather. Overall length of the lounger is 1.8m/6ft and the width is 60cm/24in.

12. Very modern, one-piece, non-adjustable lounger. This model is aluminium-framed and available in either green or white. Length is 1.95m/6ft 5in and width 65cm/25½in.

13. For comfort and ease of use, this very functional-looking, fully adjustable sun lounger has been raised well off the ground. The frame is made of lightweight aluminium and covered with a weatherproof elasticated synthetic webbing. Length is 1.9m/6ft 3in and the width is 63cm/25in. It is available in either white or brown.

CONTAINERS

Pots and baskets

1. Terracotta or clay pots with matching saucers, either glazed or unglazed, in diameters of 8–45cm/3–18in.

2. Square plastic pots with matching saucers available in sizes of 5–15cm/2–6in.

3. Geranium pot with textured finish, 40cm/16in diameter.

4. Flat-sided baskets for hanging against a wall, made of plastic-coated wire.

5. 'Swallow's nest' wall pot in reconstituted stone or terracotta, 43cm/17in high.

6. Terracotta wall pot about 15cm/6in deep.

7. Highly decorative wall pot 25cm/10in deep and made of stone.

8. Traditional wire or plastic-coated wire hanging basket 23–38cm/9–15in diameter.

9. Solid plastic hanging basket with clip-on drip tray, 23–38cm/9–15in diameter

10. Quarter-segment plastic container. Four of these form a round tub with a 90cm/36in diameter.

11. Basket-weave design pot in reconstituted stone, 25cm/10in high.

12. Attractive reconstituted stone pot with lattice-work and rope design, standing 38cm/15in high.

13. Tall container in the style of a chimney pot, 60cm/24in high. Genuine chimney pots can also sometimes be found.

14. Clay parsley pot, 23–45cm/9–18in high.

15. Terracotta strawberry pot available in sizes up to 75cm/30in high.

16. Square plastic pot with built-in water reservoir, 36cm/14in high.

17. Spiral planter made of white plastic. Each tier is 25cm/10in high.

Large containers, tubs and troughs

18. Regency style urn made of reconstituted stone, standing 38cm/15in high. Matching reconstituted stone pedestal 43cm/17in high.

19. Highly decorative, glazed earthenware pot, approximately 43cm/17in high, including integral 'feet'. This style of pot is available with a range of different motifs.

20. For a modern setting, this cone-shaped planter made of reconstituted stone stands 25cm/10in high.

21. Solidly made hardwood tub, slightly tapering, and available in either a natural wood or painted finish. Height is 38cm/15in.

22. Half-barrel usually made of oak and available in heights ranging between 23–45cm/ 9–18in. These barrels can be sealed to make very attractive water gardens.

23. Leaf-patterned terracotta trough, floor-standing or for the window sill. Approximately 25cm/10in high and 50cm/20in long.

24. Flat-sided plant trough made of elm, slightly raised on integral supports. Trough stands 23cm/9in high and is available in two lengths: 90cm/ 36in and 120cm/48in.

25. Ornate plant trough made of reconstituted stone and decorated with a grape vine motif, 38cm/15in high. Heavy stone supports, also patterned, stand 39cm/15½in high.

26. Plastic window box with drip tray, available in lengths between 38–106cm/15–42in. Can usually be found in either green or brown.

27. Alpine trough made of reconstituted stone, 26cm/ 10½in high. Available in two sizes: 109 × 66cm/43 × 26in and 80 × 56cm/32 × 22in.

BARBECUES

Small, portable barbecues

1. Compact charcoal grill, ideal for meals on the patio or picnic lunches. Legs fold away to hold the lid in position for carrying and storage. Cooking area 1032cm²/160in².

2. Rapid start-up electric unit. Re-usable volcanic rock gives food a charcoal flavour and there is a four-position variable heat control. Comes supplied with 10m/33ft of cable.

3. Gas-fired aluminium barbecue with stainless steel burner. Gas heats up the re-usable volcanic rock for authentic flavour.

4. Portable charcoal unit that folds away into a neat, attaché-sized case. The 40 × 25cm/16 × 10in grill plate can be placed in three cooking positions.

5. and 6. Double and triple Hibachi-type charcoal barbecues. Both have wooden handles and legs and three-position grill heights. Double grill measures 43 × 25cm/17 × 10in, and the triple grill 68 × 25cm/27 × 10in.

7. Adjustable-height charcoal barbecue with telescopic extension pole that allows the 40cm/16in diameter fire-bowl to be positioned at heights between 60cm/24in and 90cm/36in from the ground.

8. Cylindrical charcoal grill in attractive enamelled steel, available in black, white and red. A convenient rail for tools surrounds the grill.

9. Charcoal barbecue with stand and wheels, ideal for the patio or picnics. Unit stands 56cm/22in high and has a 34cm/13½in diameter grill plate. An accessory shelf can be fitted between the legs.

10. Barbecue kettle for cooking joints of meat. Available in red, black, brown, blue and green.

11. Cast aluminium gas-fired unit. Grill height 84cm/33in.

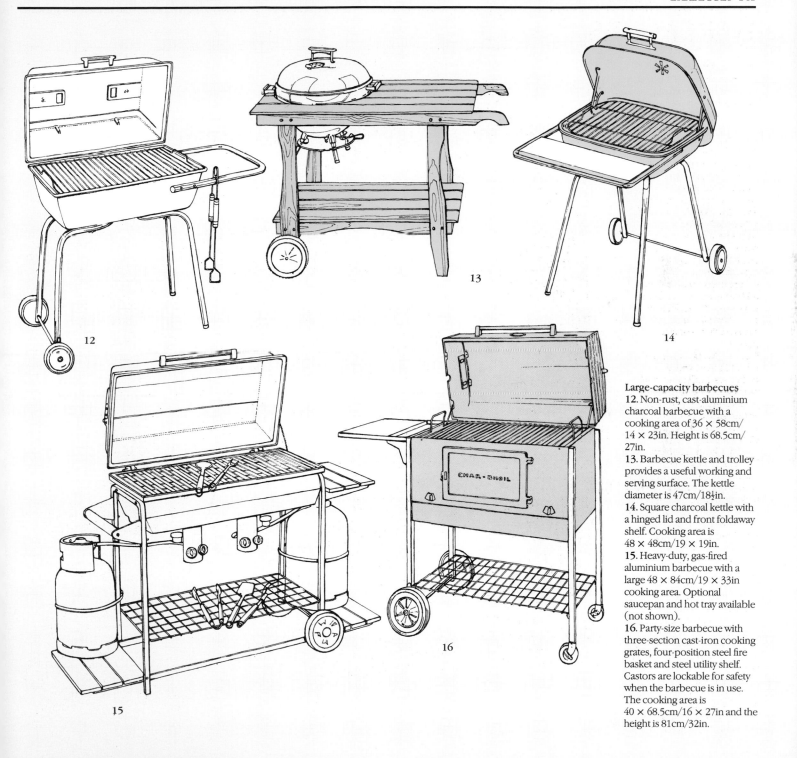

12

13

14

15

16

Large-capacity barbecues
12. Non-rust, cast-aluminium charcoal barbecue with a cooking area of 36 × 58cm/ 14 × 23in. Height is 68.5cm/ 27in.
13. Barbecue kettle and trolley provides a useful working and serving surface. The kettle diameter is 47cm/18½in.
14. Square charcoal kettle with a hinged lid and front foldaway shelf. Cooking area is 48 × 48cm/19 × 19in.
15. Heavy-duty, gas-fired aluminium barbecue with a large 48 × 84cm/19 × 33in cooking area. Optional saucepan and hot tray available (not shown).
16. Party-size barbecue with three-section cast-iron cooking grates, four-position steel fire basket and steel utility shelf. Castors are lockable for safety when the barbecue is in use. The cooking area is 40 × 68.5cm/16 × 27in and the height is 81cm/32in.

LIGHTS

1. Anodized aluminium 60W wall light with brass trim and hand-cut star glass. Height 40cm/16in.

2. Aluminium 100W wall light, available in black with a textured finish. Height 43cm/ 17in.

3. Recessed 100W wall light made of aluminium and stainless steel, fitted with safety glass.

4. Globe-shaped 60W wall light with black frame and amber-coloured glass.

5. 60W bulkhead light with porcelain lampholder, heavy-duty glass and protective cage. Available in red, yellow, white, green, black, blue and brown.

6. Round 100W bulkhead light with a 20cm/8in diameter. Available in the same colours as **5.** above.

7. Temporary floodlight with screw clamp for fixing to objects up to 5cm/2in round. Available with 75W, 100W and 150W lamps.

8. Garden flares available in a range of colours and lengths between 60cm/24in and 70cm/ 28in. Flares burn for about two hours.

9. Portable 60W garden light with textured glass and ground mounting spike. Available either in single lights or in chains of four.

10. Portable 40W and 60W garden light with a ground spike and shielded by a cylindrical lens.

11. Double 75W–150W floodlight with ground spike. Lights feature an anti-dazzle ring and 160° vertical movement.

12. Aluminium garden light and pole; allows light to be adjusted to a variety of heights.

13. Party candles available in a variety of shapes and colours. Each candle burns for about 40–75 hours.

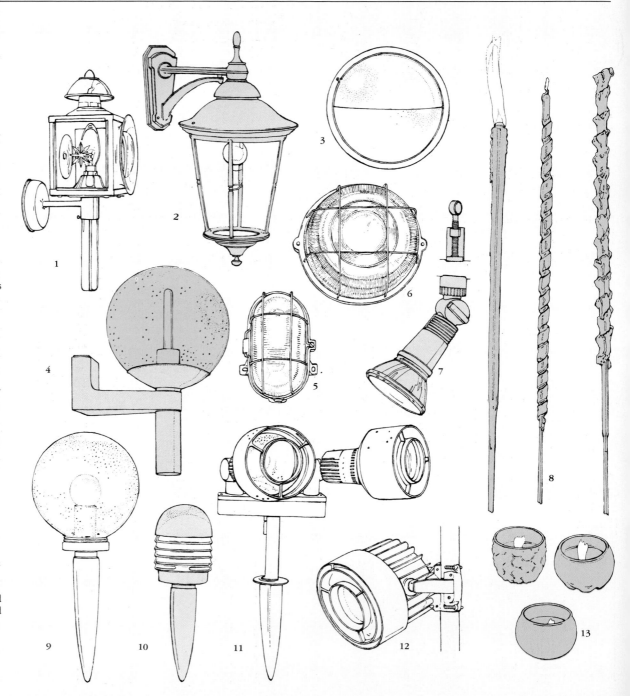

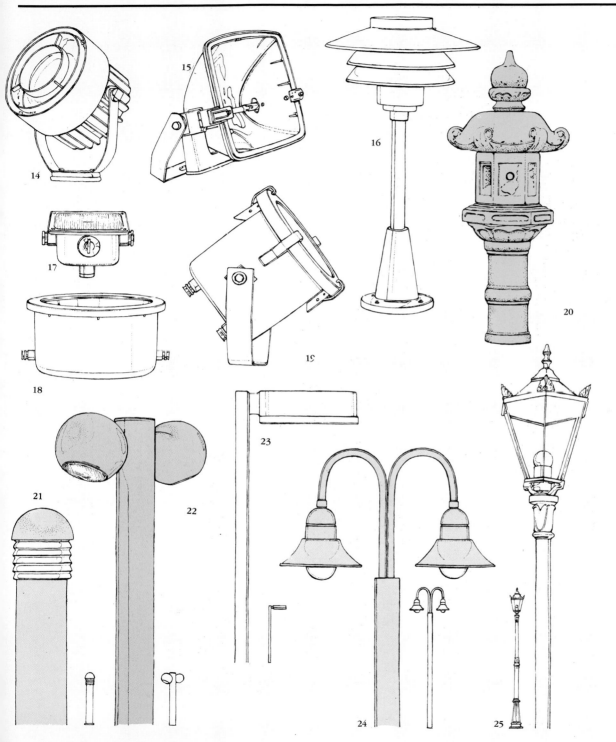

14. Cast aluminium, 300W garden light with bracket for screwing to any stable surface. Safety glass and anti-dazzle ring.

15. Totally enclosed 300W or 500W floodlight, which can be wall or pole mounted and is made of aluminium.

16. Cast aluminium 100W pedestal light. The frame has a slight textured finish and the glass is smoked coloured.

17. Watertight stainless steel distribution box for recessing into the walls of pools.

18. Underwater, flush-fitting 125W floodlight made of stainless steel.

19. Underwater floodlight suitable for 75W, 100W and 150W lamps and available with green, blue, yellow and red, as well as clear, safety glass.

20. Available in a variety of sizes, stone Japanese lanterns are best used as an attractive focal point rather than as a practical lighting alternative. You can instal either a candle or electric light in the flame box and use paper or frosted glass to diffuse the light.

21. 100W garden light with cylindrical lens. Made of aluminium and stainless steel, the light is supplied with a baseplate for screwing on to a stable foundation or a ground spike. The light stands 1m/3ft above the ground.

22. Pole-top double lights with a sunken pedestal base. Each light between 75W and 150W and the unit stands 1m/3ft above the ground.

23. Angular pole-top light containing three 60W lamps. The pole stands 1m/3ft high.

24. Aluminium and stainless steel pole-top double light. Available with ground spike or baseplate. Tall light standing 2.6m/8ft 6in high.

25. Elegant lamp post made of cast aluminium with a rough iron-like finish. Light stands 2.3m/7ft 6in high.

STATUES AND ORNAMENTS

Animals

1. and **2.** Concrete garden animals available in a wide variety of subjects. The owl stands 25cm/10in high and the alligator is 45cm/18in long.

3. Suitable for a large patio or garden only, this imposing heron, made of lead, stands 1.2m/4ft high.

4. Concrete or reconstituted stone lion, 45cm/18in high. Lions with traditional heraldic shields are also available.

Figures

5. Figure of Mercury, made of lead and standing 1.2m/4ft high.

6. Classical nude figure, which could look charming on a heavily planted patio or near a water feature. The figure is 60cm/24in high and an optional pedestal (not shown) adds an extra 82cm/32in of height.

7. Traditional stone Buddha available in heights from 40–60cm/16–24in. This type of religious figure is best not highlighted, but positioned where the eye can fall on it quite naturally.

Other ornaments

8. Reconstituted stone bird bath and pedestal 50cm/20in high. A gradually sloping bath is best for small garden birds.

9. Usually found in Japanese gardens, stone towers can stand well over 2m/6ft and are available from some specialist suppliers. For the smaller garden, a 5-storey tower is a better size.

10. and **11.** For an open aspect a sun dial can be both useful and attractive. You may need to reorientate the dial so that the shadow indicates the correct time. These examples are made of reconstituted stone and are 91cm/36in high.

GENERAL CARE AND MAINTENANCE

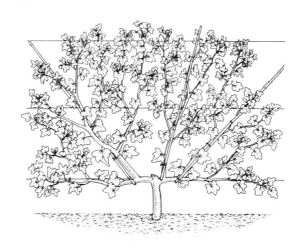

PATIO MAINTENANCE

A patio needs only a bare minimum of equipment to keep it looking good, unless it forms part of a full-scale garden. A hand fork and trowel are invaluable. A wide range of other small-scale tools are now available, and these are ideal for small beds and containers; many have 60cm/24in handles. There are special forks for grubbing up weeds, mini-rakes, hoes and even a small tool with a spiked wheel to till the soil. Only if there are permanent beds will a standard-sized lightweight fork and spade be required for a patio garden.

A watering can with two roses, one fine and one with larger holes in it, is a necessity. Choose one that is well balanced, especially when full, and make sure it will fit under the tap when being filled. Other watering equipment will depend on which method of watering you adopt (see p. 156).

A pair of secateurs and a garden knife are useful for pruning and trimming, and another invaluable piece of equipment is a really good quality, stiff-bristled broom that doubles duty as a scrubbing brush and a leaf sweeper. If the patio is really large, then some form of outdoor vacuum sweeper might be a good investment, provided there is somewhere to store it. A collapsible carrying sheet will be required to transport leaves, twigs and cuttings to the dustbin.

Do not be seduced into buying elaborate or expensive tools – electric hedge trimmers, for instance – unless you are sure you need them for, in a small space, storage is a great problem. Sometimes it is better to have two small separate tools to do a job than one large one that needs a huge storage area.

With a little cunning, storage areas can be incorporated into the overall patio design and still be unobtrusive. For instance, against the house wall build a wooden-lidded locker in bricks matching those of the house, or make an all-wood locker to blend in with a nearby timber fence. Plywood is another suitable locker material.

The locker should be either front opening, like a door, or top-hinged, when it can double as a seat or shelf, depending on height. Set ceramic tiles on it, and you can then use it as a shelf from which to serve hot food. A useful locker size is one that is longer and wider than it is deep. One with a large top-opening lid, for example 1m/3ft square, could be hinged in the middle; the back half, propped up, is then a seat back.

Whatever the style and form of storage locker, instal divisions and clips inside to keep each tool in a special place, thereby reducing the necessity of disembowelling the entire locker to find one object.

SURFACES

Keep the patio flooring and steps clean and sweep them regularly with a good quality brush. After brushing, wipe any dust off leaves and flowers. One way to reduce dust is to use an industrial vacuum cleaner that is suitable for outdoor use – some will even suck up water. If leaves are a problem, a purpose-built leaf sweeper might be the answer, if you have storage space for it.

Remove marks left by birds and other stains by scrubbing with plain water. To remove obstinate marks, add bleach to the water. Scrape off any algae and moss and then finish off with a stiff bristle, nylon or wire brush, or use a patent moss-killing compound. York stone, which acquires a patina of age in time, may also need to be brushed over occasionally with a stiff brush.

Keep surfaces free from weeds by applying a chemical herbicide such as those containing paraquat, diquat, simazine and/or aminotriazole. Use these chemicals with great care, following the manufacturer's instructions, making sure that they do not contaminate neighbouring plants.

Concrete

A concrete surface tends to give most trouble. Small cracks appear, seeds are blown into them, and the resulting weeds enlarge the cracks and make them look worse.

When repairing concrete always add one-quarter part PVA adhesive to a mortar mix of three parts sand, one part cement and one part lime. Make the mix just moist enough to allow it to be spread over a surface.

To repair cracks in the slabs, cut away the loose concrete, using a hammer and cold chisel, to provide a clean surface. Wash the inside of the crack and then paint it with PVA adhesive. Insert the mortar and level off.

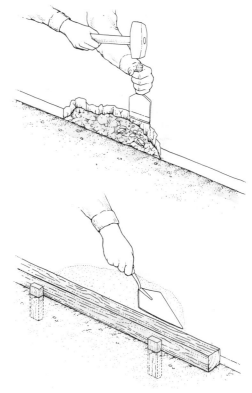

When mending concrete edges and cracks, always undercut the break to keep the new concrete in position. Level with a straight edge and finish with a steel trowel. Leave the wood for at least a month.

Hollows in the surface of concrete can be filled with the PVA and mortar mix mentioned above, once the surface has been cleaned and painted with adhesive. If the hollow is very shallow, make it deeper.

Should the edge of a concrete patio start to crumble, cut it back to sound material with a hammer and cold chisel. Check the foundation hardcore, adding more if necessary. Then wash the broken surface thoroughly. Put a length of timber alongside the broken edge, lining it up with a sound edge at both ends. Peg it in place. Brush PVA adhesive onto the broken edge and apply the PVA and mortar mix. Trowel to a finish.

Bricks, granite setts and paving stones

Hard surfaces made with these materials and grouted with mortar do not need much maintenance as they should remain weed-free and firmly in position, especially if set on mortar. Patios that have sand or earth grouting between the bricks or slabs often grow an untidy crop of weeds or grass, which should be sprayed with a powerful herbicide. Then remove the dead weeds and old grouting. Brush a mix comprising three parts dry sand to one part cement down all the joints, pushing it well into the cracks. Remove the surplus mix and then water the patio to set the new mortar grouting.

Slabs and bricks tend to get damaged if they have been incorrectly set above or below surrounding slabs so that they rock when you walk on them. To re-lay a slab, gouge out any grouting that surrounds it before lifting it out. A broken or cracked slab that will not budge should be broken up with a heavy hammer and removed in small pieces. If the slab has been bedded on sand, simply remove or add more sand as necessary to get it to the height of the surrounding slabs. Then replace the slab. Check its level with a straight edge and ensure that it is firm.

If the slab has been set on mortar, chip out the old mortar. Make up a new mix of three

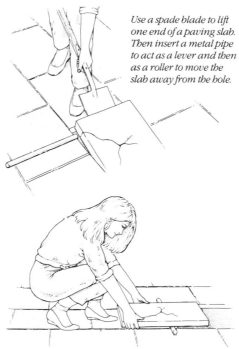

Use a spade blade to lift one end of a paving slab. Then insert a metal pipe to act as a lever and then as a roller to move the slab away from the hole.

parts of sand, one part of cement and one part lime, and add sufficient water to make a stiff mortar that is wet enough to be spread like butter. Place a blob of mortar at each corner of the hole and in the middle. (The amount of mortar required depends on whether the slab needs raising or lowering compared with surrounding ones.) Then reset the slab and check the level with a straight edge across two adjacent slabs.

Gravel

Areas of gravel can be kept tidy by regular raking over to make them level and to restore any patterns. Occasionally, top up the surface with new gravel.

Wooden decking

Wooden decking should be treated regularly with a preservative, as it is liable to rot. It also hosts algae, lichens and mosses, which can prove very slippery in wet weather. Scrape and brush these off, then apply a mixture of mosskiller and commercial algicide.

WALLS

Repointing

Patio and garden walls often need repointing where the old mortar is crumbling or dropping out. Always try to repoint the whole wall and not part of it, as a wall repointed in patches will be much weaker and is potentially dangerous.

To remove the old mortar, use a jointing chisel to clean out the joint to depth of 1cm/½in. Finish off with a wire brush to get rid of any dust. Make up a standard mortar mix of three parts sand, one part cement and one of lime. Add sufficient water to make a firm but not sloppy mix. Wet each section of wall just before pointing it. This will reduce suction from the bricks and give time to force the mortar into the joint, using a pointing trowel. Form 'weathered' pointing, which slopes downwards and throws the rain away from the joint.

Should only part of a wall be repointed, check the age of its mortar by running a stiff brush over the wall. Good mortar will remain firm whereas old mortar will crumble into bits. Most old walls are pointed with a weak mortar mix, and so must be repointed with a similarly weak mix, otherwise the new mortar will break away from the old as it sets, and may fall out of the joint, bringing the old mortar with it. A suitably weak mix is seven parts of sand, one part of cement and one of lime. To make a stronger mix, cut down on the sand. To make it weaker, increase the amount of lime. Match the existing pointing on the wall – for example, flush, keyed or weathered.

Rendered walls

These must be checked regularly for any cracks appearing in the surface: neglected cracks let in the rain. When this freezes, the ice so formed behind the rendering forces large lumps off the wall. Therefore rake out and fill any cracks as soon as you can with matching mortar (see above).

FENCES, SCREENS AND OVERHEAD SHELTERS

Wood

Post bottoms are very vulnerable to rotting, so, if you have painted posts, the base of these should be treated with preservative. Most wood preservatives are toxic to plant life; therefore, before using them, cover grass, other low-growing plants and wall shrubs with plastic sheeting. Plants growing up fences, screens or pergolas should be unfastened and lowered to the ground away from the area to be painted. Scrub the wood thoroughly. Then apply liberally a horticultural preservative, using a thick paint brush. Allow at least 48 hours for the preservative to dry before putting back the climbers.

Timber fences and screens should also be treated with a horticultural preservative. This should be done once a year, preferably during a dry spell at the end of summer. Clear away some soil from the base of fences, for example, and protect all nearby plants. Thoroughly clean the area to be treated, then brush the preservative well in, using the same paint brush as for the posts. Do not use a spray as the preservative is less easy to control in this form. Apply preservative generously to end grain.

Gates, picket and other painted wood fences should have a coat of gloss paint every two or three years. Wash the area well before rubbing it down with abrasive paper. Then remove all dust and apply the gloss paint. To prevent a build-up of paint, strip it off every second or third painting. Then apply a primer, undercoat and gloss coat.

Metal

Every two to three years, all painted metal requires repainting. Wash down the paint and then roughen it with abrasive paper to provide a key to which the new paint can adhere. Wipe the area clean before applying a proprietary rust killer to the metal and then a high-quality gloss paint.

Plastic

Plastic fences quickly look scruffy if not regularly maintained. Cracked or damaged plastic should be mended using a special repair kit produced by the manufacturer. If such a kit is not available, the damaged section will have to be replaced.

Perspex coverings should last a long time and will keep their good looks as long as they are not scratched in any way. So, when cleaning, go over the surfaces with the hose of a vacuum cleaner before washing them with several clean cloths, shaking or rinsing these frequently to get rid of any grains of dirt or grit that might damage the surface.

HEDGES AND TOPIARY

Frequent clipping of hedges and topiary will encourage good dense growth and also means that only fleshy young shoots rather than tough branches will have time to grow in between clippings. Use electric hedge trimmers, not hand shears, for the general cut and heavy-duty secateurs for large-leaved plants, such as laurel, and straggly branches, pruning them well back into the topiary shape or hedge. To keep a hedge solid at the base, give it a conical profile.

Repair any gaps in a hedge by taking cuttings from the hedge itself in late summer (see p. 155). For roses and cotoneasters, remove the old soil and replace with fresh before planting the rooted cuttings in the hedge. This is vital for successful establishment and for avoiding soil sickness.

PONDS

If a pond liner springs a leak, or a concrete pond cracks in frost, or if you want to give the pond a good clean-out, it will be necessary to remove the plants. Have a series of waterproof containers to hand, filled with water that has been allowed to stand until it has reached a temperature similar to that of the pond water. Scoop out the containers or plants, separating them into deep aquatics, surface growers and so on, and transfer them to their temporary home as fast as possible. As with other plants in the garden, they should not be shifted in very cold weather, though in an emergency – if the pond lining is punctured, for example – this may be unavoidable. In this case it is best to keep the plants in containers of water in a cool but sheltered place until they can be replanted in the pond in the normal way.

To repair a leak in the plastic liner, clean the area surrounding the hole thoroughly and roughen it. Cut a suitably sized patch of plastic, making its edges rounded. Then apply the patch to the hole, using a glue approved by the manufacturer. Allow to dry for at least two days before refilling the pond with water and replacing the plants. To repair a crack in a concrete pool, see p. 146.

After a time, fountains and submersible pumps tend to become clogged with weeds or decaying vegetation, so clean them regularly. It is essential to keep their filters clean otherwise water may not reach the pump from the pipe, and it may then overheat and burn out. The smaller and flimsier the pump, the more likely it is to expire. Good quality underwater pumps should be used and returned to the manufacturer regularly for an overhaul.

ELECTRICAL FITTINGS

All electrical wires and fittings in the patio should be checked once a year by a fully qualified electrician. Patio lights should be looked over to make sure that they are not letting in damp and any broken bulbs should be substituted by new ones. Rubber gaskets that are cracked or leaking should be replaced. If the lighting system runs off 12 volts, check the transformer to make sure it is not unusually hot and examine the lights themselves for leaks. All wiring should be checked for any damage to the plastic coating and should be renewed if hardened or split.

CONTAINER CARE

Containers must have adequate drainage holes and be absolutely clean before they can be planted up with your selected plants.

DRAINAGE

The most common problem encountered with container-grown plants is that the soil in which they are grown becomes waterlogged and they therefore wilt and sometimes die. To prevent this, it is vital always to check a container carefully to ensure that water can escape freely. The holes should preferably be at or near the base and should have a diameter of at least 6cm/¼in. Pots deeper than 23cm/9in require larger drainage holes, of about 2cm/¾in diameter, 15cm/6in apart.

CLEANING

New as well as previously used containers must always be cleaned thoroughly before use. New porous or non-glazed containers may, for example, conceal harmful salts which must be dissolved and removed by soaking the pots in clean water. A good soak will also ensure that the containers are fully rehydrated, since dried-out pots will absorb moisture from the soil, to the detriment of the plants.

Remove dust and old soil particles from containers that have been used before. Any cracked or broken containers should be discarded or set aside for repair. Examine wooden containers for rot – for instance, in knotted or split wood – and repair any damage before washing. Any badly crusted containers can be submerged in water for up to a day to help to loosen the dirt. Apply a brand-name stain remover to any stained containers.

Capillary matting and reservoirs must also be washed very well. Clean out any automatic watering systems and check they are in good working order, with no blocked nozzles or pipes.

BEFORE FILLING CONTAINERS

Containers must stand firmly with the base level, so that water can percolate evenly throughout the soil. Position containers for plants that are to be trained up a wall or trellis no more than 2cm/¾in in front of the support.

Large containers should be filled with potting compost and be planted up in situ, as once filled they are too heavy to be moved around easily. Small- to medium-sized containers, however, can be shifted to their final position on the patio after planting, using boards on pieces of pipe acting as rollers. Alternatively, drag the container on a piece of strong sacking or carpet.

Once planted, a container should be moved as little as feasible to avoid damaging the plant and container. If a container does have to be moved after planting, protect trees and shrubs by tying their branches with twine or soft netting.

To steady a heavy container while it is moved on rollers, tie a strong rope around it. A container placed on strong sacking must be dragged carefully.

GROWING MEDIUMS

To grow successfully a plant takes in food and nutrients from its growing medium. It is therefore essential that an appropriate plant is chosen to grow in a particular type of soil. To test the type of soil on your patio, that is, its acidity or alkalinity (its pH level), use a simple soil testing kit. A pH of 7 indicates neutral soil, and soils below 7 become progressively more acid, whereas those with a pH above 7 become more alkaline. The normal range is between pH4 and pH8, the change from one pH level to the next representing a tenfold increase in acidity or alkalinity.

Garden soils gradually become more acid, as rainfall washes out the calcium, whereas potting composts become more alkaline. Acid soil need not be corrected, unless the soil looks sour with moss growing on the surface. To raise the pH level, sprinkle ground limestone on the soil.

For plants grown in containers or raised beds, use special potting composts rather than ordinary garden soil, as it will compact less. You can also be sure that the growing medium is sterile and that the plants will have no competition from weeds. Another great advantage of using potting compost is that it can be tailored to individual plant needs. In a garden that is mainly alkaline, plants such as rhododendrons that thrive only in acid soil can also be included, provided you grow them in purpose-made compost in separate tubs or raised beds. Eventually the natural acid balance of the potting mix may diminish but a dose of chelated iron (sequestrene) will soon reinvigorate such acid-loving plants.

Soil-based potting composts

There is a vast array of potting composts to choose from. The best known are probably the original potting composts from the John

Innes Horticultural Institute of Great Britain, which are soil-based. They are available in three standardized formulations, the main difference between them being the amount of fertilizer they contain: John Innes no. 3 has treble the amount of no. 1. Use John Innes no. 1 for seeds and very small plants; John Innes no. 2 for most houseplants; and John Innes no. 3 for 'greedy' feeders, such as sweet peas or tomatoes, and small trees and shrubs.

Soil-less potting composts

Soil-less potting composts are now very popular since they are cleaner to handle than soil-based ones, and lighter too. They are therefore ideal for roof-top patios or hanging baskets, where weight is a problem. Most are peat-based with added nutrients. Because they contain peat it is essential that they are not allowed to dry out, for they are very difficult to remoisten properly. Soil-less potting composts have less than half the life of soil-based ones, lasting only a year. Like John Innes soil-based composts, soil-less potting composts are available in special mixes for seeds and seedlings, medium- and large-sized plants, and there are also all-purpose mixes that will do for all three categories. Some soil-less composts have tiny white granules in them. These minute pieces of polystyrene keep the soil well aerated, even if accidentally overwatered.

Soil-less potting composts are also sold in growing bags. These special plastic bags can be planted with spring and summer crops, such as cucumbers. They are clean and simple to use as separate containers and messy potting mixes are not involved.

Home-made growing mediums

Make up your own growing medium for raised beds. For most purposes you need a mixture containing equal parts of coarse sand, sphagnum moss peat and a good quality soil-based potting compost. Shallow rooting shrubs and perennials need a 30cm/12in layer of this growing medium; a layer 60cm/24in deep should be sufficient for even quite large trees. Under this layer use pea gravel or vermiculite, to provide bulk and to improve drainage. Up to 15 per cent of this home-made growing medium may be lost each year because of decomposition. Therefore, every autumn, apply a 5cm/2in layer of pure organic material, such as well-rotted manure, over the surface of the raised bed to top up the soil.

POTTING AND PLANTING

Correct potting and planting techniques are vitally important not only to the young plant but also to the way in which the plant subsequently grows and produces flowers and fruit. Timing is also crucial and should be related to season, age, condition and type of plant. Most established perennials should be repotted once a year, when dormant. Quick-growing and short-lived plants such as salad crops, vegetables or bedding plants should be potted on as soon as they show signs of outgrowing their existing containers (see below).

Choosing a container

A plant grown in a pot that is either too large or too small will suffer unnecessarily and even die. Plants grown in excessively large containers may, if quick growing, make too much leaf growth, which delays and even prevents flowering and fruiting. In slow growers, the roots cannot fully permeate the potting compost, which therefore stays cold and wet and eventually becomes sour, causing root problems.

Plants grown in containers that are too small quickly fill the pot with their roots and exhaust the soil. Such pot-bound plants dry out very fast and obtain insufficient food supply, resulting in stunted growth, poor or premature flowering and fruiting, loss of leaves and buds, and hardening of plant stems and leaves.

The correct container size for a particular plant is best judged by eye, taking in the balance of the top growth to the pot. As a general rule, the rootball of the plant, when first put into a pot, should have about 2.5cm/1in of soil all around it.

Another consideration when choosing a container is its weight. If your patio is on a roof or balcony, use lightweight pots and window boxes made of plastic or fibreglass and position them around the edge.

Crocking

Any container, once absolutely clean (see p. 149), must be crocked properly. Place a zinc gauze over large holes. Then cover holes of any size with cleaned and disinfected flat stones or shards concave-side down. Sprinkle a 1–5cm/½–2in layer of chippings over the stones or shards. Use limestone chippings for lime lovers such as clematis. Such chippings must not, however, be used for acid-loving plants such as rhododendron; substitute granite chippings or other neutral aggregates such as fired-clay granules instead.

Plants that are to remain permanently in containers should have added a 1cm/½in layer of fine, granulated sphagnum peat, pulverized bark or leaf mould.

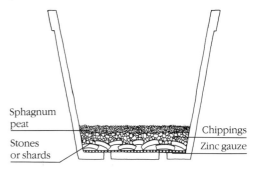

Sphagnum peat

Chippings

Stones or shards

Zinc gauze

A container must be crocked properly to encourage good aeration and drainage in the soil and to prevent fine soil from being washed out of the container. For permanent container-grown plants, add a layer of sphagnum peat to retain moisture in the soil.

Basic potting techniques

Before potting a plant, make sure the area in which you are working is clean and disease-free. Crock the container (see p. 150) and then half fill it with a suitable potting compost (see p. 149). Press the mix gently. (For bulbs, place a handful of sharp, coarse sand or grit in the centre of the container on the potting compost, to improve drainage.) Stand the plant in the soil and then fill the pot with further potting compost until it is level with the container rim. Tap the base of the container to settle the mix. Then firm it gently around the stem of the plant. Water the newly potted plant, using the fine rose on a watering can. Then position the plant in a cool site, while it establishes itself. Avoid exposed positions as these may cause the plants to dehydrate and even die.

Most plants should be repotted regularly in progressively larger pots, filled with fresh potting compost. Quick-growing plants, such as coleus, should have their roots checked once a fortnight to see whether they need repotting. Slow growers, such as palms and yuccas, generally require repotting only once a year. Very slow growers, such as camellias, can last two years, provided they are topped up with fresh compost after a year or so.

To establish whether a plant is pot-bound and therefore needs repotting, water it thoroughly and then remove it from its container, supporting the stem between the middle and forefinger of one hand. If the rootball does not readily slip out, gently tap the side of the pot before reinverting the pot and trying again to remove the plant. Alternatively, roll the pot over a few times, ensuring there are no obstructions in the way to damage the plant itself. If the roots are encircling the outside of the rootball, the plant should be repotted in a larger container. If no roots show, the plant should be replaced carefully in its original container, topping up the potting compost if necessary.

To determine how large a container to use when repotting an established plant, select one with a diameter approximately 2.5cm/1in larger than the original pot. Crock the new pot and part fill it, using a suitable fresh potting compost (see p. 149). Gently remove any crocks buried in the rootball, and prune back any damaged roots to sound tissue. Then set the plant in the new container at about the same depth as in its original pot. Cover the roots with more fresh potting compost, firming it down gently around the rootball. Leave a 2cm/¾in space at the top of the container, for watering. Then water the plant.

Eventually it will not be feasible to repot a plant in a still larger container, and the same container may have to be reused. In this case, thoroughly clean the container before crocking and partially filling it with fresh potting compost. Tease out as much of the old compost as possible from the plant's rootball, taking care not to damage the plant, and cut back any dead, damaged or diseased roots, using secateurs or a gardening knife. Follow the procedure for repotting given above, except that the potting compost should be 13mm/½in higher than previously to allow for settlement.

Large containers

Large containers such as those that are likely to remain permanently in situ on the patio can be planted up either by setting individual pots or liners inside the main container or by growing the plants directly in the potting compost in the large container. The great advantage of the former technique is that the changeover from, say, spring to summer plants can be achieved relatively easily, without disturbing other plants in the same container. However its disadvantage is that this method does not suit most circular containers, as the plants cannot be set as close together as in a long, narrow container such as a window box or a trough.

Suitable mini-containers to set within the large container are standard plastic pots. Open-mesh baskets, of the type used in garden ponds and lined with nylon gauze, are also excellent. Such liners and pots should be surrounded in the large container by moist peat or bark, to retard any possible drying out. Choose your planting design and excavate the holes for the pots and liners using the techniques given below.

When growing plants directly in a large container, follow the procedure for crocking given on p. 150. Then fill the entire container with fresh potting compost, firming it down to 2.5cm/1in below the container rim. If the compost is very dry, water it thoroughly and leave to drain for 24 hours.

It is important to work out the final position of each plant in the container before any actual planting is done. Once a satisfactory design has been worked out, water the plants thoroughly. While they are draining, make holes of an appropriate size in the potting compost, starting with the

Ensure each plant is positioned in the container to its best advantage. Set the plants on the soil surface, placing the taller ones in the middle if the pot is circular, or at the back if the container is to be wall mounted.

larger ones. Check the cavity size using either the appropriate plant's pot or one of a similar size. Excavate some more or twist the pot round in the hole until the correct size and shape have been formed. Remove one plant at a time from its pot and set it in the compost slightly deeper than in the original pot. Firm the compost gently around its roots. Continue in this way until all the plants have been set in their new position, leaving the smallest plants until last. For a mixed planting of permanent and bedding species, cover the potting compost with gravel, peat or fresh green moss. For an entirely permanent planting, use fine gravel chippings or pulverized bark to reduce rain compaction and dehydration. Finally, water the plants.

Tall pots and barrels
The techniques for planting up tall pots and barrels, such as potato or strawberry barrels, are slightly different from the standard potting techniques given on p. 151. This is to enable them to crop heavily from such a confined space.

Before planting up a proprietary or home-made strawberry barrel, place it on bricks or castors so the water can drain away freely. It is also vital that the barrel is absolutely level, otherwise, when you water, some plants will be missed out while those on the other side will almost drown.

Place a layer of gravel and small pebbles in the bottom and in this layer stand a piece of 8–10cm/3–4in-diameter plastic drainpipe on end in the centre of a 45cm/18in-diameter barrel. Then fill the barrel with a suitable potting compost (see p. 149), and at the same time fill the pipe with pebbles, pulling it up, gradually, as you go. Stop this inbuilt drainage system about 15cm/6in below the surface of the compost. Carefully poke the strawberry plants into place from the outside as you fill up to each hole level. Finish with two or three plants at the top of the strawberry barrel.

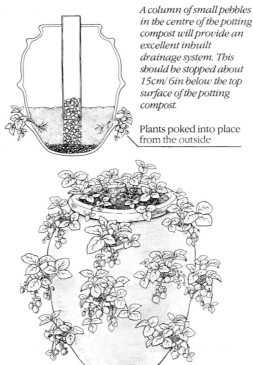

A column of small pebbles in the centre of the potting compost will provide an excellent inbuilt drainage system. This should be stopped about 15cm/6in below the top surface of the potting compost.

Plants poked into place from the outside

Potatoes cannot be planted straight into a barrel until they have been sprouted in a frost-proof room. Buy special seed potatoes and arrange them with the eyes uppermost in a shallow box. After a month, when the eyes are well grown, they can be planted outside in the barrel. Sit them on 13cm/5in of all-purpose soil-less potting compost or John Innes no. 3 (see p. 150) in the bottom of the barrel, cover them with a further 15cm/6in of potting compost and water them. As shoots appear about 13cm/6in above soil level, cover them with more potting compost so that only the tips of the leaves show. Continue to do this, keeping the potting mix watered, until the tips reach the top of the barrel. Then, add some temporary bedding plants so that the container looks attractive. Harvest early potatoes when the plants flower; maincrop potatoes when the foliage starts to yellow.

Growing bags and boards
A growing board is a block of dehydrated sphagnum peat in a polythene bag and it is light to carry. Once rehydrated, it is used like a growing bag.

Such bags and boards should be used only for spring and summer plants, otherwise drainage problems will occur. Outdoor varieties of tomatoes, courgettes and cucumbers do particularly well in these containers.

Place the growing bag in its final position on the patio, ensuring that it is level so all parts will be watered equally. Cut three separate or one large rectangular hole at the top of the bag and water it if the compost has dried out. Insert supports into the compost (see p. 157) if tall plants are to be grown. Make suitably sized cavities and insert each plant, firming the soil gently around each stem, which should be tied loosely to the support, if appropriate.

The best way to water growing bags and boards is using a simple proprietary drip feed, which has three or six nozzles. This works much better than a capillary system.

Hanging baskets
Plastic non-drip hanging baskets and wall-mounted containers can be crocked and planted up in the normal way (see p. 151). However, yet another planting technique is required for hanging and wall-mounted wire baskets, which tend to dry out rapidly as they have large surface areas and not much soil depth. Such baskets should be lined with circles or strips of green plastic foam. When filling, rest the base of the basket on a large pot or bucket. Line the basket base with the plastic foam, green side outward, and a suitable soil-less potting compost (see p. 150). Work the liners up the edges and fill the centre with the compost, planting as you go. At the top, insert the tallest plants in the centre of a hanging basket or at the back of a wall-mounted basket. Water and cover the surface with more liners.

Water gardens

Open-mesh baskets filled with special proprietary heavy loam are most suitable for aquatic plants as they are easily lifted from the water for repotting and root trimming. Plastic window boxes are also suitable for marginals, which need a container depth of about 15cm/6in, as do pygmy varieties of aquatics. Most other aquatics require a container depth of about 20cm/8in. Line open-mesh baskets with a piece of nylon gauze. Partially fill each container with a special heavy (i.e. soil-based) potting compost. Insert the water plant, firming the roots gently. Then fill the container to within 2.5cm/1in of the rim, making sure the growing point shows above the surface. Mask the surface with a thin layer of gravel or stones, to prevent the soil from muddying the water. Set oxygenators and deep water plants, such as water lilies, on the pond bottom and stand marginals on a pile of bricks at the edge in about 10cm/4in of water.

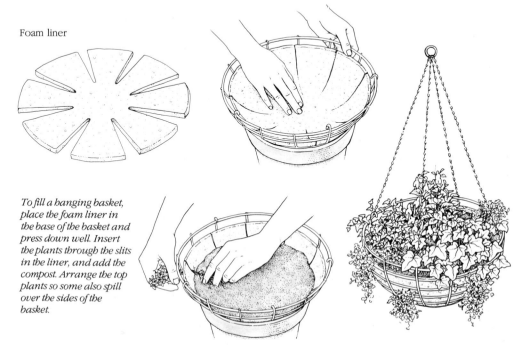

Foam liner

To fill a hanging basket, place the foam liner in the base of the basket and press down well. Insert the plants through the slits in the liner, and add the compost. Arrange the top plants so some also spill over the sides of the basket.

ROUTINE CARE AND MAINTENANCE

To extend the life of containers, regular care and maintenance is extremely important. For example, to prevent containers cracking or bursting from frost damage, protect them by moving them indoors or under cover when severely cold weather is forecast. If this is not practical, place a 30cm/12in layer of straw, bracken, sacking or old clothes around the sides and top; tie on or hold in place with boards or netting. Lie pots on their sides and cover with a 60cm/24in layer of straw, but do not leave them in this position for long otherwise the potting compost will dry out as rainwater cannot reach it.

Wood

Wooden containers are liable to rot, so prevent this by cleaning them thoroughly and then painting all surfaces with a horticultural wood preservative, which is available in a range of colours. Never use creosote, because its fumes can harm plants, particularly in warm weather.

Replace any rotten and badly worm-eaten patches with new wood and prime with a lead-based paint. To conceal the resulting patchwork of new and old wood, apply two coats of exterior-quality paint to the container.

Concrete

Repair concrete containers using a PVA and mortar mix. A suitable mix is four parts of soft sand, one part cement, one part of lime and a quarter part of PVA adhesive. Thoroughly clean the broken edges of the container. Then add sufficient water to make up a fairly stiff mortar mix. Paint the broken edges with PVA adhesive before applying the mix. Support the edges being filled with a 'bandage' of wood, metal or even cardboard, held in place with masking tape or string, until they have completely dried. This will usually take up to two days.

Clay

Protect the rims of clay containers as these are particularly susceptible to frost damage. Twist wire tightly under the rim, thereby giving added support.

Containers that do split must be discarded immediately, because they may harbour disease. Alternatively they must be broken along the split so they can be cleaned thoroughly and then glued back in position, using an impact adhesive or latex glue.

Plastics and fibreglass

Repair kits are available for each of these materials, although plastic containers that have gone brittle and have cracked do not repair satisfactorily. Fibreglass, on the other hand, can be mended successfully by sticking a patch of glass fibre material over the crack with special resin. Such kits are sold at builders' suppliers and shops specializing in glass fibre boats.

PLANT CARE

To include an imaginative selection of plants in the patio, it is well worth buying from specialist nurseries where the particular plants that interest you are raised. Fuchsias, clematis, rhododendrons and alpines, in particular, are best bought in this way. Most nurseries will dispatch by post, so delivery should not be a problem. With herbs, a basic range of thyme, marjoram, sage and mint should be available in most garden centres, but a herb farm can give you a much wider selection – tricolour sage, for instance, with leaves splashed with olive green, pink and white, instead of the ordinary variety, or a special golden, curly-leaved marjoram.

When buying plants from a garden centre or nursery, there are several points to watch, especially with plants in containers.

Make sure that your plant is actually container-grown: that is, raised from seed and grown on in pots, rather than simply dug up and jammed into a pot ready for sale. If you pull gently on the stem of a tree or shrub, provided it is sturdy, it should move in the container complete with its surrounding soil ball. If it moves without the surrounding soil, then it is almost certainly not container-grown, and the disruption of being hastily potted up before sale will not augur well for its future growth. Moss on the surface of the soil in a container is a good, rather than bad, sign, for it shows that the plant is well established in its pot. However, a plethora of weeds is evidence of neglect.

The plant itself should look healthy with glossy leaves and sturdy growth. Heavily pruned shoots could indicate that the plant failed to sell the previous season and has been cut back, and may not necessarily be a good buy.

Do not choose the largest plant you can see – always a temptation with trees, shrubs and climbers – unless it looks really well grown and healthy. The larger the plant, the

bigger the shock to its system when planted and the more likelihood that you might lose it. Always select a short, plump, sturdy plant rather than a tall, spindly one. Once in the ground, a short one will soon catch up.

The root system is the most important part of a plant, and this is a particular area to watch. Roots growing out through the bottom of the container, especially into the ground below, show that the plant has either outgrown its container or has exhausted all the nutrient in the pot and is seeking more. Roots within the container wrapped around the edge of the soil ball are nothing to worry about and should be left undisturbed when planting; sinister signs are: roots actually growing out through the sides or bottom of the pot and roots exposed on the surface of the potting compost.

Having bought your stock, take care when you transport it home. Always cover the plants with plastic to prevent them drying out during the journey. There is always the temptation to squeeze a large tree or shrub into the car in order to take it home as quickly as possible, but you may do untold damage that way, especially to standard grown trees. Ask the garden centre to deliver instead.

If you order trees and shrubs from a nursery that you are unable to visit, or if you pick up a pre-packaged bargain in your local supermarket, then you may be buying bare-rooted plants. Those packed in a plastic display carton need special scrutiny – any signs that buds are beginning to open and leaves appear, or of white hair-like roots growing from the main ones, indicate that the plant has been stored for some time, possibly in warm conditions, and is probably not a good buy. Look out, too, for blackened or shrivelled pieces of stem – a sealed plastic container can be a hothouse for spreading disease.

PROPAGATION

As space is at a premium in the patio, there is unlikely to be much opportunity to propagate plants that are slow to root. Therefore, only the quickest methods of plant propagation are given below.

Seeds

You may find the only way to obtain some stock for your patio is to raise your own from seed. For there is no doubt that, if prepared to do so, you have a much wider choice of varieties. The easiest way to start off seeds in a small way is in an electrically heated propagator, which will keep the seeds at the correct temperature and atmosphere. Be careful, however, where you site the propagator, for an indoor window sill with the sun beating down on it can create near-scorching temperatures in the propagator.

For ease of transplanting, sow your seed in soil blocks. These can be formed from honeycombed polystyrene seed-raising kits. Each cell is filled with fresh seedling potting compost and a seed is inserted. When moistened, the potting compost forms a neat cube of soil around the seed, and it is eventually held together by the seedling's roots. When ready to be transplanted, remove the seedling together with the soil block. Always harden off seedlings before they are taken outside: put them in a cool but light room indoors for a while. If the light comes from only one source, for example, a window, turn the seedlings regularly so that they do not strain towards the light.

If there is insufficient space in the house to provide adequate light for all the seedlings to grow on, it is relatively simple to transform a raised bed against a patio fence or wall into a temporary nursery. Drape a tent of clear polythene over the entire bed and fix it at the back to the fence. This should provide the same sort of warmth and shelter as an unheated frame. Gradually harden off the seedlings and then transplant into their final position on the patio.

Stem cuttings

Another method of increasing plant stock is to take stem cuttings. There are three main types of stem cuttings: hardwood, semi-ripe and softwood. Hardwood cuttings are taken in early autumn from fully mature, leafless stems of trees and shrubs. Semi-ripe cuttings are made in late summer when the stems of plants such as camellias still carry leaves. Softwood cuttings are taken in spring from the fast-growing tips of plants such as fuchsias and geraniums.

Choose a non-flowering, vigorous tip that looks plump and healthy. Cut it from the parent plant about 10cm/4in down the stem, just below where a leaf joins the stem. Dip the stem in a hormone rooting powder, which will disinfect the cutting and also encourage root growth. Then set it in a pot filled with seedling potting compost (see p. 150) or in a soil block. If using a wide-diameter pot, set several cuttings around the edge of the pot. To keep the right micro-climate around the cuttings, place the pot in a propagator. Alternatively, make a tent from a large, clear, plastic bag, using a twig to keep the plants clear of the sides. Secure the bag over the pot with an elastic band.

To raise a standard or half-standard from your favourite ordinary plants, so they can be highlighted in the patio, is also relatively straightforward. Take a healthy-looking stem cutting from the plant to be propagated and raise it following the method given above. Once established, tie the stem to a stake the next time it is repotted (see p. 151). Eliminate side shoots as they appear. When the plant has reached the height you require, nip off the growing tip, so that the plant will bush out, and remove any side leaves lower down the stem. Eventually you may be able to remove the stake.

Division

Perennials that have grown too large for their pots or beds can be divided either in late autumn or before they start to make fresh growth in early spring. Ease the plant from its pot or lift it from the bed. Tease the roots gently apart with your hands, or, if the plant is too tough for this treatment, use a knife to complete the separation. The sections of the plant around its outer edges are the young healthy ones, so remove any dead old wood from the centre of the plant before repotting or planting.

Bulbs and corms can be lifted and stored once they have finished flowering and the foliage has died down – never lift a bulb that still has green leaves since this is when food is being returned to the bulb ready for next year's flowering. If the bulbs have produced small bulblets, gently detach these and plant immediately in the ground – it will be two years before they start to produce flowers. Store bulbs and corms in a cool, dry place, out of the way of mice, until planting time comes again. Inspect them regularly to check that none have become diseased.

Layering

Pot, or tip, layering is the form of layering that produces roots quickest, as plants propagated using other methods, such as simple layering or air layering, can take up to two years to root and often the plants should also be kept indoors during this time.

Pot layering is a specialized technique for clematis and cane fruits such as black-berries and loganberries. In mid-summer, position a 15cm/6in pot containing the plant to be layered inside a 20cm/8in pot that has been crocked and filled with a little potting compost. Fill the area between the two containers with more potting compost and then peg down the tips of stems of the current year's growth in this compost. In autumn, sever the new plants from the parent and replant.

Runners

Some plants, such as strawberries and sax-ifrages, produce embryo plants on long, thin stems, or runners. To establish some runners as new plants, in summer pin down the runners in individual pots of potting compost. Once the runners have rooted, sever them from the parent plant.

Protect the cutting until it has established, ensuring the growing tip is not nipped until the plant has reached the height required. Cut only the side shoots not the side leaves, which are needed to provide food until the plant's final height is achieved.

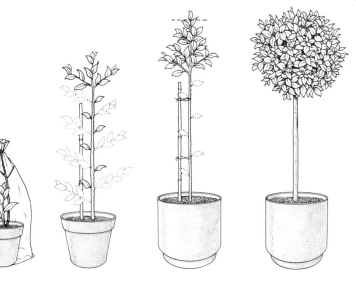

WATERING

Correct watering is a vital aspect of growing plants on a patio, especially if the plants are under cover, in containers or in raised beds. Like caged birds, their food and water must be controlled much more carefully than for plants grown in open ground.

Watering depends entirely upon the weather and the air temperature – the drier and hotter it is, the more water your plants will require. In cool conditions, watering should be cut down. In exposed conditions the wind will tend to dry out the soil, so plants in such an area should be given more water than those in a sheltered spot. The usual time to water plants is at one end of the day never in the full mid-day sun, because droplets on the leaves will act like a magnifying glass and scorch them. Another danger is to water the plants too little, too often. It is better to give an occasional good soaking.

Ideally, on the patio use an overground watering system based on copper pipes with holes in them or a 'drip' irrigation system with plastic tubing and special emitters, or a hose that has perforations at regular intervals. The latter can be left snaking among the plants, to which it supplies water on a trickle system. An ordinary unperforated hose is less satisfactory as it can be time-consuming to use, and it may damage the more delicate flowers or bedding plants.

To protect small container-grown plants while you are away, and to reduce water loss, place the plants in individual, perforated, clear plastic bags. Seal them and leave in a cool, shaded place.

Hand watering at ground level should be done with a watering can fitted with a rose, to prevent the jet washing away the soil. Sprinklers can be more of a nuisance than a help on a patio, as they tend to splash the windows of the house, wet the surface of the patio itself, and, if the plants are crammed together in a clutch of containers, douse some and miss the rest.

Containers with built-in water reservoirs should be checked regularly to ensure they are fully topped up. To devise your own built-in watering system, rest containers in bowls of shallow water. The potting compost should act like a syphon and absorb moisture as needed – but it does not always do so. To be certain, make a wick of capillary matting by poking one end up into the potting compost and setting the other in the bowl of water – but ensure the potting compost is thoroughly moist before you do as otherwise this technique will not work.

For watering hanging baskets and high containers, tie a bamboo cane to the end of an unperforated hose to keep the pipe rigid. An adjustable spray fitted on the end is also invaluable.

FEEDING

For sucessful balanced growth, plants need to be fed regularly with fertilizers. The main nutrients are nitrogen, phosphorus and potassium. Nitrogen is necessary for general growth, especially of leaves and shoots; potassium increases the intensity of flower colour and improves the formation and ripening of fruit; and phosphorus promotes healthy root development, especially in young plants. Complete balanced fertilizers contain all three nutrients in varying quantities, so for each of your plants pick a product with a relevant balance, for example, for a plant grown for its flowers use a fertilizer high in potassium.

Fertilizers may be organic – that is, of animal or plant origin – or inorganic – that is, made from mineral sources. Organic fertilizers tend to be slower acting but longer lasting than inorganic ones. Of the organic fertilizers, nitrogen can be found in dried blood, bonemeal, farmyard manure (not recommended for a patio near a house) and fish meal. Dried blood also has traces of potassium. Phosphorus is in bonemeal and can be found in quantitiy in leaf mould. Of the inorganic fertilizers, a source of nitrogen is sulphate of ammonia, that of potassium is sulphate of potash, and that of phosphorus is superphosphate of lime.

The most common forms in which plant food are available are: liquids; pellets and spikes; and granules and powders. Liquid feeding is the easiest way to apply fertilizer on the patio. Make up the mix in a bucket, following the instructions on the packet. Always use tepid, rather than ice-cold, water. As an easy back-up for containers, look out for slow-release fertilizers, which are available in plant spikes and pellets. Insert these into the potting compost in the container; they will gradually release the chemicals as the plant needs them. Granules or powders of base fertilizers can be used when making up individual potting composts or top dressings, for application, for example, at the beginning of the growing season on well-established plants in large containers.

During their first season, plants growing in containers in proprietary potting composts should not need feeding. After that, the nutrients in the compost will require topping up with an application of general fertilizer when each plant is in its peak growing season and when it is forming flowers or fruit.

Finally, to spruce up plants, a complete foliar feed is useful for all but hairy-leaved plants. It can be sprayed on the leaves any time when the sun is not shining. Such feeds are absorbed quickly when applied with a watering can. They take only about three days to act, whereas a liquid fertilizer applied to the plant's roots will take about double that time.

KEEPING PATIO PLANTS TIDY AND MANAGEABLE

Patios always look much more attractive when kept tidy, especially since dead leaves and vegetation lying around on paving may discolour it, encourage the growth of moss and algae and even, at times, provide a slippery hazard underfoot.

Cut off any dead flower heads and dying foliage promptly, unless you are planning to save seed from a particular plant or require fruit or berries from it. For some flowers, this deadheading will encourage a fresh crop of flowers; for others, bulbs for instance, it will save a great deal of energy that should have been directed towards next year's growth from being wasted in setting seed.

It always helps to keep plants looking at their best if you provide some method of support for them or train them up a wall.

Supporting and training plants

A well-chosen support should not only enhance the appearance of a plant but also protect it from flopping and from wind damage. Stakes should ideally be of plastic or specially coated metal. Wooden ones need treating with a good horticultural preservative, and bamboo canes should be disinfected after each use, since they can harbour insects.

Use soft twine or wire ties covered in tar-impregnated paper for soft-stemmed plants, and plastic-coated metal wire for woodier stems. For standards or tree stems, use plastic tree ties.

Insert the stake – of the same width as the plant's final width – at the same time as the plant is potted or planted in the ground. For most plants, the height of the stake should be about two-thirds of the plant's final height. Tie the plant stem loosely to the stake as soon as it is tall enough to place the twine around it. Remember that all plants become heavier as they mature so fix the support securely.

Single-stemmed plants These need usually one support. However, if the site in which they are to grow is particularly exposed, it is best to provide two supports, one either side of each stem. Make sure that there is space between stake and stem, to prevent chafing.

For a standard tree, the stake top should be 3–5cm/1–2in below the lowest branches. Secure the stem with two adjustable ties, one about 4cm/1½in from the stake top, the other about half way down the stake.

To tie a soft-stemmed perennial, use a proprietary stake that will clip onto a cane.

Multi-stemmed plants Soft-stemmed annuals, such as love-in-a-mist (*Nigella*), can be supported simply with twiggy sticks, such as pea sticks, pushed into the soil around them, avoiding the plants' roots.

All climbing plants need some support until they become established, even the so-

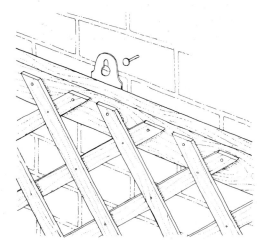

Wooden supports are far less likely to rot if they are nailed to a batten or, at intervals, to wooden blocks, and if they are positioned a few centimetres above the soil. If the wall needs to be painted, then the best support is a trellis that is held on small hooks, so that you can unhook it and gently pull it, complete with climber, away from the wall while you do the decorating.

called self-clinging climbers, such as Virginia creeper, that cling to a wall with little self-adhesive pads. The easiest way to support climbers is with pliable horticultural plasticine. Roll a piece of this adhesive material into a ball, put it between the plant and the wall surface, and press the plant onto it. It can be re-used and moved about the wall if you want to train the climber in a different direction. An alternative method of support is old-fashioned lead-headed nails, hammered into the wall or fence. The lead tag is then wrapped around the stem. However, the head tends to separate from the rest of the nail if hammered too hard. A modern version of this nail is the plastic binders, fixed to a wall with masonry nails or to a fence with galvanized nails. These plastic strips are slotted, and therefore adjustable for any thickness of stem.

Plants, such as convulvulus, that climb by twining will twist around polypropylene twine. Peg the twine into the ground at one end and fix it to the wall at the other.

Plants, such as *Vitis*, that cling by tendrils need a framework for support. This can be a trellis, free-standing and made of wood, or one of expandable PVC fixed to a wall. Leave a 3–5cm/1–2in gap between the wall and trellis as rooting too close to the wall may damage it. Rigid plastic mesh can be fixed to the wall with plastic mesh supports, wooden battens or blocks, whereas loose plastic mesh will first need to be stapled to a frame. Mesh supports are T-shaped, and they carry the mesh in a groove or slot.

Long-term climbers, such as wisteria and roses, are best trained up a wall on a system of horizontal wires 45cm/18in apart, supported by galvanized vine eyes. These are available either as special nails that have sharp triangular-shaped heads with holes in them or as screws that have circular heads with holes in them. These latter are safer. Hammer or screw the vine eyes into the wall and thread them with galvanized or green plastic-coated wire. Then stretch the wire until taut and fix in position.

Really lightweight annual climbers, such as sweet peas, that need attaching to a fence should be fixed with 'ties' of string or raffia held by a domestic staple gun or a zigzag network of string.

Fruit trees on a patio must be trained correctly. This will enable far more specimens to be included, and trees grown in this way often produce more fruit as well. A fig thrives if its root run is restricted and will only produce fruit under such conditions. It can also be trained flat against a hot, sunny wall with its branches fanned out, so that its fruit is easy to pick.

To grow a fan, buy a partially trained three-year-old tree with six to eight shoots. Tie the shoots onto canes and anchor these in their fan shape to the wall with wires. In early spring, shorten each leader by about one-third, cutting to downward buds. In summer, tie two evenly spaced shoots on the upper side of each leading shoot to individual canes, and one shoot on the lower side of each leading shoot. Remove all other extension growth. Continue training and cutting back each year until the wall is covered with well-spaced branches. Once established, remove the cane supports.

Follow a similar technique with Morello cherries, which are ideal for a cold wall – ordinary sweet cherries are too large for fan training. Plums, nectarines and apricots can also be very successfully fan-trained and will appreciate a warm wall to host them.

Single-stemmed trees that produce hard fruit, such as apples and pears, thrive when trained as cordons. Plant cordons 75cm/30in apart. Tie a bamboo cane 2.5–3m/8–10ft long to each tree, using a soft twine. Then wire the canes to horizontal wires, fixing them at an angle of 45° to the ground if diagonal cordons are required. In late summer, cut back mature laterals to three leaves from the main stem and cut back mature side shoots from the laterals to 2.5cm/1in from the lateral. Once the tree stem reaches the top wire, remove the cane and, in early summer, cut back new growth on the leader to 1cm/½in from the top wire.

Fans, with their branches radiating from the base, are best trained on horizontal wires tied to canes. Cordons can be arranged upright or better still diagonally where they need less height and are easier to prune as their growth is more even. A row of cordons can make a very useful free-standing screen.

Pruning

Plants need pruning for three reasons: to form them into attractive shapes; to improve the health of the plant by letting in air and light around its centre; and to encourage flowers and fruit. Pruning is carried out at different times of year, depending on the type of plant and the reason for pruning. Always cut branches back flush with the main stem; prune shoots and stems by making a clean, slanting cut just above a bud that is upward- or outward-facing; do not leave an end of dead or ragged wood, which could eventually become diseased and affect the rest of the plant.

Climbers and shrubs should be pruned routinely once a year, thinning out overcrowded, weak, dead, diseased and crossing shoots and branches on established plants. It is worth while taking a little extra trouble with climbers grown around the patio, as they are much more likely to be seen at closer quarters than if they were in a larger garden. Climbers can be trimmed into any shape, but if the plant is destined to produce attractive flowers and fruit rather than just foliage, as in the case of ivy (*Hedera*) or Virginia creeper (*Parthenocissus*), it should not be cut back ruthlessly.

Tackle deciduous climbers and shrubs in autumn, when the leaves have dropped and you can see the basic skeleton of the plant. Prune evergreens as late as possible in spring but before they start making fresh young shoots. Most plants that flower in spring or in early summer do so on growth made in the previous year, and they should therefore be pruned when they have finished flowering. Forsythia and winter jasmine (*Jasminum nudiflorum*), for example, have this growth habit. Climbers and shrubs that flower in summer and autumn, such as summer jasmine (*Jasminum officinale*), usually do so on shoots made in spring, so these plants, like evergreens, should be pruned in spring before new growth starts.

Clematis comprises such a large group of climbers that there is no one pruning season. Most of the species clematis, including the *C. montana* group, do not require much pruning; only dead and weak stems need to be removed once flowering has finished in early summer. All other clematis, including the large-flowered hybrids such as 'Nellie Moser' and the late-flowering *C. jackmanii* group, should be pruned in early spring.

Roses, with the exception of climbers, should be pruned in early spring. The true climber, on the other hand, should be cut back in autumn, removing those stems that have produced blooms for two seasons.

Young deciduous trees, especially fruit trees, should be pruned so that a well-balanced framework of branches is formed. (To train a fruit tree, see p. 158.) Thereafter they should have just a routine prune once growth has stopped for the season, when overcrowded, dead or diseased branches and so on are thinned out, as for climbers and shrubs. Cordons, however, should continue to be pruned back each year as in their initial training (see p. 158).

Overhanging branches should also be cut back in the dormant season, unless the trees are of the prunus species – flowering plum, for instance – which should be cut back in early summer to avoid a risk of bacterial canker.

Tree branches are always heavier than they appear, so, to save accidental damage, pass a length of rope over a nearby, higher branch and then yoke it to the branch to be pruned. Leave plenty of spare length of rope so the severed branch, once cut, can be lowered easily and slowly to the ground. If the branch is particularly large or heavy, cut it off a bit at a time, to avoid damaging paving stones on the patio. Do not leave an unsightly stump – the branch should be cut right back to the trunk and then treated with a compound containing cresylic acid, which will prevent disease, rot and canker.

Both garden walls and patio paving can be disturbed by rampant roots from neighbouring trees. However, root pruning must be carried out carefully to avoid killing the tree, and it should take place in winter. To find the root ends, dig up the ground directly below the ends of the branches, then work your way inwards towards the trunk to find the main tap roots. Cut these through with a hand or chain saw, but do not cut more than half of the root system in one season. Some support by guying might be necessary for big trees. Root pruning can be beneficial, improving flowering and fruiting.

PROTECTING PLANTS

Cloches

These are a convenient way to warm up the soil prior to planting and to protect tender plants. Cloches are made from a wide range of materials, including glass, fibreglass, rigid and semi-rigid plastics and polythene film. They vary in size from low, classical 'tents', suitable for low-growing plants, to the taller plastic tunnels, which can accommodate larger plants such as tomatoes and dwarf beans. Cloches can be used either singly over a plant or in multiples end-to-end over numerous plants. Their great advantage for a patio is their mobility. All except glass cloches are small and light. However, their drawback is that they have to be moved every time the plants underneath them need weeding, watering and so on.

Strong winds

The best way to protect patio plants from strong winds is to stake them and provide some sort of screening. Another plant, a shrub for instance, or a solid fence may shut out too much light, but mesh or netting stretched on a frame is extremely good at reducing prevailing wind.

Cats

Cats may be deterred from crushing plants or digging them up by the use of proprietary fend-off dusts and lozenges attached to shrubs. However as these are not always effective, another method, if the cats are not your own, is to stretch some wobbly netting above the boundary fence or wall. Cats are unable to get a hold on it and so cannot vault over the wall.

Birds

An old-fashioned bird scarer– for example a cat face made out of tin – or strips of tinfoil fluttering in the wind can keep birds at bay. Less obtrusive, however, is cotton zigzagged over plants to be protected or, in the case of small trees, a covering of fine netting.

Other pests

Plants that are crammed together in containers, as often happens on the patio, should be inspected regularly for pests, because, once attacked, the trouble will spread rapidly throughout the patio in such crowded conditions. The pests listed below are those most likely to occur in the patio. However, should other pests appear, consult a specialized book for a suitable treatment.

The main pests that are likely to invade the patio can be controlled comparatively easily with a little prevention, rather than an expensive cure. Slugs are a fact of life in the garden, but on the patio they are particular nuisance, not only eating lush young greenery but also leaving a tell-tale trail over the paving stones. To tackle this pest, there are plenty of proprietary granules, which you can scatter among your plants, and they are produced in earth-coloured granules as well as the more usual bright blue shade. Some are more toxic than others, so, before you buy, consult the instructions on the packet carefully should children or pets be likely to inhabit the patio. A liquid slug and snail killer is also now available, small amounts of which are dotted at intervals in a ring around the plants. Although the liquid appears to soak into the soil, it is very effective against slugs and snails. Another deterrent, which is slightly more difficult to use, is an anti-slug-and-snail tape, which you lay out around the plants and anchor with small stones. If you prefer to try an old-fashioned remedy, then beer attracts both slugs and snails and drowns them when put in a small beaker sunk into the ground. Alternatively, you can buy a 'Slug Pub', which does the same job rather more decoratively.

Mice and other vermin can be a great nuisance. To prevent them nibbling container-grown bulbs, lay a sheet of glass, plastic, slate or fine gauze over the container. Remove it immediately the plant breaks through the soil surface. Cover young plants growing in the ground with a cloche (see p. 159).

Greenfly and blackfly are also attracted to young, green shoots, especially on roses and herbs such as borage. The best way to tackle such aphids is to spray plants at risk with a systemic pesticide, which is taken up in the sap of the plant and kills off the insects as they take their first bite of the season. Never use a systemic pesticide on or near edible plants unless the instructions specifically note that it can be used in these conditions.

Whitefly, rising in what look like clouds of cigarette ash, not only look unattractive but also damage plants as they can stunt and on occasions even kill off tender plants. Like aphids, they also leave 'honeydew' on the leaves – a sticky coating that attracts dust and dirt and allows moulds to grow on it. Both aphids and whitefly, if they appear unexpectedly in the patio, can be dealt with by giving the plants a good spray containing malathion. If the plant victims are in separate small containers, after spraying them cover with an up-ended bucket or plastic refuse sack for an hour, to make sure the deadly chemical does its work.

A pest that is peculiar to patios, although better known in the conservatory or greenhouse, is the red spider mite – a creature that is so minute that it can scarcely be seen by the human eye. It signals its presence by contorting leaves by weaving a minute spider's web on their underside. Part or all of the leaves may also turn a mottled brown. If you rub the underside of a leaf you suspect to be infected, a reddish rust-like stain may appear on your hand. Suspect red spider mite if normally brilliant flowers look sick and faded. This spider thrives in hot, dry conditions, so try to prevent it by frequent misting, especially in hot, dry spells. Tackle any red spider mites that do appear with a compound containing malathion, and be particularly careful to repeat the dose again and again, even if nothing more can be seen.

Diseases

Like pests, the range of diseases that can attack your garden is enormous, so only those most likely to threaten patio plants are discussed below. If in doubt as to the identity of a plant disease and therefore how to treat it, consult a specialized book.

There is no short cut to controlling diseases, but it is important that you should be able to recognize a disease and know how to treat it. Paying attention to hygiene and cleanliness, such as scrubbing old containers and always using sterilized potting composts, is also important as it will help control the risks of disease.

The airless, often clammy conditions on a patio are ideal for the spread of mildew and its fellow traveller, black spot, which attacks roses. To prevent such diseases, spray patio plants with a systemic product at ten-day intervals throughout the summer. Should mildew still break out, dust or spray the plants with benomyl. To tackle black spot on roses, use a general-purpose rose cocktail that will treat all diseases likely to attack them.

APPENDIX

GLOSSARY

Acid Term applied to soil with a pH content below 7.0; such soil is mostly peaty or very sandy.

Alkaline Term applied to soil with a pH content above 7.0; such soil has a high lime or calcium content.

Annual Plant that grows from seed and completes its lifecycle in less than twelve months.

Bedding plant Plant used for short-term display, then promptly removed, e.g. wallflowers in spring.

Biennial Plant with a lifecycle of two years.

Bulb Usually an underground part of a plant composed of thick, fleshy leaves or leaf bases packed tightly together. It stores food reserves for winter.

Bulbil Tiny bulbs that grow in the leaf axils of the stems of some lilies.

Conifer Class of primitive plants, mainly trees, that bear woody seed clusters known as cones, e.g. pine, fir, spruce.

Cordon Single-stemmed fruit tree.

Corm Swollen base of a solid stem, which is surrounded by short, thick, fleshy leaves. It stores food reserves.

Cultivar Short for cultivated variety and referring to a distinct variant of a species (q.v.) maintained in cultivation. Such a plant does not usually come true from seed and is maintained only by vegetative propagation (cuttings, divisions, etc.)

Cutting Severed piece of leaf, stem or root used for propagation.

Deciduous Term used mainly of trees and shrubs that are leafless for part of each year, usually from autumn to spring.

Dormant Term applied to the natural resting stage in the annual cycle of a plant's growth.

Double Flower with extra petals derived from stamens and sometimes also from pistils.

Espalier Tree trained with a vertical main stem and horizontally trained branches in tiers to either side of the main stem.

Evergreen Plant that retains its leaves for at least one whole year.

Fan Tree or shrub in which the main branches are trained like the ribs of a fan against e.g. a wall or fence.

F₁ hybrid Plant grown from seed resulting from the controlled crossing of carefully selected true-breeding parent plants. F_1 hybrid plants have greater vigour and uniformity than ordinary seed-raised cultivars. Seeds saved from F_1 hybrids have to be recreated each time by crossing the same parents or parent stocks.

Genus (pl. genera) Category of plant classification in which are placed all species (q.v.) with characteristics in common.

Habit Overall shape and structure of a plant.

Half-hardy Term applied to plants that will survive moderately low temperatures in a sheltered position.

Half-standard Tree or shrub grown with 0.9–1.2m/3–4ft of clear stem.

Harden off Gradual acclimatization to the open air of plants grown in warmth.

Hardwood Woody stem on a tree or shrub that has matured fully by the end of its first growing season.

Hardy Term applied to plants that survive outdoors without protection through the year.

Herbaceous Term applied to perennial plants whose stems die back each winter.

Hybrid Plant created by crossing two separate varieties, species or genera.

Lateral Buds, shoots or stems that arise on the side of an existing stem.

Leaching Used of soluble fertilizers and such substances as lime that are washed deep into the soil out of the reach of roots or out of the bottom of containers, by rain or continual watering.

Loam Fertile soil of good texture containing balanced mixture of nutrients.

Offset Lateral shoot that develops from a leaf axil at the crown of a plant and becomes a plant in its own right.

Perennial Non-woody plant that lives longer than two years.

Pinching out Removal of the tip of a stem to encourage the growth of lateral stems and a bushy habit.

Potting compost, mix or soil Growing medium, containing minerals essential for growth, formulated for growing plants in various types of container.

Runner Long, more or less prostrate slender stem, each leaf node rooting quickly and forming a new plant, e.g. strawberry.

Semi-hardwood Partially mature stem a bit more than halfway through its first growing season, distinguished by its firm, woody base and soft, sometimes still growing, tip.

Shrub Plant formed of woody, persistent stems, usually with most of the main branches arising near to or below ground level, and not much above 4m/13ft tall.

Single Opposite of double (q.v.); used in plant groups such as roses where most cultivars have double or semi-double flowers. It then refers to the wild species or one of similar form having a normal complement of petals, stamens and pistils.

Softwood Soft, sappy, actively growing stem near the beginning of the first season's growth.

Species Plant type within a genus with distinct characteristics that breed true from seeds or spores.

Standard Tree or shrub grown with 1.5–1.8m/5–6ft of clear stem.

Tender Term applied to plants that cannot survive outdoors during the winter.

Tuber Enlarged root or stem, which functions as a storage organ and is usually, but not invariably, underground.

Twiner Climber that coils around its supports using its growing tips.

Variegated Term applied to leaves or flowers patterned with at least two colours.

Variety Distinct form of a species (q.v.) that occurs as a true-breeding entity in the wild.

PLANTS FOR SPECIAL SITUATIONS

The following comprise a selection of those plants that require, or do well in, special conditions, such as full sun, damp shade or by cool walls, as well as some perennials, annuals and bulbs in their appropriate flowering seasons. A selection of accent plants and basic background plants for the patio is also listed.

CLIMBERS AND WALL SHRUBS
For sunny walls
Abutilon vitifolium
Acacia dealbata
Aristolochia macrophylla
Bougainvillea glabra
Campsis grandiflora
Ceanothus × 'Autumnal Blue'
Clematis montana
Ecremocarpus scaber
Fuchsia
Lathyrus odoratus
Lonicera × *brownii* 'Fuchsioides'
L. × *tellmanniana*
Passiflora caerulea
Phygelius capensis
Trachelospermum jasminoides
Tropaeolum
Vitis vinifera 'Brant'
Wisteria sinensis

For cool walls
Celastrus orbiculatus
Chaenomeles speciosa
Clematis hybrids
Cotoneaster horizontalis
Euonymus fortunei
Forsythia suspensa
Garrya elliptica
Hedera canariensis
Hydrangea petiolaris
Jasminum nudiflorum
J. officinale
Kerria japonica
Lonicera × *americana*
Parthenocissus quinquefolia
Polygonum baldschuanicum
Pyracantha rogersiana
Rosa

SUN-LOVING PLANTS
Artemisia arborescens
Ceanothus
Clematis
Dianthus
Escholtzia
Gypsophila
Helichrysum
Hibiscus syriacus
Hippophae rhamnoides
Kniphofia
Lavandula
Marjoram
Nerine bowdenii
Pelargonium
Phaseolus multiflorus
Phlomis fruticosa
Potentilla
Rosa
Rosmarinus
Tamarix
Thymus
Viola

PLANTS FOR DRY SHADE
Ajuga
Alchemilla mollis
Althea
Arundinaria
Berberis
Bergenia
Calendula
Cotoneaster
Euonymus
Hedera
Hippophae rhamnoides
Hypericum calycinum
Ilex
Mahonia
Malcolmia maritima
Pachysandra terminalis
Pittosporum tenuifolium
Salvia
Santolina
Vinca major

PLANTS FOR DAMP SHADE
Acer palmatum 'Atropurpureum'
Astilbe
Begonia
Camellia
Cyclamen
Elaeagnus angustifolia
Fatsia japonica
Fern
Hamamelis mollis
Helleborus
Hosta
Hydrangea
Impatiens
Nephrolepis exalta 'Bostoniensis'
Primula
Rhododendron

FLOWERS ALL YEAR ROUND
Spring
Alyssum
Anemone blanda
Aubretia
Camellia
Chaenomeles speciosa
Cheiranthus cheiri
Chionodoxa luciliae
Clematis armandii
Convallaria
Crocus chrysanthus
Eranthis
Erica carnea
Forsythia
Galanthus nivalis
Helleborus niger
Hyacinthus orientalis
Impatiens sultanii (I. walleriana)
Iris reticulata
Jasminum nudiflorum
Magnolia stellata
Muscari
Narcissus
Polyanthus
Primula denticulata
Prunus cerasifera
Rhododendron
Saxifraga granulata
Scilla sibirica
Tulipa

Summer
Alyssum
Aster
Aubretia
Begonia × *tuberhybrida*
Campanula carpatica
Centaurea cyanus
Cheiranthus cheiri

Chrysanthemum frutescens
Clematis
Dianthus × *allwoodii*
D. barbatus
Dicentra spectabilis
Endymion nonscriptus
Fuchsia hybrids
Gypsophila
Hesperis matronalis
Impatiens sultanii (I. walleriana)
Ipomoea purpurea
Lathyrus odoratus
Lavandula
Lilium
Lobelia erinus
Matthiola incana
Nemesia strumosa
Pelargonium
Petunia × *hybrida*
Rosa
Rosmarinus officinalis
Salvia splendens
Wisteria
Zinnia angustifolia

Autumn
Begonia × *tuberhybrida*
Chrysanthemum
Clematis
Colchicum autumnale
Cyclamen neopolitanum
Dahlia
Dianthus × *allwoodii*
Erica
Fatsia japonica
Fuchsia hybrids
Hibiscus
Impatiens sultanii (I. walleriana)
Lathyrus odoratus
Lobelia erinus
Nerine bowdenii
Pelargonium
Petunia × *hybrida*
Salvia splendens
Schizostylis coccinea
Sternbergia lutea
Viburnum × *bodnantense*

Winter
Chimonanthus praecox
Daphne mezereum
Erica carnea
Galanthus nivalis
Hamamelis mollis
Helleborus orientalis
Hyacinthus orientalis
Iris unguicularis
Lonicera fragrantissima

BASIC BACKGROUND PLANTS
Acer palmatum 'Senkaki'
Buxus
Camellia armandii
Ceanothus
Chaemaecyparis
Choisya ternata
Cistus
Cornus alba 'Westonbirt'
Fatsia japonica
Ilex
Malus sargentii
Pachysandra
Picea abies (*P. excelsa*) 'Clanbrassiliana'
Pieris formosa forrestii
Populus balsamifera
Prunus
Rhododendron
Rubus cockburnianus
Sorbus 'Joseph Rock'
Spiraea arguta

ACCENT PLANTS
Acer palmatum 'Atropurpureum'
Araucaria araucana
Arundinaria viridi-striatus
Betula pendula 'Youngii'
Buxus
Chrysanthemum
Coleus blumei
Cordyline australis
Cotoneaster
Fuchsia
Hibiscus syriacus
Laurus nobilis
Lonicera nitida
Magnolia × *soulangiana*
Pelargonium
Phormium tenax
Prunus 'Cheals Weeping'
P. subhirtella 'Autumnalis'
Rheum palmatum
Taxus baccata
Trachycarpus fortunei
Wisteria
Yucca gloriosa

GENERAL INDEX

A
Accent plants 98–9, 162
Access 10
Arab design 25
Autumn flowers 93–5, 162
Awnings 131

B
Background plants 88–9, 162
Backyard patio 36
Barbecues 65, 131, 140–1
  see also Furniture
Benches 134–5
Berries *see* Autumn flowers, Winter
  flowers
Birds 160
Bricks *see* Paving
Bulbs 93, 112–13, 155

C
Candles *see* Lighting
Cats 160
Climbers 10, 20, 46, 66, 86–7, 88, 102,
  109–11, 148, 158, 159, 162
Cloches 93, 159–60
Cobbles *see* Paving
Colour 36, 81, 88, 93, 95, 124
Compost 151
Concrete 50, 60, 146–7
  care and repair 146–7
  paving 50
  walls 60
Containers 69–71, 84, 93, 95, 98, 101–3,
  138–9, 149, 150–3
  planning 69–71
  planting 101–3
  types 138–9
Crocking 150

D
Damp-proof course 48–50
Decked patio 26
  see also Wooden decking
Dining furniture
  see Tables and chairs
Diseases 160
Drainage 71, 103, 149, 150
Drought 96

E
Edible plants 102–3, 120–1
Electrical fittings 148
  see also Lighting, Lights
Espaliered trees 103, 158
Evergreens 88, 104–9
Excavation 52

F
Feeding 156
Fences 46, 58–63, 148
  construction 61, 62
  maintenance 148
  types 61
Fertilizers 156
Flares *see* Lighting
Foliage 14, 84–92, 104–11
  see also Climbers 104–8
Fruit 102, 109, 121, 158–9
Furniture 64–5, 124–44
  built-in 64–5
  construction 64–5
  types 124–44
  see also Tables and chairs, Benches,
  etc.

G
Granite setts *see* Paving
Gravel 51–2, 147
Ground cover plants 90–2, 116–18
Growing bags 129, 152
Growing medium 149–50

H J
Hanging baskets 152, 156
Herbs 95–8, 103, 122, 154
Japanese garden 13, 16, 30, 125

L
Layering 155
Levels 20, 22, 38, 46, 47, 48, 52, 53, 71
  raised beds 22, 71
Lighting 11, 76–80, 124, 130
  see also Safety, Underwater lights
Lights 142–3
Lounging furniture 136–7

M
Maintenance 44, 45–6, 146–60
Marginal plants 101, 153
Mirrors 81
Moated patio 37

O
Overhead shelter 42, 66–8, 131, 148
Oxygenators 100, 119–20, 153

P
Patio, definition of 8
Pavers *see* Paving
Paving
  brick 50–1
  cobbles 51
  concrete 50
  granite setts 51
  maintenance 146–7
  pavers 51
  techniques for laying 52
  tiles 52–3
  York stone 50–1
  see also Ground cover 90–2
Peat 46, 108, 150, 152
Pergola 26, 40, 68
  see also Overhead shelter
Pests 160
Planning 8–17, 42–7
Plant care 154–60
Pollution 97
Ponds 30, 32, 34, 75, 100–1, 148
  see also Water features
Potting techniques 150–2
Privacy 11
Propagation 154–5
Pruning 146, 159

R
Raised beds 11, 22, 45, 70–1
Roof garden 46, 47
Runners 155

S
Safety, lighting 79–80, 148
Salad plants 102, 121–2
Screens 36, 42, 62–3, 82, 97, 130–1, 148
  types 63
  see also Overhead shelter
Seasons, flowers for 162
Seeds *see* Propagation
Shade, plants for 162
Shrubs 84–9, 106–11, 159
Site, choice of 10, 42
Soil 18, 87, 90, 96, 104, 107, 149, 150
Special conditions, plants for 96–7, 162
Special effects 14, 81
Spring flowers 93–5, 162
Statues and ornaments 131, 144
Stem cuttings 155

Style 12–14
Submersible pump 75
Summer flowers 93–5, 162
Sun, plants for 40, 96–7, 162
Supporting and training plants 157–8
Surfaces 42, 48–57, 146–7

T

Tables and chairs 132–3
Terrace 34, 38
Tiles 25, 52
    see also Paving
Tools 51–2, 98, 146, 151
Topiary 98, 148
Trees 84–8, 99, 158
Tropical look 25, 88, 96, 98, 129

U V

Umbrellas 131
Underwater lights 79, 80, 130, 143
Vegetables 102, 121

W

Walls 58–60, 86, 88, 147
    concrete blocks 60
    construction 60
    maintenance 147
    types of wall 59
Wall shrubs 109–10, 162
Water features 11, 13, 17, 18, 21, 25,
    30–1, 32–3, 34, 37, 72–5, 147
    construction 72–5
    maintenance 147
    making a pond 75
    see also Ponds
Watering 70, 146, 156
Water plants 100–1, 119–20
Weeds 46, 90, 92, 146
Wind screen 97, 159
Winter flowers 93–5, 162
Wooden decking 26, 30, 45, 54–7, 75,
    82, 147
    construction 54–7, 75
    maintenance 147
    materials 54
    modules 57, 75
    patterns 56

PLANT INDEX (ENGLISH NAMES)

Plants are indexed under their Latin names on pp.165–6

A

Accent plants 98–9, 162
Alpine phlox see Phlox amoena
Apple see Malus sylvestris
Arrowhead see Sagittaria
Aubretia see Aubrieta deltoidea
Autumn crocus see Colchicum
    autumnale

B

Background plants 162
Balsam see Populus balsamifera
Bamboos see Arundinaria
Barberry see Berberis thunbergii
    atropurpurea
Bellflower see Campanula carpatica
Berberis 97
Bleeding heart see Dicentra spectabilis
Bluebells see Endymion nonscriptus
Box see Buxus
Brandy bottle see Nuphar lutea
Bridal wreath see Spirea arguta
Buffalo currant see Ribes odoratum
Bugle see Ajuga reptans
Busy Lizzie see Impatiens

C

Cabbage palm see Cordyline australis
Californian lilac see Ceanothus
Canadian pondweed see Elodea
    canadensis
Cardoon see Cynara cardunculus
Carrots 102
Chamomile see Chamaemelum nobile
Chicory see Cichorium intybus
Chicory 'Rossa de Verona' see Radicchio
Chilean glory flower see Ecremocarpus
    scaber
Chives see Allium schoenoprasum
Christmas rose see Helleborus niger
Chusan palm see Trachycarpus fortunei
Clematis see Clematis armandii
Climbing bittersweet see Celastrus
    orbiculatus
Climbing rose see Rosa
Common lilac see Syringa vulgaris
Conifers 87, 88
Cornflower see Centaurea cyanus
Corsican mint see Mentha requieni
Cotton grass see Emophorum

Cotton lavender see Santolina
Crab apple see Malus sargentii
Creeping Jenny see Lysimachia
    nummularia
Creme de menthe mint see Mentha
    requienii

D

Daffodil see Narcissus
Dogwood see Cornus
Drumstick primrose see Primula
    denticulata
Dutchman's pipe see Aristolochia
    macrophylla
Dwarf reedmace see Typha minima

E

Easter lily see Lilium longiflorum
Edible plants 102, 121
Elephant ears see Bergenia × schmidtii
Espaliered trees 103, 158
Evergreens 88, 104–9

F

'Fairy changeling' rose 92
'Fairy damsel' rose 92
Fairy moss see Azola carolinian
Fennel see Foeniculum vulgare
Firethorn see Pyracantha rogersiana
Flowering rush see Butomus umbellatus
Flowers 93–5
Foliage 14, 84, 86, 104–8
Forget-me-not see Myosotis
French and African marigold see Tagetes
French bean see Phaseolus vulgaris
Fruit 102, 109, 121

G

Geranium see Pelargonium
Globe artichoke see Cynara scolymus
Glory of the snow see Chionodoxa
    luciliae
Gold dust see Alyssum saxatile
Grape hyacinth see Muscari
Grape vine see Vitis vinifera
Ground cover plants 90–2

H

Herbs 95–8, 103, 154, 122
Hibiscus see Hibiscus syriacus
Holly see Ilex
Hollyhock see Althaea
Honeysuckle see Lonicera

Hornwort see Ceratophyllum demersum
Hybrid tea roses see Rosa

I J

Iris see Iris kaempferi, I.laevigata
Ivy see Hedera
Japanese angelica see Aralia elata
Japanese quince see Chaenomeles
    speciosa
Jasmine see Jasminum officinale
Jerusalem sage see Phlomis fructicosa
Judas tree see Cercis siliquastrum

K L

Kaffir lily see Schizostylis coccinea
Lady's mantle see Alchemilla mollis
Lamb's ears see Stachys lanata
Lavender see Lavandula
Lawson's cypress see Chamecyparis
    lawsoniana
Lettuce see Lactuca sativa
Lily of the field see Sternbergia lutea
Lily of the valley see Convallaria
Lobelia see Lobelia erinus
London pride see Saxifraga × urbium
Lungwort see Pulmonaria

M

Magnolia see Magnolia stellata
Maiden pink see Dianthus deltoides
Marginal plants 101, 153
Marguerites see Chrysanthemum
    frutescens
Marigold see Calendula
Marsh marigold see Caltha palustris
Meadow saxifrage see Saxifraga
Mexican orange blossom see Choisya
    ternata
Mimosa see Acacia dealbata
Mint see Mentha
Mock orange see Philadelphus
Monkey musk see Mimulus luteus
Monkey puzzle see Araucaria
    araucana
Monterey cypress see Cupressus
    macrocarpa
Morning glory see Ipomoea purpurea

N

Nasturtium see Tropaeolum
New Zealand burr see Acaena
    microphylla
New Zealand flax see Phormium tenax
Norway spruce see Picea abies

O

Old English lavender *see Lavandula angustifolia*
Ornamental plum *see Prunus cerasifera*
Ornamental rhubarb *see Rheum palmatum*

P

Pampas *see Cortaderia*
Parsley *see Petroselinum crispum*
Pasque flower *see Pulsatilla vulgaris*
Passion flower *see Passiflora*
Peach *see Prunus persica*
Pennyroyal *see Mentha pulegium*
Periwinkle *see Vinca major*
Pernettya 97
Petunia *see Petunia* × *hybrida*
Polyanthus *see P.* × *Polyantha*
Potatoes 102, 122, 152

R

Rock rose *see Helianthemum nummularium*
Rosemary *see Rosmarinus*
Rose of Sharon *see Hypericum calycinum*
Runner beans *see Phaseolus multiflorus*
Runners 155
Russian vine *see Polygonum baldschuanicum*

S

Sage *see Salvia*
Salad plants 102
Scarlet trumpet honeysuckle *see Lonicera*
Scilla *see Scilla sibirica*
Sea buckthorn *see Hippophae rhamnoides*
Seakale *see Crambe maritima*
Snowdrop *see Galanthus nivalis*
Spanish broom *see Spartium junceum*
Spindle tree *see Euonymus fortuneii*
Spotted deadnettle *see Lamium maculatum*
Stock *see Matthiola incana*
Strawberries 103
    see also Fragaria
Strawberry tree *see Arbutus andrachne*
Sweet bay *see Laurus nobilis*
Sweet flag *see Acorus*
Sweet pea *see Lathyrus odoratus*
Sweet William *see Dianthus barbatus*
Swiss chard *see Beta vulgaris*

T

Thyme *see Thymus*
Tomato *see Lycopersicon lycopersicum*
Tomatoes 102, 121
Trailing lobelia 103
Trees 84–9, 99, 158 *see also* Espaliered trees
Trumpet vine *see Campsis grandiflora*
Tulip *see Tulipa*

V

Vegetables 102, 121
Virginia creeper *see Parthenocissus quinquefolia*
Virginia stock *see Malcolmia maritima*

W

Wallflower *see Cheiranthus cheiri*
Wall shrubs 107–9, 162
Water buttercup *see Ranunculus*
Water crowfoot *see Ranunculus aquatilis*
Water forget-me-not *see Myosotis palustris*
Water hawthorn *see Aponogeton distachyus*
Water hyacinth *see Eichhornia crassipes*
Water lilies *see Nymphaea*
Water soldier *see Stratiotes aloides*
Wattle *see Acacia dealbata*
Weeping cherry *see Prunus* 'Cheals Weeping'
White clover *see Trifolium repens*
Wild strawberry *see Fragaria vesca*
Wild thyme *see Thymus*
Winter aconite *see Eranthis*
Winter iris *see Iris unquicularis*
Winter jasmine *see Jasminum nudiflorum*
Wisteria 93
Witch hazel *see Hamamelis mollis*
Worm weed *see Cotula squalida*

Y

Yellow skunk cabbage *see Lysichiton americanus*
Young's weeping birch *see Betula pendula* 'Youngii'

PLANT INDEX (LATIN NAMES)

A

Abutilon vitifolium 109, 162
Acacia dealbata 104, 162
Acaena microphylla 116
Acer japonicum 34
Acer palmatum 'Atropurpureum' 97, 104, 162, 163; *A.p.* 'Senkaki' 89, 163
Acorus 119
Ajuga 97, 162; *A. reptans* 116
Alchemilla mollis 91, 97, 116, 162
Allium schoenoprasum 122
Althaea 48, 162
Alyssum 95, 162; *A. saxatile* 116
Anemone blanda 112, 162
Anethum graveolens 122
Anthemis cupaniana 116
Aponogeton distachyus 119
Aralia elata 97
Araucaria araucana 98, 163
Arbutus andrachne 104
Aristolochia macrophylla 109, 162
Armeria maritima 116
Artemisia arborescens 96, 162; *A. brachyloba* 116
Arundinaria 84, 97, 162; *A. viridi-striata* (syn. *Pleioblastus viridi-striatus*) 106, 163
Astilbe 162; *A. chinensis pumila* 119
Aubrieta 95, 162; *A. deltoidea* 116
Azola caroliniana 119

B

Begonia semperflorens 95, 162; *B.* × *tuberhybrida* 112, 162
Berberis thunbergii atropurpurea 106
Bergenia × *schmidtii* 116
Beta vulgaris 97
Betula pendula 'Youngii' 104, 163
Bougainvillea glabra 109, 162
Brunnera macrophylla 116
Buddleia 'Lochinch' 106
Butomus umbellatus 119
Buxus 88, 98, 163; *B. sempervirens* 106

C

Calendula 48, 162
Caltha palustris 101, 119
Camellia 106, 162, 163
Campanula carpatica 112, 162; *C. portenschlagiana* 116
Campsis grandiflora 109, 162
Ceanothus 163; *C.* × 'Autumnal Blue' 109, 162

Celastrus orbiculatus 109, 162
Centaurea cyanus 93
Ceratophyllum demersum 119
Cercis siliquastrum 104
Chaenomeles speciosa 93, 97, 109, 162
Chamaecyparis 88, 163; *C. lawsoniana* 97, 104
Chamaemelum nobile 116
Cheiranthus cheiri 93, 112, 162
Chimonanthus praecox 95, 162
Chionodoxa luciliae 112
Choisya ternata 88, 106, 163
Chrysanthemum 163; *C. frutescens* 95, 162
Cichorium intybus 121
Cistus 163
Clematis armandii 88, 93; *C. balearica* 95; *C. montana* 93, 162; *C. viticella* 95; hybrids 109, 162
Colchicum autumnale 95, 112, 162
Coleus blumei 99, 163
Convallaria 93, 162
Convolvulus sabatius 117
Cordyline australis 98, 104, 163
Cornus 89; *C. alba* 28, 106, 163
Cortaderia 84
Cotoneaster 162, 163; *C. horizontalis* 109
Cotula squalida 117
Crambe maritima 103
Crataegus × *grignonensis* 97
Crocus chrysanthus 112, 162
Cupressocyparis leylandii 97
Cupressus macrocarpa 97
Cyclamen hederifolium (C. neapolitanum) 112, 162
Cynara cardunculus 84; *C. scolymus* 103, 121

D

Daphne mezereum 95, 162
Deutzia monbeigii 106
Dianthus 162; *D.* × *alwoodii* 112, 162; *D. barbatus* 113, 162; *D. deltoides* 117
Dicentra spectabilis 113, 162

E

Ecremocarpus scaber 110, 162
Eichhornia crassipes 100, 119
Elaeagnus angustifolia 97
Elodea crispa 100, 119; *E. canadensis* 119
Emophorum 101
Endymion nonscriptus 93, 162
Eranthis 93, 162
Erica 95; *E. carnea* 113, 162
Escallonia 'Donard Radiance' 107

Escholzia 162
Eucalyptus gunnii 97
Euonymus fortunei 110, 162

F

Fatsia japonica 46, 88, 95, 97, 107, 163
Ficus carica 121
Foeniculum vulgare 122
Forsythia suspensa 110, 162
Fragaria × *ananassa* 121; *F. vesca* 117
Fuchsia 162, 163; *F.* hybrids 110; *F. magellanica* 107

G

Galanthus nivalis 95, 113, 162
Garrya elliptica 87, 110, 163
Geranium renardii 117
Glyceria aquatica 'Variegata' 119
Gypsophila 162

H

Hamamelis mollis 48, 95, 162
Hedera 86, 97; *H. canariensis* 110, 162; *H. colchica* 'Variegata' 87; *H. helix* 'Goldheart' 87
Helianthemum nummularium 117
Helichrysum 162
Helleborus 162; *H. niger* 95, 113; *H. orientalis* 162
Hesperis matronalis 162
Hibiscus syriacus 96, 107, 162, 163
Hippophae rhamnoides 96, 97, 162
Hosta 117, 162
Hottonia palustris 119
Hyacinthus orientalis 162
Hydrangea macrophylla 48, 107; *H. petiolaris* 28, 36, 86, 162
Hypericum calycinum 48, 107, 162

I

Ilex 88, 162, 163
Impatiens 48, 95, 162; *I. walleriana* 'Holstii' 113
Ipomoea purpurea 113
Iris kaempferi 119; *I. laevigata* 34, 120; *I. reticulata* 93, 113, 162; *I. unguicularis* 95, 162

J

Jasminum nudiflorum 93, 110, 162; *J. officinale* 87, 162
Juniperus horizontalis 34; *J. pyramidalis* 46

K

Kerria japonica 162
Kniphofia 162

L

Lactuca sativa 121
Lamium maculatum 117
Lathyrus odoratus 10, 86, 95, 113, 162
Laurus nobilis 105, 163
Lavandula 162; *L. angustifolia* 'Munster' 92; *L.* × *intermedia* 107
Lilium auratum 95; *L. longiflorum* 114
Liriope muscari 117
Lobelia erinus 114, 162
Lonicera 86, 87; *L.* × *americana* 110, 162; *L.* × *brownii* 'Fuchsioides' 110, 162; *L. fragrantissima* 95, 162; *L. nitida* 98, 163; *L.* × *tellmanniana* 162
Lycopersicon lycopersicum 121
Lysichiton americanus 120
Lysimachia nummularia 117

M

Magnolia stellata 93, 162; *M.* × *soulangiana* 163
Mahonia 162
Malcolmia maritima 48, 162
Malus sargentii 105, 163; *M. sylvestris* 121.
Matthiola incana 114, 162
Mentha 122; *M. pulegium* 120; *M. requieni* 92, 117
Mimulus luteus 120; *M. ringens* 120
Muscari 93, 162
Myosotis 92, 120

N

Narcissus 114, 162
Nemesia strumosa 114, 162
Nerine bowdenii 114, 162
Nuphar lutea 100, 120
Nymphaea 120; *N. odorata* 'Froebelii' 120

P

Pachysandra 163; *P. terminalis* 118, 162
Parthenocissus quinquefolia 46, 86, 111, 162
Passiflora caerulea 82, 87, 103, 111, 162
Pelargonium 48, 95, 99, 103, 114, 162, 163
Petroselinum crispum 122

Petunia × *hybrida* 114, 162
Phaseolus coccineus 122; *P. multiflorus* 102; *P. vulgaris* 102, 122
Philadelphus 'Lemonei Erectus' 107; *P.* 'Virginal' 108
Phlomis fruticosa 96, 162
Phlox amoena 118
Phormium tenax 20, 84, 98, 108
Phygelius capensis 162
Picea abies (syn. *P. excelsa*) 'Clanbrassiliana' 163
Pieris formosa forrestii 163
Pittosporum tenuifolium 162
Pleioblastus viridi-striatus see *Arundinaria viridi-striata*
Polygonum baldschuanicum 36, 46, 86, 87, 107, 162
Populus balsamifera 89, 103
Potentilla 162; *P. fruticosa* 108
Primula denticulata 115, 162; *P.* × *polyantha* 115, 162
Prunus 163; *P. cerasifera* 93, 162; *P. laurocerasus* 37; *P. persica* 121; *P. subhirtella* 105
Pulmonaria 118
Pulsatilla vulgaris 118
Pyracantha 108; *P. rogersiana* 38, 97, 110, 162

R

Radicchio 102
Ranunculus 101; *R. aquatilis* 120
Rheum palmatum 98, 163; *R. rhaponticum* 103
Rhododendron 108, 162, 163
Ribes odoratum 108
Robinia 28
Rosa 108, 110, 162; *R.* 'Max Graf' 118
Rosmarinus 96; *R. officinalis* 108
Rubus cockburnianus 89, 163
Rugosa (roses) 97

S

Sagittaria sagittifolia 120
Salix caprea 'Pendula' 105
Salvia 115, 122, 162
Santolina 48, 162
Saxifraga 162; *S. granulata* 115; *S. moschata* 118; *S.* × *urbium* 92
Schizostylis coccinea 115, 162
Scilla sibirica 115, 162
Sedum spurium 118
Senecio compactus 118
Solanum tuberosum 122
Sorbus 89; *S. aria* 97, 105; *S.a.* × *hostii* 105

Spartium junceum 97
Spiraea arguta 89, 163
Stachys lanata 92
Stephandandra incisa 28
Sternbergia lutea 115, 162
Stratiotes aloides 120
Syringa vulgaris 108

T

Tagetes 95
Tamarix 162; *T. gallica* 97
Taxus baccata 98, 163
Tellima grandiflora 118
Thuya plicata 'Atrovirens' 97
Thymus 122, 162; *T. herba-barona* 118; *T. serpyllum* 118
Trachelospermum jasminoides 110, 162
Trachycarpus fortunei 98, 163
Trifolium repens 'Purpurascens Quadriphyllum' 118
Tropaeolum 10, 95, 162; *T. majus* 118
Tulipa 115, 162
Typha minima 120

V

Viburnum × *bodnantense* 95, 108, 162
Vinca major 48, 90, 162; *V. minor* 90, 118
Viola 162; *V. labradorica* 'Purpurea' 118
Vitis vinifera 36, 87, 111, 121

W Y Z

Weigela florida 108
Wisteria 163; *W. sinensis* 111
Yucca gloriosa 46, 98, 163
Zinnia angustifolia 115, 162

USEFUL ADDRESSES

SUPPLIERS OF GARDEN FURNISHINGS, LIGHTING AND ACCESSORIES

Allibert Garden Furniture, Sommer Allibert UK Ltd, Berry Hill Industrial Estate, Droitwich, Worcestershire WR9 9AB
Andrew Grace Designs, Bourne Lane, Much Hadham, Herts SG10 6ER
David Arbus, The Granary, Railway Hill, Barham, Nr Canterbury, Kent
Barlow Tyrie Ltd, Springwood Industrial Estate, Rayne Road, Braintree, Essex CM7 7RN
W. C. Bradley Enterprises Inc, Box 1240, Columbus GA 31993 USA
Brambley Garden Furniture, Crittal Drive, Springwood Industrial Estate, Rayne Road, Braintree, Essex CM7 7QX
R. V. Branson & Co Ltd, East Road, Sleaford, Lincs
The Charles Verey Garden Furniture Collection, Green Brothers (Geebro) Ltd, Hailsham, East Sussex, BN27 3DT
Chilstone Garden Ornaments, Sprivers Estate, Horsmonden, Kent TN12 8DR
Concord Lighting Ltd, Concord House, 241 City Road, London EC1V 1JD
The Country Garden, Binns Close, Coventry, CV4 9UJ
Robin Eden, Pickwick, Corsham, Wilts
Eibis International, 3 Johnson's Court, Fleet Street, London EC4A 3EA
Emess Lighting (UK) Ltd, 6 Anderson Road, Roding Lane South, Woodford Green, Essex IG8 8ET
Frank Odell Ltd, 70 High Street, Teddington, Middlesex, TW11 8JE
Garden Crafts, 158 New Kings Road, Fulham, London SW6
Gloster Leisure Furniture Ltd, Universal House, Pennywell Road, Bristol B55 0TJ
Grosfillex (UK) Ltd, Planters division, 10 Chandos Road, London NW10 6NF
Hoffmeister Lighting Ltd, Units 3 & 4, Preston Road, Reading, Berks RG2 0BE
Jardine Leisure Furniture Ltd, Rosemount Tower, Wallington Square, Wallington, Surrey SM6 8RR
Loga Möbel, 8621 Untersiemau, Schlossstrasse 22
Neyrat Peyronie, distributed in the U.K. by King Easton Garden Leisure, The Green, Station Road, Winchmore Hill, London N21 3NB
The Olive Tree Trading Co Ltd, Church Wharf, Pumping Station Road, London W4 2SN
Osram (GEC) Ltd, PO Box 17, East Lane, Wembley HA9 7PG
Rausch KG Fabrication Internationaler Möbel Collectionen, An der Tagweide 14, D-7500 Karlsruhe 1, West Germany. Licensed Product of Brown Jordan – U.S.A. Exclusive Distribution for Europe Rausch
Stewart Plastics Ltd, Purley Way, Croydon CR9 4HS
Triconfort, distributed by Witbourne (Leisure Products Ltd), 23 Upperton Lane, Eastbourne, East Sussex, BN21 2DB
Weber Distribution Ltd, 64 London Road, Wheatley, Oxon (for Weber Stephen Products Co, 200 East Daniels Road, Palatine, Illinois 60067, USA)
Zenith International Ltd, Selecta House, Charing Hill, Ashford, Kent TN27 0NL

AUSTRALIA

OUTDOOR FURNITURE

Barracks Trading Centre, 3a Anzac Highway, Keswick, South Australia
Freedom Furniture, 625 South Dowling Street, Surry Hills, NSW
French's Pine World, 396 Hobart Road, Youngtown, Tasmania
Greenwood Industries, 493 Main Road, Montrose, Tasmania
Inside Out, 1055 High Street, Armadale, Victoria

BARBECUES

Barbeques Galore (state branches):
    138 Silverwater Road, Silver Water, NSW
    18 Ipswich Road, Woolloongabba, Queensland
    95 Hobart Road, Kingsmeadow, Tasmania
    13 Main Road, Moonah, Tasmania
    41 Anzac Highway, Ashford, South Australia
    504 Charles Street, North Perth, Western Australia
    313 Bridge Road, Richmond, Victoria

OUTDOOR LIGHTING

Atkins Carlyle, 1 Milligan Street, Perth, Western Australia
R. J. Brodie Lighting Co., Pacific Highway, Chatswood, NSW
Cassaway Lighting, 151 Hobart Road, Kingsmeadow, Tasmania
Group Trading Services, 134 Giles Street, Adelaide, South Australia
Illumination Design, Waterworks Road, Ashgrove, Queensland
Lights 'n Lamps, 85a Harrington Street, Hobart, Tasmania
Outdoor Lighting Centre, 123 Smith Street, Fitzroy, Victoria

PUBLISHERS' ACKNOWLEDGMENTS

The publishers would like to thank the following individuals and organizations for their help in preparing this book.

For allowing their gardens to be photographed: Peter Baistow, Mr and Mrs Michael Becher, Alan Bermen, Mrs Chilton, Mrs Susie Cummings, Ian Mylles, Mrs Riggall, Edward Samuels, Rodney Slatford, Mike and Debbie Staniford, Martin Summers, David Tierney and Mrs Wardroper. For helping us locate suitable gardens: Mrs Nancy Pattenden. Thanks also go to Don Evemy and David McClintock for identifying and/or checking plant lists, Janet Turner of Concord Lighting Ltd for checking information on lighting and to Robin Williams for help with garden designs.

Text editors   Jonathan Hilton, Joanna Chisholm
Art editor   Louise Tucker
Designer   Anne Fisher

Picture researcher   Anne Fraser

Series editor   Susan Berry
Art direction   Steven Wooster

Typesetting
Vantage Photosetting Co. Ltd.,
Eastleigh and London

Reproduction
Hong Kong Graphics Arts Ltd

Photographers
Agence Top 8, 13
Agence Photographique Top (Roland Beaufre) 8
(Hinous) 13
ARCAID (Richard Bryant) 96
Peter Baistow 86
Michael Boys 2, 12, 16, 79 (via Susan Griggs Agency 25)
Karl-Dietrich Bühler 9, 18, 19, 40, 62, 65B, 73, 89, 99
Geoff Dann 1, 4, 20, 21, 22, 23, 24, 28, 29, 34, 35, 36, 38, 39, 45, 49, 50, 53, 58, 59, 63, 65T, 69, 70, 77, 85, 87, 88, 94, 95, 100, 103R
Ken Druse 47
Michael Dunne 55
Daniel Eifert 56
Inge Espen-Hansen 14, 37, 44, 46, 67, 71, 74, 75, 89, 90, 98
Derek Fell 68
Jerry Harpur 32, 33, 60, 78
Jacqui Hurst 93
Pat Hunt 48
Joy Larkcom 103L
Sylvia Martin 92
Mike McKinley 17, 64
Ken Muir 102
Hugh Palmer 81, 101
Ron Sutherland 26, 27, 30, 31, 43, 51, 82, 97
Louise Tucker 10
Elizabeth Whiting 57, 72
George Wright 91

Illustrators
Ken Baker 125–30
Will Giles/Sandra Pond 21, 22, 24, 29, 30, 48–80, 146–58
Ros Hewitt 104–20
Liz Pepperall (Garden Studio) 11, 15
Christine Robins (Garden Studio) 132–44
Robin Williams 18, 25, 26, 33, 34, 38, 40

Garden designers
Diane Baistow 34
Mackenzie Bell 32
Anthony Paul 26, 30
Pat O'Brien 92
Ruben de Saavedra 56
Robin Williams 81
Wendy Wright 59